The Ethics of Liberal Democracy

State, Law and Society

Series Editor: Andrew Altman

This series presents major authors in the continental, and particularly the German, tradition of legal and political theory. It is concerned with recent comparative work in the field of legal and political history, but it also makes available in translation some of the classics of this tradition.

Ernst-Wolfgang Bockenforde, *State, Society and Liberty: Studies in Political Theory and Constitutional Law*

Franz Neumann, *The Rule of Law: Political Theory and the Legal System in Modern Society*

Anthony Woodiwiss, *Rights v. Conspiracy: A Sociological Essay on the History of Labour Law in the United States*

Petra T. Shattuck and Jill Norgren, *Partial Justice: Federal Indian Law in a Liberal Constitutional System*

Alan Hunt, *Reading Dworkin Critically*

Forthcoming:

Mortimer Sellers, *An Ethical Education: Community and Morality in the Multicultural University*

The Ethics of Liberal Democracy

Morality and Democracy
in Theory and Practice

Edited with an Introduction by

Robert Paul Churchill

BERG
Oxford / Providence, USA

Published in 1994 by

Berg Publishers, Ltd.

Editorial offices:
150 Cowley Road, Oxford OX4 1JJ, UK
221 Waterman Street, Providence, RI 02906, U.S.A.

© Robert Paul Churchill

All rights reserved.
No part of this publication may be reproduced
in any form or by any means without the permission
of Berg Publishers.

British Library Cataloguing in Publication Data
A CIP catalogue record for this book is available from the British Library.

ISBN: 0 85496 099 6

Library of Congress Cataloging-in-Publication Data
A CIP catalogue record for this book is available from the Library of
Congress.

ISBN: 0 85496 099 6

Printed and bound by WBC, Bridgend, Mid Glam.

Dedicated to the memory of Alfred Emil Koenig, 1915–1988,
philosopher and founder of
The Institute for Advanced Philosophic Research

Contents

Acknowledgments

Earlier versions of all but one of the essays published here were among the forty-four papers presented at a conference on "The Ethics of Democracy" and held in August 1991 at Estes Park, Colorado. This conference was sponsored by REALIA: The Institute for Advanced Philosophic Research, and I am grateful to REALIA for making possible a stimulating but collegial and supportive environment in which philosophical arguments could be presented and discussed. I am grateful as well to all of those who gave unselfishly of their time and energy to make the conference a success, and I wish to recognize especially the help of Walt Koenig, Jane Koenen, Jack Weir, Dale Wilt Evans, Larry DeSaulniers, and Peter Redpath, and my wife, Eileen Churchill, whose help with the final editing was a godsend. Finally, special mention must be made of the invaluable assistance of Rebecca Churchill, an Oberlin student and my daughter, who worked as my research assistant for the summer of 1991, and without whose sound judgment and good cheer it would have been impossible to organize the conference.

Versions of eleven of these essays have appeared in *Contemporary Philosophy*, the journal of REALIA, and I am grateful to Jack Weir, editor-in-chief, and to the editorial board for permission to reprint some articles and to publish others following further revision. Although Gordon Graham did present his paper at the conference, a revised version was first published in the *International Journal of Moral and Social Studies*, Vol. 7 no. 2 (Summer 1992). I am grateful to both Gordon Graham and to the journal's editor, Dr. Sybil Wolfram, for permitting it to be reprinted in this collection. Lisa M. Heldke was not able to attend the conference on "The Ethics of Democracy," and her article was first published in *Social Theory and Practice*, Vol. 17 no. 3, pp. 349–368. I am grateful to Lisa Heldke, to Peter Dalton, editor-in-chief, and to the editorial board of *Social Theory and Practice* for granting permission to reprint the article in this anthology. Special thanks also to two of my colleagues in the department of philosophy, Andrew Altman and David DeGrazia, who read and commented on many of the manuscripts before a book proposal was sent to Berg Publishers and who offered technical assistance in transforming a multitude of word processing programs into a single electronic file. Finally, I am grateful for the constructively critical review of the entire manuscript arranged by Andrew Altman as Series Editor for Berg Publishers.

WASHINGTON, D.C.
APRIL 1992

Introduction

In the last several years, we have witnessed, indeed, continue to witness, momentous victories on the world stage for liberty, for human rights, and for market economies. Historically all of these have been associated with democracy, so it is hardly surprising that democracy is also emerging as the political system of choice around the globe.

Does the development of liberal democracy represent the "end of history," in the sense that this form or system of government is the only one free from the internal contradictions that have caused all previous systems to be supplanted by alternatives? Is it true that there can be no improvement upon the *ideal* of liberal democracy? These are the controversial claims Francis Fukayama seeks to defend in his *The End of History and the Last Man* (1992, p. xi). Whether or not Fukayama's extreme claims are justifiable (or even meaningful), it is undeniable that democratic government has sprung beyond the boundaries of its North America and Western Europe strongholds into new, and formerly alien domains of society and culture. People in increasing numbers are turning to democracy as the "best" system of government. Some have fairly realistic expectations about what democracy may be able to accomplish in their countries, others seem to be turning to it unthinkingly, as a panacea for all of their social and political ills, or alternatively, as simply the governmental system of last resort. Obviously these processes of democratization are of vital concern to those in the "second" and "third worlds" who stand to gain or lose from them. But friends of liberty and democracy in the "first world" – concerned laypersons, academicians, theorists, policy-makers; indeed, anyone with a keen interest in the prospects for democracy and the stability of regional and international politics – also will be watching these developments with great interest.

It is to be expected that the historical processes presently at work will give rise to an even more pressing need for intellectual and theoretical discussions of democracy, both for those experimenting with democracy and for witnesses of change who consequently feel more keenly the need to reexamine the democratic systems in their homelands. Such concerns over the merits and demerits of democratic systems can be divided conveniently into two kinds: the concern with the theoretical *justification* of democracy, that is, the demonstration of its rightness, and secondly, with the *vindication* of particular institutions and processes – the demonstration

that desirable states of affairs are the probable consequences of their operation (Cohen, 1972, p. 609). It is precisely in the spirit of such a reexamination of the issues of democracy's justification and vindication that the
essays making up *The Ethics of Liberal Democracy* have been written. It is
fortuitous that as political changes pointing toward democracy have
swept across Eastern Europe, the former Soviet Union, and much of the
rest of the world, a vigorous debate on the foundations of liberal democracy has been taking place on its "homefront." This debate has been
sparked by the rising influence, both within and without traditional
social and political theory, of the methodologies and views of postmodernism and feminism, as well as by the formation of communitarianism
and the communitarian and feminist critiques of liberalism. Some of the
sharpest points in this debate over the justification and vindication of liberal democracy have been captured in this collection of essays.

Before proceeding to issues of justification or vindication, however, a
reader might be warranted in asking for a straightforward description of
democracy. Shouldn't we distinguish the descriptive, conceptual aspects
of democracy from normative, prescriptive arguments about its value? In
fact, unless some attention is given to what democracy is before turning
to its assessment, we can hardly be confident that those debating its ethical status will be attacking or defending the same thing. In addition,
greater clarity about the definitional conditions for democracy will help
to remove some glaring but nettlesome confusions. Indeed, perhaps we
can dispose of three common errors at the outset.

One error concerns the confusion over democracy and its outcomes.
Despite the temptation, it is no more reasonable to judge a decision, or
outcome, right and legitimate *just because* it was arrived at democratically
than it is to pronounce a political system democratic because of the quality of the outcomes it produces – unless, of course, we wish to adopt
some senseless tautology to the effect that a law or policy is good for the
people because it was made by the people. But such a claim is foolishness
in the extreme. Democratic polities do make bad laws, and disastrous
decisions on occasion, even if, in general, self-rule may have some salu-
tary effect on character. Whatever set of institutions, processes, capacities
and attitudes, liberties and rights make up democracy, democracy is not
the same thing as the end results of these in action. It is always an open
question whether the outcomes of democratic government are wise or
foolish, moral or immoral, and so forth.

A second common confusion concerns the relationship between
democratic polity and the economic order associated with it. It is certainly true that many, if not most, democracies exist in countries also

possessing, to a greater or less degree, free enterprise capitalist economies. But there is no inherent contradiction involved in a democracy having a socialist economy, or some other non-market economy, unlike the inherent contradiction involved in a democracy with a dictatorial ruler, for example, or a democracy without any freedom of participation. Alec Nove (1983), Joseph Schumpeter (1950) and Charles Taylor (1971), among others, have argued strenuously for the justification of democratic socialism over liberal democracy.

Finally, a third confusion concerns the relationship between the concepts of democracy and of limited, or constitutional government. No doubt, we might refer to a people's self-rule, or to the representation of their interests by elected officials in terms of certain rights of speech, press, assembly, vote, and so forth. It is quite reasonable to suppose, therefore, that a minimum of participation rights is necessary before democracy exists. But possession of these *participation rights* is not incompatible with majoritarian decisionmaking or even with a majoritarianism that enacts legislation invasive of other human rights or that seeks to deny the rights of members of various minorities. (Such a majority might even try to remove the rights of participation of a minority, thereby attempting to redefine the "people" entitled to self-government.) For this reason there is no inherent contradiction in the concept of a democracy unlimited in power; indeed, as John Stuart Mill ([1859] 1976) aptly noted, a democracy could become a "tyranny of the majority." There is to be sure, a logical contradiction in the conception of a *liberal democracy* as involving a tyranny of a majority, but that is because this conception of government, about which I shall say more below, adds to democracy certain justifying principles of liberty, of limited power, or justice, generally associated with liberalism.

But even after disposing of these errors and returning to the task of defining democracy, we find that the way ahead is studded with difficulties more subtle in their challenges. Of course, everyone knows that democracy means "rule by the people," but this shibboleth seems ambiguous at best, and vacuous at worst. It is not at all easy to say exactly what "rule by the people" allows or prohibits, or whether this "definition," even if elucidated, could capture the conditions either necessary or sufficient for democracy. Part of this difficulty results from the significant differences among the systems that have historically been regarded as democratic – the difference, for example, between the Athenian Assembly meeting on the Pynx and the representative body known as Parliament. Robert Dahl identifies four different sources for democracy: the governing assembly of classical Greece, a republican tradition derived from Rome and the Italian city-states of the Renaissance, the modern ideas and institutions of representative government, and the logic of political equality (1989, p. 13). But, of course, recognizing these different sources of democracy does not get us closer to identifying its necessary and sufficient conditions.

Fortunately, or unfortunately, there has been no dearth of theorists who have sought to identify the "essence" of democracy. Even a cursory review of candidates for necessary attributes produces such differences as the following: the opportunity of every citizen to contribute to government decisions (e.g., Lindsay, 1929); rule in accord with the consent of the majority (Ely, 1980); institutional arrangements according to which the only persons permitted to make political decisions are those who have acquired this power by means of a competitive struggle for the people's vote (Schumpeter, 1950); a form of government in which citizens participate equally in making decisions which concern them all (Cohen, 1972); a process of making collective and binding decisions in which citizens have equal opportunities to express their preferences and equal weight in determining the outcomes (Dahl, 1979); and the holding of regular elections, universal suffrage, and the provision of civil liberties essential to the election process itself (Bowie and Simon, 1977).

The essential, or necessary conditions of democracy have even been thought to be certain personal capacities or attitudes and dispositions: the voluntarism and disposition to form "voluntary associations" identified by Alexis de Tocqueville ([1835–40], 1945), for example, or the "participant" attitudes that constitute a "frame of mind" or a "civic culture" (e.g., Barbu, 1956; Almond and Verba, 1965); the capacity and will of citizens to engage in deliberative processes determining the public good (e.g., Tussman, 1960); or even a way of life, as Dewey believed, encompassing "a faith in the capacities of human nature; faith in human intelligence and in the power of pooled and cooperative experience" (Dewey [1940] 1972, p. 578).

If we wish to know whether democratic institutions have much chance of surviving in newly proclaimed "democratic" countries, then some help may be found in efforts to single out, from the category of putative "necessary conditions," those that are truly *preconditions* or *prerequisites* in the sense that the absence of even one would spell the doom of democratic reform. Thus some of the characteristics and attitudes identified by de Tocqueville and Dewey, or those comprising a "civic culture" may constitute at some level, at least, such preconditions. Likewise, many empirical studies purport to establish correlations between economic development and the incidence and stability of democratic systems

(Beitz, 1981), although there is much debate over the validity of these studies (e.g., Lively, 1975).

But even if some conditions can be isolated as necessary prerequisites, this will hardly end the debate over what other institutions, processes, capacities or freedoms and abilities are necessary and sufficient for "true" democracy. My point is that, despite the need to recognize that questions about the "descriptive" and "normative" aspects of democracy often raise different concerns, and therefore often require different answers, we cannot develop an empirical "science" of democracy sanitized from the infection of value. At the conceptual level we cannot disentangle our notions of democracy from such logically related notions as those of freedom, participation, representation, and self-reliance. And embedded in notions of the latter kind are value-laden assumptions about the self-perceptions we believe persons should have of their own influence and efficacy as well as the ways in which individuals should interact in social settings. Thus, both at the most rudimentary stages of inquiry and at the furthest reaches of debate, we realistically cannot expect to separate completely an understanding of what democracy is from our beliefs about what democracy ought to be. The question, then, is this: can we proceed to issues of the justification and vindication of democracy without tripping continually over problems of definition? I believe that we can if we are willing to employ a simple strategy and to accept a certain amount of definitional uncertainty.

Surely some readers surveying the above list of putative conditions must have been thinking that there may be a number of different ways for a polity to be democratic. A theorist's insistence that some feature, to the exclusion of others, *truly* defines democracy, may say more about that author's *ideal* vision than her acuity as a political analyst or observer. Hence, we might well get around the problem of definition by employing a stratagem familiar to philosophers since Wittgenstein articulated the notion of "family resemblances" in *Philosophical Investigations* (1958, p. 32e). The members of a family can resemble each other in a variety of ways: facial features (blue eyes, cleft chin, dimpled cheeks, ruddy complexion), height, hair color, voice, way of laughing, gestures when talking, gait, and so on. Yet, in a family of say, eight members, not all of these features will be present in each individual. And possibly the members of the family will have no single distinguishing feature in common. Nevertheless, they could all be unmistakably members of the same family. Likewise, democracies need have no distinguishing feature in common (unless we hold onto the vacuous "rule of the people"), nor need they share exactly the same central features. Nevertheless, I think we would want to say that a political system must have at least one – and probably two or three core features – from among those identified in the list above (or a list improved by a more scrupulous survey), before we would recognize it as a member of the "family" of democracies. We would need to recognize, of course, that unlike human families, membership in the family of democracy can be a matter of degree and that, again unlike the human case, there is nothing like a final genetic test for membership. Nevertheless, this stratagem allows us to proceed with a general, if vague, consensus over which states have democratic governments, and it places the burden where it belongs: anyone who insists that one or more features are *essential* for democracy must base that claim on something more than a definition or descriptive account of democracy. This person must enter the arena of "justification" and show why a political system possessing those particular features better instantiates, or better serves, the values we believe democracy should protect or promote in the first place. (This is the course undertaken by Robert Dahl who in *Democracy and Its Critics* – the most comprehensive study of recent decades – frankly appeals to "ideal standards" in setting forth his "criteria for a democratic process" (1989, pp. 108–114)).

Having considered these definitional and conceptual issues, it is important to add that the authors of the essays published here are interested primarily in what may be called *liberal democracies*, that is to say, democratic systems that incorporate additional features presumably justified by a set of moral precepts and assumptions known generally as liberalism. Thus those concerned in Part I with foundational issues, especially the ethical grounds for democracy, have as a target some model or theory of liberal democracy. And the authors in Part II concerned with the criticism or vindication of practical aspects of presently working democracies also have in mind either the United States or the major democracies of Western Europe.

As any adequate explanation of liberalism as a philosophy or ideology would have to be accepted as a fair characterization by its critics (e.g., C.B. Macpherson 1977, Alasdair MacIntyre 1981, and William M. Sullivan 1982) as well as its latter day formulators and defenders (e.g., Rawls 1971, Ackerman 1980, and William A. Galston 1991), it is an undertaking too large and hazardous for a mere introduction. Nevertheless, we can identify the salient features of the social and governmental systems most often spoken of as "liberal democracies," provided that we recognize that the full realization of these represents aspiration for the *ideal* as much as actual practice. Thus, liberal democracies all incorporate, to some extent, virtually all of the "defining" features of democracy identified above. They add to these, however, several important features: (1) explicit limitations on majoritarian power and increased protection of individual rights, both civil and political; (2) a strong association with a capitalistic economy, either through explicit government policies and institutions that abet and support market mechanisms, or alternatively, through regulations that redistribute profits in support of some aspects of a welfare state, or (most likely) some mixed combination; and (3) neutrality among competing conceptions of the good life, that is, equal respect for citizen efforts to freely pursue individual interests up to the point at which the pursuit of private preference may conflict with the rights or protected liberties of other members of the polity. It is some ideal of liberal democracy toward which most democratic reformers in Eastern Europe, Asia, and Latin America aim, and it is the advance of liberal democracy, Fukayama claims, that is bringing about the end of history (1992).

The essays in Part I, "Justifying Democracy? De/Reconstructing Democracy?", raise directly the issue of the justification of democracy. They consider either the ethical principles that have been thought to provide the moral foundations for democracy, or they examine fundamental assumptions that ground arguments for democracy as the best form of government. Thus the essays of Part I are concerned with the broadest possible, or most inclusive basis for justifying democracy, and thus, are representative of the best of the late twentieth-century debate over democratic theory. The authors of Part I draw variously on the insights and theoretical perspectives of feminism, postmodernism, and communitarianism, as well as the most recent research in political theory and social philosophy. Specific introductions for each article will be found in the Foreword for Part I.

Rather than evaluate the broadest principles of democratic theory, the essays of Part II, "Democracy, the Individual, and Moral Community," direct our attention to serious problems with some aspect of democracy understood as crucial to the successful practice of liberal democracy. The critical issues address the social role of institutionalized rights and freedoms, such as popular participation, voting, freedom of speech, and freedom of conscience, as well as institutional efforts to increase rational deliberation in the political process and to reduce discrimination based on gender. Some essays in this part are informed by salient scholarship in feminism, postmodernism, and the communitarian debate; some are informed, as necessary, by personal experience with the limitations of democratic processes, or by specialized knowledge in a domain such as legal opinion on first amendment freedoms.

The essays in Part III are concerned with the making of public policy in liberal democracies, ranging from the regulation of drugs to the decision to wage war, and the protection of environmental quality. The authors of these essays are troubled either by the defects of standard, accepted practices for making public policy (e.g., the economistic model of utility maximization) or by the absence of any policy process that meets even minimal standards of rationality and coherence. Each author accepts the assumption (acceptable as well to the authors of the essays in Parts I and II) that liberal democratic policymaking processes should meet ethical criteria in terms of process itself, and not merely in outcome. Some consider the opportunities for, and difficulties in the way of, making the policy process both more democratic and more ethical; others present proposals for the improvement, ethically, of the policies with which they are concerned.

The essays of Parts I, II, and III thus represent concern and controversy over the three main areas in which liberal democracy needs reappraisal: the morality of its theoretical foundations, the quality of its key institutions and processes, and the morality of its public policy. The authors address these various issues with their own respective styles and voices, as befits the ideal of open and diverse debate in the spirit of liberalism. One will find here much sustenance for intellectual hunger about liberal democracy, and sufficient provender for rich debates over the form of democracy for the future. Read in good spirit.

References

Ackerman, Bruce. 1980. *Social Justice in the Liberal State*, Yale University Press, New Haven.

Almond, Gabriel A. and Verba, Sidney. 1965. *The Civic Culture: Political Attitudes and Culture in Five Nations*, Little, Brown, Inc., Boston.

Barbu, Zevedei. 1956. *Democracy and Dictatorship*, Grove Press, New York.

Beitz, Charles. 1981. "Democracy in Developing Societies" in Peter G. Brown and Henry Shue (eds.) *Boundaries*, Rowman and Littlefield, Totowa, NJ, pp. 177–208.

Bowie, Norman E. and Simon, Robert L. 1977. *The Individual and the Political Order*, Prentice-Hall, Englewood Cliffs, NJ.

Cohen, Carl. 1972. "The Justification of Democracy" in Carl Cohen (ed.) *Communism, Fascism, and Democracy*, Random House, New York, pp. 608–628.

Dahl, Robert A. 1979. "Procedural Democracy," *Philosophy, Politics and Society*, Peter Laslett and James Fishkin (eds.) Yale University Press, New Haven.

______ 1989. *Democracy and Its Critics*, Yale University Press, New Haven and London.

de Tocqueville, Alexis. [1835–40] 1945. *Democracy in America*, ed. by Phillips Bradley, trans. Henry Reeve and revised by Francis Bowen. Alfred A. Knopf, New York

Dewey, John. [1940] 1972. *The Philosopher of the Common Man*, excerpted in Carl Cohen (ed.) *Communism, Fascism and Democracy*, Random House, New York, pp. 581–584.

Ely, John Hart. 1980. *Democracy and Distrust*, Harvard University Press, Cambridge, MA and London.

Fukayama, Francis. 1992. *The End of History and the Last Man*, Basic Books, New York.

Galston, William A. 1991. *Liberal Purposes*, Cambridge University Press, Cambridge and New York.

Lindsay, Alexander D. 1929. *The Essentials of Democracy*, 2nd ed., The Clarendon Press, Oxford.

Lively, Jack. 1975. *Democracy*, Basil Blackwell, Oxford.

MacIntyre, Alasdair. 1981. *After Virtue*, University of Notre Dame Press, Notre Dame, IN.

Macpherson, C.B. 1977. *The Life and Times of Liberal Democracy*, Oxford University Press, Oxford and London.

Mill, John Stuart [1859] 1976. *On Liberty*, Gertrude Himmelfarb (ed.) Penguin Books, Harmondsworth, UK.

Nove, Alec. 1983. *The Economics of Feasible Socialism*, George Allen & Unwin, London.

Rawls, John. 1971. *A Theory of Justice*, Harvard University Press, Cambridge, MA.

Schumpeter, Joseph. 1950. *Capitalism, Socialism and Democracy*, 3rd ed., Harper & Brothers, New York.

Sullivan, William M. 1982. *Deconstructing Public Philosophy*, University of California Press, Berkeley.

Taylor, Charles. 1971. "The Agony of Economic Man," *Essays on the Left*, L. Lapierre, Jack McLeod, Charles Taylor and Walter Young (eds.) McClelland and Stewart, Toronto.

Tussman, Joseph. 1960. *Obligation and the Body Politic*, Oxford University Press, Oxford.

Wittgenstein, Ludwig. 1958. *Philosophical Investigations*, 3rd ed. trans. by G. E. M. Anscombe, Macmillan Co., New York.

Justifying Democracy?
De/Reconstructing Democracy?

FOREWORD

In the opening essay, "The Moral Basis of Democracy," Gordon Graham examines efforts to ground the preference for democracy in morality. More specifically, Graham examines the moral basis for the democratic claim that everyone is entitled to a say in government. There are two versions of this entitlement claim, Graham believes. One version, populism, maintains that everyone's say on social and political questions is equally valuable. But the most plausible arguments for populism, Graham finds, including utilitarian appeals to preferences as the basis for political choice, are clearly wanting. The second version of the entitlement claim, self-determination, Graham interprets as a claim about the right of citizens to equal political participation. But under Graham's scrutiny, arguments for this claim also fail to provide a moral basis for democracy. Nevertheless, Graham concludes on an optimistic note about the beneficial effects of the dispersal of power through universal suffrage.

Ardent supporters of liberal democracy are unlikely to be consoled by Graham's conclusion. But they will be hard-pressed to find a more defensible interpretation of the entitlement claim or to find weaknesses in Graham's arguments. Thus Graham poses a serious challenge for theorists who argue that democracy is the natural form of government for autonomous citizens. Yet, it might be objected that, even if we find insupportable the claim that everyone is entitled to participate in government, as Graham claims, nevertheless democracy might be justified as the system that best promotes the development of individuals capable of autonomous choice or best protects the autonomous choices individuals make in the various dimensions of their lives.

In the very next selection, "To Rule in No Matters, To Obey in All," Russell Hardin questions the fit between autonomy and government in libertarian, contractarian, and utilitarian democratic theories. He finds that autonomy is problematic in each theory, but in distinctively different ways. All of these theories do presume, however, that democracy is justified, at least in part, as the system of government that gives greatest play to personal autonomy. But, Hardin argues, there is no direct connection between the outcomes of democratic processes, which result necessarily from collective choice, and individual autonomy. In effect, the exercise by some citizens of their individual autonomy, understood as the opportunity to direct one's life by effecting significant political decisions, may adversely effect the opportunities for autonomous choice on the part of other members of the *demos*. In an ironic comment that foreshadows his conclusion, Hardin notes that "the autonomy, the self-governance that arises from the moral self has little room to play in politics."

It may be that, as a matter of fact, democratic polities generally do better than other systems of government in protecting, or even developing, individual autonomy. But can political theorists rely on autonomy as a justification for democracy? In each case – with libertarianism, social contract theory, and utilitarianism – Hardin argues that democracy can be justified only by fulfilling what he calls "institutionalist" requirements. Theorists must be concerned with the *design of government structures* in ways that best protect rights, result in just outcomes for citizens, or maximize preference satisfaction, depending on the political outcomes each theory regards as paramount. In each case, Hardin argues, theorists cannot demonstrate a connection – either conceptual or causal – between individual autonomy and the required institutional design for democracy.

For example, libertarian democrats claim that autonomy justifies the respect we accord liberty rights and that a democratic polity is justified insofar as it protects these rights. But in Hardin's view the libertarian's model of social interaction is oversimplified and fails to take the problem of collective interactions into account. When we try to straighten out the complex ways interests compete in collectivities we discover that there are no a priori correct rights to stipulate, Hardin claims. Instead, we find that rights are collectively determined, and therefore contingently derived, and subject to change. Thus, while Hardin does not deny that a state's protection of rights affords it some legitimacy, he denies the libertarians' claim that rights mark out and thus guarantee *a priori* realms of autonomous action for individuals.

Turning to contractarian theories, such as those of Rawls (1971) and Beitz (1989), Hardin argues that they are resolutely "institutionalist." That is, contractarian theories attempt to specify principles of justice that define the overall structure of institutions. An interest in autonomy may influence the selection of principles in the hypothetical contract situation, Hardin notes, but contractarians tend to believe that once principles are selected, the institutions justified by them possess a "monopoly" on autonomy. Contractarians thus are not open to the appeals of solitary individuals who complain that the resulting institutions infringe on their autonomy.

As for utilitarian democratic theories, Hardin distinguishes between the utilitarian interest in accurately representing aggregate interests and the interest in enhancing individuals' understanding of their interests – to make them more effectively autonomous. With respect to the first interest, Hardin notes that public choice theory does not support the belief that democratic procedures accurately represent aggregate interests. Next Hardin subjects to exacting scrutiny the utilitarian claim that democratic participation develops in us greater capacities for autonomous choice. Tracing this interest back to the political philosophy of Mill (1859; 1861), Hardin argues that the interest in participatory democracy is institutionalist, not individualist, for Mill's concern is with the *design of government institutions* that will draw people into participating.

Hardin does not deny the utilitarian's claim that we can enhance autonomous choosing by creating opportunities for it. On the contrary, the upshot of Hardin's criticisms is that individual autonomy cannot be used to justify democracy as the best political system. Democratic institutions may support or even produce autonomy, or they may require sacrifices of autonomy – after all, successful institutions must require or proscribe behaviors needed to maintain themselves. In any case, the connection between democracy and autonomy is only contingent and never necessary. Still, Hardin admits that democracy may be practically the best available form of government, both in offering the possibility of exercising one's citizenship to affect one's fate and (as Graham also notes) in reducing the threat of government to autonomy in those other spheres of our lives in which we do most of our living.

It is difficult to predict what specific responses autonomy theorists might make to Hardin's challenges. Some may contest the use Hardin makes of collective decision theory to support his conclusion that, because democracy is grounded on collective choices, "autonomy is [also] an institutional creation" in democratic polities. Some may try to show that Hardin has missed the conceptual connections between self-government and autonomous choice, and still others may argue that Hardin errs in claiming that the institutions arising from contractual procedures will betray the autonomy that partly defines the conditions under which individuals would contract for principles of justice. Whatever the response, ensuing debates will be greatly enriched by Hardin's critique.

Liberal democrats not yet prepared to accept social contract theory as a justification for democracy will take a keen interest in the next selection in Part I, "False Stability and Defensive Justification in Rawlsian Liberalism," by David Anderson. Anderson focuses specifically on the work of arguably the most famous advocate of liberalism since John Stuart Mill. Since the publication in 1971 of the now classic *A Theory of Justice*, the social contract theory of the philosopher John Rawls has been thought by many to offer the best ethical foundation for democracy. The principles of justice derived from Rawls's "original position" – the equal liberty principle and the equal opportunity and difference principles – have been thought both to necessitate and to justify democratic institutions and procedures.

Drawing on the extensive literature of feminist scholarship in a broad range of disciplines, David Anderson subjects Rawls's philosophy to detailed and searching criticism and he finds Rawls's philosophy to be inadequate both practically and theoretically. Anderson begins his attack with an explication of a major condition of injustice he calls "false stability." This condition occurs when a society is politically stable and yet, despite egalitarian ideals, perpetuates the systematic domination of some members by others. Such a society, Anderson notes, will be stable and inhumane at the same time.

Anderson proceeds on the factual basis that conditions of domination, oppression, and exploitation are sufficiently severe to warrant the ascription of false stability to present social life; and furthermore, that Rawls's principles, even as amended by the 1980's essays and even if perfectly applied, could not overcome sexism and other forms of domination. This part of Anderson's argument – his practical critique of Rawls – is conditional, since he must assume that the feminist, and predominately "socialist feminist," accounts of injustice are true or at least highly plausible.

At the second, theoretical level, Anderson scrutinizes the way Rawls has attempted to incorporate facts of moral psychology and data from the social sciences into his theory of justice. Here Anderson finds serious methodological difficulties in Rawls's arguments. The brunt of Anderson's criticism is that the supposedly neutral decision-procedures by which principles of justice are selected actually perpetuate the practices of domination and oppression prevalent in present society. For support in his criticism, Anderson discusses the ways in which dominating and exploitive relationships distort the capacities and personalities of both victims and victimizers. Indeed, one of the most intriguing parts of Anderson's argument is his claim that fear and anxiety would motivate the selection of principles even

14

behind a "veil of ignorance," and therefore, that the very structure of Rawls's argument denies the feminine in the original position. Thus Rawls cannot explain how the principles of justice needed to end the injustice of "false stability" could be derived from his theory.

Readers will judge for themselves, of course, how damaging are Anderson's criticisms for a justification of democracy based on Rawls's theory of justice. They will find that Anderson offers brief retorts to the most likely of "Rawlsian" responses. But readers also may be troubled by Anderson's exposure of deeper difficulties facing attempts to justify democracy through social contract theory. Anderson's argument shows that if the justification of democracy requires neutrality in its strictest sense – that is, that political institutions, policies and laws not be biased in favor of any particular conception of the good life – then it will be extremely difficult to devise decision procedures capable of according to each citizen the equal respect required by neutrality. One possible response to this difficulty might be to subject the broadest principles of liberalism to reexamination and possible reformulation. Indeed, this is the project, in varying ways, of the two remaining essays in Part I.

In "The Self, Difference, and Democratic Theory," Michael Howard investigates the relationship between conceptions of the self that define what is most fundamentally important for individual persons, and democratic theory as a theory of how we, as a collectivity, ought to govern ourselves. How do shared visions of justice arise from the diversity of individual interests when these interests reflect not just preferences but our deepest commitments? Adequately answering this question is a major task for any democratic theory grounded in ethics.

Howard takes the view that in the public domain, at least, each person defines his or her own self in terms of what appears as most fundamental and compelling: what counts for each person as "the good." What, then, is to be done about the reality of difference and the specter raised by irreconcilable interests and incommensurable ends? Given pluralism, is there any normative basis for a non-coerced and shared conception of justice?

Howard accepts many of the communitarian, postmodern and postmodern feminist critiques of political liberalism. He acknowledges that former efforts to forge "consensus" in liberal democracies have been based largely on efforts – through classism, racism, and sexism, for example – to suppress the effects of difference in the public arena. Yet Howard rejects the relativism and pessimism toward which these critiques incline. Even if traditional political liberalism is unsatisfactory as an ethical basis for democracy, Howard believes that we can move from pluralism to a shared conception of justice.

Thus Howard advocates a new approach he calls "ontological liberalism." It is "ontological" because it attempts boldly to face the challenge of basing a theory of justice on an account, claims Howard, of "the kind of being a self is, and the goods that are real for it." Recognizing that the magnitude of this project requires much more than a single essay, Howard devotes the remainder of his contribution to outlining, through critical and insightful commentary, the work lying ahead for those democratic theorists who would follow his lead. Howard's discussion here, as elsewhere in the essay, is highly provocative as he suggests how "ontological liberalism" would mediate between respect for individual differences and the need for political consensus in a democracy.

In "A (Somewhat) Communitarian (Partial) Reformulation of Liberalism," Maurice Wade also is concerned with the adequacy of liberalism as a moral foundation for democracy. More specifically, Wade is troubled by what he sees as the corrosive effects of public policymaking on the capacity of deontological liberals to defend democratic institutions. Indeed, Wade goes so far as to aver that the predominant economistic conception of public policy impoverishes liberalism's "definitive moral commitments." How can liberalism recover those moral commitments? Interestingly enough, by adapting itself to two of the crucial insights of communitarianism, Wade claims.

Drawing on Michael Oakshott's (1975) distinction between a *societas* and a *universitas*, Wade argues that deontological liberals are strongly attracted to the vision of social life as *societas*: a society organized to facilitate the purposes of individual members and neutral toward different individual values and ends. The theoretical perspective dominating public policy, Wade argues, reinforces this view of social life as *societas*. The economistic theory of public choice, with its vision of the individual as *homo economicus* and its emphasis on efficiency, maintains that individuals will support political parties and vote for candidates for the same reason that they expend resources in the market – to maximize personal satisfaction.

Yet, Wade asks, why should deontological liberals insist on political neutrality or on the provision of institutions to assist individuals in meeting their goals? Can it be denied that the "definitive commitment underlying liberalism's social ideal" is the commitment to the "special moral status for rational self-determination"? Indeed, Wade argues that the commitment to neutrality makes little sense without a deeper commitment to autonomy as a "meta-value." Thus, at the level at which principles of justice apply, liberalism must presuppose a conception of social life as a *universitas*: liberal society as bound by the pursuit of some minimal, communal purposes. Liberal democracies must therefore accept two communitarian theses, Wade believes. First, society must protect conceptions of the good that are rationally self-determined, but discriminate against conceptions of the good that are not freely chosen or that undermine autonomy. Second, contrary to the view of individuals in society as atomistic units, the link between individuals and society is partly constitutive in nature. The upshot of this, Wade claims, is that if we are to value human capacities, then we must value to the same degree the social arrangements that are necessary for their development, protection, and nurturance. But, Wade points out, this is precisely why deontological liberals should reject the economistic conception of public policy. The economistic conception emphasizes maximizing preference satisfaction even when doing so may subvert the social conditions that ground and make possible the abilities of individuals to freely pursue their conceptions of the good.

1
The Moral Basis of Democracy

Gordon Graham

What is the moral basis of a preference for democratic institutions? Though most people unhesitatingly suppose that there must be an answer to this question, it is in fact rather difficult to find. To begin with there is the problem of going beyond the popular use of "democracy" (meaning simply "the most desirable form of government"), and providing a substantial characterization of a distinguishable form of election, representation and decisionmaking. The difficulty is to find a precise formulation for two very general ideas at work in the democratic ideal, namely, that everyone is entitled to a say in government and that the will of the majority should prevail. Both of these ideas generate further difficulties. Those who believe in the first must answer the question, "everyone of whom?" This is the familiar "problem of inclusion." Those who believe in majority rule must resolve its potential conflict with rationality. If, in weighing up the pros and cons of an issue, the individual voter may, through ignorance or prejudice, arrive at a demonstrably mistaken conclusion, can a majority of voters not also do so? And if so, how could their being in a majority improve matters? This is the basis of the familiar, much discussed, paradox of democracy, and closely connected with nineteenth century fears about the tyranny of popular government.

Important though these problems are, they are not directly my concern here. Since these two leading democratic ideas are connected, what we say about one will have a bearing upon the other, but I want to focus upon just one aspect of the first of them, and ask what the moral basis of everyone's entitlement to a say in government might be. There are at least two familiar contenders, populism and self-determination, which need to be examined in turn.

Populism

By "populism" I shall mean the belief that at the most fundamental level everyone's say on the social and political questions of the day is equally valuable. If this is correct, it follows that no one has any special claims to political wisdom, and hence that everyone is entitled to an equal say. Populism in this sense is an anti-aristocratic doctrine, closely allied to political egalitarianism. That is to say, whereas the aristocratic ideals that dominated European politics up to the end of the eighteenth century subscribed to the belief in a ruling class, i.e., a class specially fitted to rule, the French Revolution signalled a rejection of this belief, and an assertion of the fitness for everyone and anyone to take part in government. With this belief came the desire to sweep away all social distinctions as irrelevant to the proper ordering of society. In the terminology of the ancien régime, the distinction between the first and third estates was no longer politically relevant (if indeed it ever had been).

This huge change in political thinking did not occur overnight, of course, and its origins are to be found very far back in the history of ideas. But the French Revolution, or at least the popular perception of its significance, gave dramatic historical expression to it. The change in thinking is most clearly revealed, in fact, in Paine's attack ([1791–2] 1969) on Burke's response ([1790] 1955) to that revolution, where the conception of society as an organism hierarchically ordered for the better government of all, is swept aside in favor of a belief in the fundamental moral equality of all members of society. In Paine's conception of society, it is this equality alone that is politically relevant, and every attempt on the part of a self-appointed aristocracy to deny it involves a massive effort of deception and self-deception.

There are many difficulties in Paine's view of society, and Burke's organic conception is not without its modern supporters. This is not an issue to be explored here, however, because it does not touch directly on the topic of greatest concern to this paper. I shall take the incontestable truth in populism to be this: there is no social group, to be distinguished by history, race, gender or economic status, which is "naturally" or peculiarly fitted to government such that a well-ordered society will restrict political power to that group. That is to say, in whatever way rulers are to be selected or political decisions taken, no *a priori* exclusions on grounds such as these can be justified. By itself, however, this element of populism does not imply the democratic ideal that everyone is entitled to a say in the running of the country. Strictly speaking, while oligarchy – the rule of a restricted group – has been excluded, aristocracy – the rule of the best – has not. To see this consider a parallel: the government of the prereformation Church.

The prereformation Western Christian church was hierarchically governed but (leaving aside the exclusion of women) in contrast to many other religions, there was no natural or Brahmin-like priestly class. That is to say, although the princes of the church ruled without seeking or requiring the consent of the ruled, in principle they could, and regularly did, include among their number individuals from a wide variety of racial, social and economic backgrounds. The assumption, though hardly the reality, was that anyone who was spiritually fitted could be admitted to the priesthood and the most spiritually fitted would be elevated to positions of episcopal authority. In the government of the prereformation church, therefore, a certain kind of populist egalitarianism prevailed, but it did not imply that everyone was entitled to a say in church government. On the contrary, the vast majority of Christians were excluded. In the reformation this exclusion came under attack, but the rejection of episcopal government arose not from egalitarianism alone, but a certain amplification of it – the doctrine of the priesthood of all believers. What we need to inquire, therefore, is what the corresponding doctrine might be for the idea of political democracy.

It is part of the doctrine of the priesthood of all believers that everyone is equally well placed to apprehend the nature and requirements of the divine. A parallel belief in the political case might be that everyone is equally well placed to apprehend the nature and requirements of government. In other words, on matters political everyone's opinion is equally good. But how can this be? Surely countless issues in the course of political deliberation require expertise in their answering and, as a matter of fact, some people have very silly opinions on the political questions of the day. One way of responding to this objection, very much in keeping with the spirit of democratic theory, is to make use of a sharp distinction between means and ends. On questions of political means, it may be said, expertise is indeed required. How we are to accomplish the political purposes a society sets itself is a highly complex matter. But what those purposes are is a matter for popular choice, not specialist decision. On matters concerning the ends of politics, then, the deciding factor is not what is *known*, but what is *wanted*. If this is correct, an argument in favor of democracy does seem to be generated, because the expert (whether Platonic philosopher or contemporary social scientist), whose advice may be essential in deciding upon political means, has no role to play in settling upon political ends. To locate the choice of political ends in the realm of wants introduces an egalitarian base. Different groups and individuals may truthfully claim different degrees of knowledge and understanding, but what reason could there be for members of society to agree that some one individual's or group's *desires* should prevail? The knowledge of experts makes their professional opinions authoritative, but people are their own authorities on what they want. From this we should conclude, the democrat may argue, that when it comes to settling upon political ends, as opposed to political means, everyone is entitled to a say.

This conclusion clearly rests upon the applicability of two distinctions to the democratic conduct of politics – that between political ends and political means on the one hand, and knowledge and desire on the other. In order for this argument in favor of democracy to work it must be the case that democratic procedures range only over ends and not means, and that the content of these ends is specifiable in terms of desires. Clearly there are instances of collective decisionmaking when this model appears to capture the reality adequately enough. The most widely used example is that of rules on smoking in a confined space. The rightness of permitting or forbidding smoking turns on the desires of the occupants, and an appropriate decision procedure would appear to involve an equal say for all and adherence to majority rule.

Doubts may be raised about the adequacy of the model for even this simple case,[1] but once we turn to the more complex world of political government we quickly come to see that neither of these crucial distinctions can actually be applied. Consider first the distinction between means and ends and its application to the seemingly straightforward case of raising revenue and spending it. The raising of revenue might be thought of as a means to the ends upon which it is spent. Now there are certainly plenty of "technical" questions to be asked about alternative systems of taxation, having to do with their relative efficiency and the administrative organization for their collection. But equally, questions of justice and freedom enter into the issue of their respective merits, and insofar as these involve further issues about the rights of citizens and the limits of state power, it is at the very least misleading to think that the choice of a particular tax is a purely technical question. Conversely, since some of the revenue will be spent upon its collection, there is inherent competition between these "means" and other ends. Similarly, the wider context of state spending cannot be regarded purely as a matter of ends. Spending on, say, regional investment or occupational training schemes can readily be regarded as having purely instrumental value in the pursuit of some larger aim such as the combatting of unemployment or the creation of prosperity. Here, as much as in the raising of revenue, technical questions about relative efficiency must enter into a discussion of the merits of rival programs, and these are matters requiring a measure of

1. It was Brian Barry (1965, p. 312) who first introduced this example but he too has come to think its simplicity misleading for the discussion of democracy. See "Is Democracy Special?" in Brian Barry (1989, pp.24–60).

specialized knowledge and expertise. At the same time such programs obviously entail political beliefs about the proper role of the state. To attempt to demarcate means and ends, in the way required by the argument we are considering, runs counter to political practice, even in this relatively straightforward example, since disputes about how revenue is to be raised and what it should be spent on are equally matters of public debate in a democracy.

The truth is, of course, that the distinction between means and ends is not a distinction like that between "vegetable" and "mineral," but like that between "tall" and "short," that is to say, a relative one. Any one action may be both means and end, relative to other actions and states of affairs. The striking of a match may be the means to the end of lighting a fire, lighting the fire may be a means to the end of heating the room, and heating the room may be a means to drying out the carpets. And so on. This relativity of means to ends applies just as readily to politics as to any other sphere of human conduct. Even the relation between politics and military action is not susceptible to explanation in terms of isolated means and ends. While it may seem obvious that which wars to fight is a question for politicians and how to fight them one for military strategists, insofar as war is diplomacy by other means, the decision when to go to war will be both political and strategic.

All democracies have bureaucracies, and an account needs to be given of the proper relation between the political and the administrative in a democracy as much as in any other form of government. While it may be correct to think of this relation as one between political masters and political servants (I leave aside the further question as to whether, in a liberal democracy, the rulers are properly regarded as the servants of the ruled), it is plainly mistaken to think that this master/servant relation can be understood as a matter of exclusive concern with ends and with means.

So far we have not been able to employ the distinction between means and ends to any useful purpose in exploring the moral basis of the democratic principle that in matters political everyone should have a say. One response would be that no account has yet been taken of *ultimate* ends – those actions or states of affairs that are valued in themselves and not for any further end. That there must be ultimate ends seems plain, for the chain of means/end reasoning must stop somewhere. Even if we regard this claim as obvious, however, we might still raise difficulties about its relevance in the present context. The ultimate ends of politics may turn out to be valuable chiefly as means in the lives of individual citizens – peace, prosperity, universal literacy, and public health – are obvious examples. But even should any such further difficulties be resolved or laid aside, in politics as we know it democratic debate is not restricted to the consideration of ends, and at a minimum, therefore, there is a hiatus in the suggested justification of a preference for democracy.

Suppose, however, that we concern ourselves with ultimate ends only, and that the choice of these does not involve anything that might be regarded as a technical matter over which more expert opinion has greater authority. Let us further leave aside the important issue of whether, in the absence of technical expertise, it still makes sense to speak of the choice of ultimate ends as being better or less well informed, and accept the suggestion, outlined at the start of this section, that the choice of ultimate ends is a matter of desire or preference. There is still, it seems to me, an important gap to be bridged in the argument for democracy. It is a gap that discussions of utilitarianism have commonly revealed, and some of the points that have been raised by such discussion can pertinently be raised here.

Bentham's celebrated remark that in utilitarian calculations everyone is to count for one and no one for more than one expresses something of the same egalitarian populism that the argument for democracy we are examining aims at. But any attempt to generate principles of social distribution from a utilitarian base inevitably introduces a certain inegalitarianism. Problems with the hedonistic elements in the classical version have led to a modern day version, which seeks to maximize not pleasure or happiness, about which in any given society there may be insufficient agreement, but individual preference satisfaction. The move to preference utilitarianism, however, brings with it two important complications. First, not all preferences are equally strong. Individuals may rank some of their preferences higher than others, and different individuals may rank their preferences for the same outcome differently. If we are concerned with maximizing preference satisfaction, some way must be found of making different preferences commensurable. Secondly, preferences can change in the light of increased information, and what may figure highly in the preference schedule of an individual may fall markedly with the provision of greater information. To accommodate this second complication, most versions of preference utilitarianism concern themselves not with felt preference but with informed preference. In whatever way we deal with these complications, however, an important difficulty arises.

Let us imagine that we are possessed of some calculus by which different preference schedules can be made commensurate and that we formulate principles of social distribution on this basis. The individuals whose schedules they are will, at one level, be treated equally. At the same time, depending on the strength of those preferences, the social outcome for any individual may be markedly different to that of some other. Suppose, for instance, that we are concerned with the distribution of financial resources. To distribute them with a view to maximizing preference satisfaction while accommodating strength of preference may well result in individuals receiving substantially different amounts. No doubt within the framework of preference utilitarianism, assuming always that the method of commensuration is adequate, this is right and proper. But its application to the distribution of political power will not necessarily result in a democratic system as this is generally understood. There is no reason to believe that the maximization of political preferences will require either universal suffrage or "one man, one vote." Indeed, it need not imply voting at all. If there is some alternative method by which political preferences may be recorded and measured – a highly plausible supposition – political decisions effecting a maximal distribution of social benefits and burdens may be taken by autocrats or oligarchs, provided only that they have access to that method. In short, appeal to desires and preferences as the basis of political choice does not sustain the principle that everyone should have an equal say, or even that everyone should have a *say*.

The second complication – about informed preferences – raises a similar difficulty. We know that with the provision of relevant information the political preferences of individual voters will change. We further know that, even with the widespread availability of information, the political preferences of the denizens of a democracy will not all be equally informed. It follows that, if we are attempting to maximize informed preference satisfaction, we may not have reason to distribute votes equally. This, I take it, is the thought at work in Jean-Jacques Rousseau's conception of the general will. Those who cannot leave aside purely personal preference and interest when they enter the realm of public debate, must either, as Rousseau concluded, be "forced to be free" or be disenfranchised. Again, within the general utilitarian framework this may be right and proper, but, as many have argued with respect to Rousseau, the resulting political system may diverge strikingly from what is commonly thought of as a democratic one.

The defender of democracy might argue, with some justice, that this whole approach to its justification is fundamentally wrongheaded. Populism as it has been expounded here introduces a gap between the desires or preferences of individuals and their expressed choices. It also fails to take account of the important distinction between desires and interests. What democracy seeks to secure is the idea that in political decisionmaking everyone has a right to an equal exercise of power. If so, it does not matter, from the democratic point of view, whether an individual's exercise of that power results from belief or desire, from informed or uninformed preference, anymore than it matters whether an individual's choice of clothing issues from an educated preference or not. The choice is still his or hers to make. This way of thinking, of course, pushes the argument in the direction of the second type of justification with which this paper is concerned – the appeal to self-direction.

Self-direction

To believe in the value of self-direction is to lend value to action in itself as well as to states of affairs. That is to say, if we value individuals choosing for themselves, we must continue to attach value to their actions even when we believe their choices to result in less good outcomes. Children are given money of their own to spend in the certain knowledge that they will spend some of it less well than would adults purchasing on their behalf. But an independent value attaches to their having money of their own and choosing how to spend it, and this value can override unfortunate outcomes that may result from their choice, which is not to say that it overrides any such outcome. In this simple case the possession of money is power. The child is empowered to purchase at will. Of course, elders and betters will seek to inform the child's desires and hence influence the resulting choices, but even if this educational process fails, to respect the child's right to self-determination is to protect the empowerment, and hence the possession of money.

Spending small sums of money on objects of considered desire is a clear but hardly paradigmatic case of deliberative action. The sort of utilitarianism examined in the last section, employing the terms "desire" and "preference" in the way it does, conflates within these categories both actions that are responses to felt desires, and actions that spring from a larger, more considered reflection on longer-term interest. Individual choice need not be the expression of a felt desire (or even personal preference narrowly understood), but the rational pursuit of the individual's interest. Of course, just as autocrats and oligarchs can register the desires and preferences of their subjects, so they might pursue their interests on their behalf. The difference is that, while it does not seem to matter how the satisfaction of desire or preference is secured, the pursuit of interest allows for the antipaternalist principle that individuals have the right to decide for themselves what is in their own interest. In other words, from the point of view of self-determination, what matters is not only, and perhaps not chiefly, whether individual desires and preferences are satisfied, but whether the individual whose desires and preferences they are, is involved in choosing to have them satisfied.

It has not always been obvious to social and political theorists, still less politicians, that individuals have a right to decide for themselves what is in their own best interests. Plato, for example, would not have accepted such a principle, and Mussolini expressly rejected it. Others less extreme in their views have denied it also, on the very good ground that those who are free to go to hell on their own, sometimes do indeed end up in hell when, with a little less emphasis on individualism, this might have been prevented. But for present purposes I propose to accept the antipaternalist principle in order to explore its use as a defence of democracy.

The argument might go like this. Individuals have a right to decide for themselves what is in their own best interest. Political decisions concern the common good, but the common good is usually inextricably bound up with individual interest. Therefore, individuals have a right to a say in political decisions, and since the interests of every individual within a given society are bound up with the life of the whole, every individual has a right to political participation. In short, in a society where self-direction is valued, democratic procedures will be valued precisely because the full realization of self-direction requires them.

It is important to note one respect in which this argument for democracy differs from the populist argument considered previously. Populism approaches the problem of political decisionmaking from the point of view of the ruler, and requires neutrality on the part of the state with respect to the desires and preferences of its citizens. That is to say, in performing the appropriate social calculation, the state should not concern itself with whose desires or preferences are to be weighed in the balance. The difficulty with this, as we saw, is that it allocates no necessary role in the decisionmaking to individual preference holders. The alternative, self-determination argument proceeds from the point of view of the ruled and makes their right to self-determination the basis of a distribution of political power. As David Miller has shown (Miller, 1978), this allies the concern with democracy with a more general concern for social justice, though given its origin in a belief in the value of self-determination, there is a connection with classical liberalism here that he overlooks.

On the face of it, it seems to me, this is a more promising line of argument. An essential feature of democracy is that is disperses power through the citizenry as a whole. There is a question, one that occupied nineteenth-century liberals a good deal, as to whether arguments in favor of the dispersal of power imply that it be distributed equally. This is obviously a very important question, but let us assume here that it can be answered positively. Another question, and to my mind a more important one in the present context, is whether the dispersal of power, after a certain point, is not also its destruction. To appreciate the importance of this question we have to see that the value of self-determination is respected only where the means available to the individual provide the power to effect choices, or at least affect decisions. If they do not, then – though it may still be true that the individual has a means of expressing a preferred choice – it will not be true that he or she is empowered to make that choice effective.

Now it is fairly evident that the dispersal of power through universal suffrage does not in this sense empower the individual. How any individual votes on a given issue will not determine the outcome. There is one context in which this seems not to be true – that in which an individual holds a casting vote. But even in this case, in order to effect the outcome intentionally the voter must know the existing distribution of votes. Plainly this is at most a rare occurrence, and impossible in the operation of secret ballots. It follows that under universal suffrage there is a dispersal of power, but not a distribution of it. Consequently, even if we suppose that the importance of self-determination entitles the individual to a say in those decisions that relate to his or her interests, universal suffrage does not realize this entitlement.

It might be argued that I have overstated the case. While it is true that universal suffrage denies individuals the power to effect outcomes, which is as it should be, it does not deny them the power to affect outcomes, which is all that we can reasonably require. But even this view of democratic voting procedures is incorrect. It may well be true that my right to self-determination cannot reasonably be thought to override every other consideration on every occasion, but for it to be realized at all, there must be at least some occasions when my choice is decisive in the promotion or protection of my interests, and on every occasion my choice must be an explanatory factor in the outcome. Neither of these things is true if the only power at my disposal is a vote under a system of universal suffrage. In the real world of politics, there is never an occasion on which the outcome would have been different if I had not voted as I did. And even in the peculiar case of a single vote majority, assuming a secret ballot, we cannot attribute the outcome to the action of any one voter.

The conclusion must be that the argument from self-determination is no more successful than the populist argument in justifying a preference for democracy.

28

Checks and Balances

The discussion need not end with this very negative conclusion. Something of importance can be extracted from the argument about self-determination. The widespread belief that universal suffrage gives power to the people is a myth. It is often said, correctly, that in a democracy the government can be put out of office, but it is a mistake to infer from this that anyone has the power to put them out, and to speak of "the people" here as though it were an agent with aspirations and intentions simply compounds the myth. Nevertheless, this does not alter the fact that the dispersal of power has an effect. Its effect, however, is not to empower "the people" but to disempower any one individual or group. (I shall leave aside here the troublesome case of entrenched majorities.) From any point of view, it seems to me, this is to be welcomed, and not least from the point of view of those who value self-determination. For the dispersal of power prevents the interests of the individual, insofar as these are bound up with political decisions, from being at the mercy of the will of another. Under democratic procedures, as I have argued, no one has the power to make his or her will prevail. This carries the implication that individual voters are powerless to effect their chosen purposes with respect to their own interests, but it also implies that they are likewise powerless to effect their purposes with respect to the interests of others. The dispersal of power in a democracy is thus a check upon its use and abuse. This is, of course, an implication of democracy in theory. In practice the voting behavior of groups can be coordinated into the exercise of effective power over others. This can be done intentionally by concerted action, or it can result from the exploitation of racial division, historical association, or cultural affinity. The consequence of such groupings, and their manipulation by leaders, is that the dispersal of power is reversed and the theoretical limitations of democratic procedures subverted. This does not show that democratic procedures are worthless, any more than the ability of businesses to form cartels and monopolies tells against the merits of a free market. All it shows is that there is a need for checks on power other than that which universal suffrage itself supplies. Democratic procedures alone are no guarantee against their manipulation or abandonment.

But if other checks are needed this tells us something about the justification of democracy. In this paper I have been exploring lines of argument in the hope of finding a justification of the preference for democracy that will show it to be special. To view democratic procedures as a way of dispersing political power in order to put a check upon it, is to rank it as just one among a whole range of necessary checks and balances, the justification of which is the general protection of citizens from tyranny. There may be nothing special about democracy, but this no more shows it to be valueless than the fact that locks will not keep burglars out when the windows are open shows that it is pointless to lock the door.

References

Barry, Brian. 1965. *Political Argument*, Routledge, Kegan Paul, London.
______ 1989. *Democracy, Power and Justice*, Clarendon Press, Oxford.
Burke, Edmund. [1790] 1955. *Reflections on the Revolution in France*, J. M. Dent Publishers, London.
Miller, David. 1978. "Democracy and Social Justice," *British Journal of Political Science*, Vol. 8.
Paine, Thomas. [1791–2] 1969. *The Rights of Man*, Penguin Books, Harmondsworth, UK.

2
To Rule in no Matters, To Obey in All: Democracy and Autonomy

*Russell Hardin**

Introduction

At the beginning of the seventeenth century, well before democracy became the practice or the aspiration of the peoples of Europe, Johannes Althusius was perhaps the first thinker to work out a full-blown theory of popular sovereignty and democracy. He characterized its appeal as follows: "The nature of democracy requires that there be liberty and equality of honours, which consist in these things: that the citizens alternately rule and obey, that there be equal rights for all, and that there be an alternation of private and public life so that all rule in particular matters and individuals obey in all matters" ([1603/14], 1965, p. 200).[1] This sounds consistent with the modern concern for individual autonomy. Unfortunately, Althusius's vision of the requirements of democracy suggests, in the light of contemporary experience, that democracy may be practically impossible. The striking fact of contemporary democratic practice is that most individuals rule in no matters but more nearly only obey in all matters.

Nevertheless, autonomy and democracy are thought to be closely related in most contemporary political philosophies, most of which are generally democratic in their thrusts. Autonomy takes such precedence in libertarian theory that democracy, and certainly majoritarian democracy, is in doubt. In consent or contractarian theory, autonomy also takes central place, but in contemporary versions of such theory the desirable content of the person is a matter for rational determination. In utilitarian

* I wish to thank participants in the Wednesday evening moral and political theory seminar at the University of Chicago and at the Realia Conference (Estes Park, Colorado, August 1991) for comments on a preliminary draft. I also thank the Mellon Foundation for general support.

1. For more on Althusius, see Otto Gierke. [1913] 1957. *Natural Law and the Theory of Society, 1500–1800*, trans. Ernest Barker, Beacon Press, Boston.

political theory, democracy is a means of determining collective interests but, as is often true of means in general, a plausibly inaccurate one. Similarly, for utilitarians the protection of autonomy of choice and action is a means of securing individual welfare. Again, it may be a faulty means.

There is one exception to this commitment to autonomy to some substantial degree among contemporary theories. In the recent efflorescence of communitarian political theory, autonomy is largely derided as a meaningless notion, an arid fabrication of abstract philosophizing out of touch with actual human life. Communitarian theory is insufficiently developed as yet for us to conclude very much about its commitment to democracy, although democracy at the community level might seem to be a naturally communitarian value.

It is their opposition to the vision of the abstracted individual in these other theories that seems most to unify communitarians, who lump these other theories together under the rubric of liberalism. There is some historical justification for lumping the three strands of theory together. Liberalism owes its Anglo-Saxon origins to the discovery of self-interest and its elevation to moral status as much as it owes them to any other body of ideas, such as the development of modern secular rights theory. Libertarians commonly trace their views to the rights side of Locke's arguments – in large part, no doubt, because Locke's rights are about protecting self-interest. Utilitarianism in its Hobbesian and Humean roots similarly has a central concern with self-interest that is well articulated by J. S. Mill. And contractarians, who often trace their lineage through the contract side of Locke's theory, make individual consent the principle of political morality. My consent to a political regime is likely to turn on how that regime affects my interests, although "my" becomes very abstract in contemporary contractarian thought, as it does in the putatively contractarian theory of John Rawls (1971).

In all these branches of political philosophy, it is necessary to move to the institutional level of analysis. Although we may have concern for individual autonomy, rights, or welfare, we can address the concern in practice only through political institutions. Therefore, a coherent version of any of these theories must be institutionalist. But an even stronger claim is true: a coherent libertarian, contractarian, or utilitarian political theory is constitutively institutionalist. Communitarianism may not be institutionalist to such a strong degree.

In what follows, I will address libertarian, contractarian, and utilitarian democratic theories and the role of autonomy in them. Autonomy is problematic in each of these, but in distinctively different ways. I will not separately take on communitarian theory, in part because its thrust has largely been critical and it does not yet offer articulate answers to many of the relevant questions. Consider, for example, two issues. First, does communitarian theory have practical implications for the structure of political institutions? Opening communitarian values to democratic choice may undercut them. These values may therefore have to be protected by super-majority requirements, as in the procedure for constitutional amendment in many nations. Second, in large nations comprising many communities worthy of protection, such as the United States, should we have fully proportional representation with election by status group rather than by geographical district to accommodate the multiplicity of ethnic and other interests? Perhaps not, because a system of proportional representation might accommodate ethnic minorities by splitting them off from the more eclectic parties. As a result, virtually all issues might be addressed from ethnic perspectives, so that ethnic conflict might be exacerbated while overall effectiveness of government might decline. We might say that ethnic autonomy had increased in some – ugly – sense, but we would also have to note that all were worse off as a result.

Autonomy in democratic "self" government

Before turning to the democratic theories, let us consider the possible content of the autonomy of a citizen in a democratic polity. But let us keep the discussion relatively general and not specific to any particular notion of autonomy. Rather, we should focus on what must be common to all notions of autonomy that allow it any significant bite. At a minimum, we tend to think that *autonomy entails something like control over one's own destiny or life choices*. What control over my life can I have through the democratic politics of my society? Given that there are more than 150 million adult citizens of the United States, I must surely want the average citizen to have very little impact on national policies, and I trust that other citizens would, if they once thought about it, fully agree with my view. Almost none of us should have any significant degree of control. An individual life is volatile enough without having 150 million other people with all their odd and idiosyncratic views making noticeable impacts on it.

Fortunately, we need not worry about the intrusions of 150 million separate persons in our lives. It would be impossible for so many people taken individually to have significant effects. Max Weber notes that

The term "democratization" can be misleading. The *demos* itself, in the sense of a shapeless mass, never "governs" larger associations, but rather is governed. What changes is only the way in which the executive leaders are selected and the measure of influence which the demos, or better, which social circles from its midst are able to exert upon the content and the direction of administrative activities by means of "public opinion." "Democratization" . . . does not necessarily mean an increasingly active share of the subjects in government. This may be a result of democratization, but it [need not be]. ([1922] 1978, pp. 984–985)

Anthony Downs (1957, pp. 207–276) and numerous political scientists have argued and shown that voters are relatively ignorant of what they do and that they are not very active participants in democratic politics.

It follows that there can be very little active role for autonomy in politics for most citizens of large democratic states. At first thought, one might think this a sad or even bad fact of life. But, again, it is as one would want it, because the alternative in which everyone had significant impact would be horrendous. Perhaps someone concerned with individual morality would wish to create, stimulate, or protect autonomy. But the autonomy, the self governance, that arises from the moral self has little or no room to play in politics. This is true, of course, not only of democracy but also of any other form of centralized government of a large population.

Hence, the role of autonomy in politics may well be more akin to that advocated by several contemporary interpreters of Mill's views. Carole Pateman (1970, esp. pp. 28–35) and Jane Mansbridge ([1980] 1983, esp. pp. 244–246), among others, argue for the autonomy that comes to us from our participating and developing our characters. This is not the autonomy that enables or even provokes us to participate. It is the product, not the cause of participation. This vision of the value of autonomy at the level of character development appears to yield a clear defense of democracy: democracy allows for individually autonomous choosing. Indeed, it is even argued that it is the natural form of government for autonomous citizens. It is merely sad that autonomous choosing is individually ineffectual for political outcomes.

What does this vision of the value of autonomy say for democratic practice? Mill ([1859] 1956) defended democratic participation on the contingent claims that the individual generally knows her interests best and that participation is good for character development. On this view, a person participates from interest and then receives the extra benefit of personal character development. Unfortunately for this view, the contemporary public choice school questions the fit of individual interests with collective choice procedures, including democratic procedures (Hardin, 1990b, pp. 184–203). Hence, an intelligent grasp of contemporary politics may imply that it is not in one's interest to participate for the sake of achieving some valued policy effect.

Some contemporary advocates of personal autonomy in politics seem to argue that participation per se is valuable, as though this were the residue of Mill's view after the corrosive effects of public choice theory. Against this view, Jon Elster (1983, pp. 43–108) argues that one cannot participate well merely for the sake of character development, with no thought of achieving a political goal. If the goal falls away, participation loses its appeal and its central drive. It is that central drive – interest in a particular outcome – which produces, as a by-product, the kind of participation that can lead to character development.

Libertarian autonomy and collective constraints

Much of the libertarian criticism of modern liberalism is provoked by the following kind of problem. A large group (perhaps the majority) can achieve its members' desired end "Q" only collectively and perhaps only by attaching penalties to "free-riding" (that is, penalizing efforts to acquire Q without sharing the costs of cooperation). But then we may have insurmountable epistemic problems determining whether an apparent free-rider is someone who desires Q but wants to free-ride or is someone who does not desire Q (perhaps even opposes Q) and therefore wants not to have to contribute to the group's getting it. Or, even if I do not want Q and do not have to contribute to it, I may still suffer at least a minor loss from its provision. The libertarian typically or always supposes the individual concern trumps the collective, even though the collective concern is nothing other than a very large number of individuals' concerns taken together. The liberal, who may be as much a methodological individualist as the libertarian, often supposes the interest of the many trumps the interest of the one or the few.

Oddly, both the libertarian and the liberal in this debate can claim to ground their positions in autonomy. Their difference is simply that the libertarian insists on focusing on the individual one at a time while the liberal is willing to think of everyone at once. There is no inherent difference between denying the collective interest here and denying the individual interest. Perhaps neither can be effected except through collective institutions. The gains and the losses of the individual and of the individuals in the larger group could be reversed and the debate would still survive. The issue is therefore neither negative versus positive liberties, nor individual versus collective provisions.

There appears to be a basic intuition at stake that falls one way for libertarians and the other way for many liberals, including welfarist utilitarian liberals. But the content of this intuition is not at all clear. I have put the apparent intuition that what counts is individuals taken one at a time to several libertarians for whom it clearly was *a priori* and not subject to doubt. I can attest that my own contrary intuition – that the claim of right is not weaker just because it is the shared claim of a group of individuals – is similarly not subject to ready revision.

One response to the libertarian is that the libertarian's intuitionist rights theory cannot be articulated intelligently if it does not take strategic or collective interactions into account. There are no rights against nature, only against other people. Farmers may have rights against invasion of their farms and despoliation of their crops by neighbors. They have no right against the destruction of their land and crops by a volcano, a hurricane, or locusts.

As an example of the strategic nature of meaningful rights, consider Dutch legal property rights in the lowlands of the Netherlands, where water is always a potential threat. Through the ground water that comes virtually to the surface, how you use your property may have massive effects on the property of others. If I own a home next to yours, I will have a keen interest in what you do to your home. If you tear it down, your ground may rise while mine sinks on the side adjoining yours, and my house may crack or tumble. Lesser alterations in your building and even the ways you use it may affect the integrity of my building. Do you have an unrestricted property right to the use of your land? Not in the positive Dutch law. Is the positive Dutch law plausibly consistent with moral theory? With many it surely is consistent. For example, a utilitarian or a Kantian might readily say you are morally required to give attention to the external effects of your changing the use of your property.

The libertarian who really insists that the interests of individuals taken one at a time trump the interests of groups, such as the larger community of property owners in some quarter of Leiden or Amsterdam, now faces a difficult conceptual problem. It is evidently true that the interest that is protected by the positive Dutch law of property rights is the reciprocal interest that each individual owner most likely has in the actions of other individual owners. We protect individuals, but we do so by restricting classes of individuals. Or, one might prefer to say, we protect the class of property owners by restricting each individually. It is very hard to see a conceptual difference between these two ways of characterizing the result. Either way, individuals are constrained for the benefit of individuals. Seen *ex ante*, we might even say each individual is constrained for the benefit of each individual. And it is clear in this case that the constrained property right is inherently collectively determined – indeed, we would want it to be determined that way. We can easily enough say what the right means to an individual. But we cannot ground it in the individual alone.

Robert Nozick (1974), or a Nozickian libertarian might agree with most of this, even with the claim that rights are collectively determined. If everyone consents to changing the definition of some right, there is no rights violation involved in changing it. Hence, as the density of housing in Amsterdam increases over the centuries, we may imagine universal agreement on a new regime of rights. But the problem for the Nozickian, again, is what to do if we do not all consent to a proposed change. Suppose you are a nascent game theorist among us and you fully comprehend that, in bargaining over a new rights definition, all of the benefit is up for sharing among the group. You may hold out for as much of that benefit as possible. For most of us, the old rights definition has become a liability; for you it is suddenly an empowerment. For most of us, therefore, some of the autonomy our rights were supposed to protect may be lost. If there were *a priori* correct rights that we could stipulate, we would not face such problems. But in the world of real concern, little or nothing is a priori, and we cannot escape such problems. Without something more practical than a fairy tale about how we might have developed without rights violations into our present complex social state, we will not resolve them. Then we will want collective determinations short of unanimity.

In sum, we ground property rights in contingent facts that make the positive land law in much of North America justifiably different from that in the northwestern Netherlands. There are no *a priori* property rights that can be deduced from the nature of the individual and the individual's own relationship to external property. Property rights in political philosophy are like positive rights in the law; they must be contingently derived. And the contingencies are likely to change with time, as demography and technology change. Our property and other rights are therefore sure to be changed along the way. Perhaps political philosophers can claim better reasons for their rights in the face of various contingencies, but judges can claim richer experience for theirs.

Autonomy and contractarianism

Contractarian theory is immediately more complex than deontological and libertarian rights theory and it is tentatively institutionalist just because it must start from concern with more than one person. The simplistic model of contractarian thought is probably the classical vision of legal contract: two parties agree on some kind of exchange and then they are bound by law to fulfill the agreement. Contractarianism as a political philosophy clearly requires more and tougher analysis than this, however, because it must be undertaken in a context in which there is no law to enforce the agreement by binding the contractors. This effectuating role of law may be played by morality if the contractors are morally bound by their promises. But contractarianism needs more than this to make it a compelling theory because it is supposed to apply to people who need the agreement and what that agreement creates in order to regulate their interactions. If morality were enough, they would not need contractarian solutions (Hardin, 1990a, pp. 35–52).

But let us suppose we have resolved these issues and have before us a contractarian justification for political order, including justification for rights such as the libertarian might want and justification for democratic participation. Charles Beitz (1989) has given the best extant contractualist argument for a principle of relatively equal democratic participation. The argument is resolutely institutionalist. It goes so far as to say that we can only justify the whole package of procedures. An individual's concern for fair treatment is already incorporated in the systemic justification. Hence, an individual cannot apply the contractualist principle (the criterion of reasonable agreement) to details of procedure or outcome once the principle has defined the overall structure of institutions for democratic participation (Beitz, 1989, p. 191).

Autonomy, which originally seemed to be the driving force for the contractualist principle itself, is pushed out of view by its own institutionalization. Indeed, on this account, claims for the prior rightness of individual autonomy sound a bit like libertarian claims that individuals have *a priori* rights that trump contingent collective concerns. Concern for autonomy or respect for persons ostensibly distinguishes contractualist from utilitarian thinking. The contractualist seems to think the utilitarian is benevolent to humanity as a whole but is oblivious to single human beings and therefore lacks respect for persons. But the contractarian's respect turns out to be respect for the *idea* of persons, and the actual contractarian theory pays no attention to actual individuals and their claims.[2]

---

2. Recall the contemporary contractarian dismissal of utilitarianism on the ground that it violates respect for persons. This criticism gained its seeming force from the fact that the institutional implications of the rationalist contractarian theory had not yet been worked out. On the ground, the institutions that this theory seems to entail may bulldoze actual persons without remorse.

As Kant, the greatest of the rationalist contractarians, says, it is not necessary that our "original contract" in fact brings us all together to form a common will ("and, indeed, is utterly impossible") nor that there need have been any actual agreement by our forebears for us to be bound by such a contract. "Instead, it is a *mere idea* of reason, one, however, that has indubitable (practical) reality" ([1793], 1983, p. 77).

What is the status of autonomy in the justification of participation in a large democratic polity? In the United States, again, the odds are daunting. Surely no one can take seriously any claim that the normal citizen's personal autonomy turns very much at all on the citizen's role in politics. Yet is its fit with or contribution to our autonomy the ground on which we should justify the actual political system we have? That is what the autonomy theorists argue. Put that way, however, against the (impractical) hope for it under our conditions, the thesis of a fundamental connection between autonomy and democracy sounds very nearly absurd. In a large contemporary democracy there is little meaningful scope for substantial autonomy in or from politics. The best that can be claimed is that, through democratic procedures, we will likely be protected against various depredations and harms and that our general interests will be furthered. This will enable us more readily and freely to exercise and develop our autonomy in other spheres of our lives, the spheres in which we do almost all of our living.

Autonomy in utilitarianism

There are two ways in which autonomy comes into utilitarian discussions of politics. First, utilitarian theory is a theory of aggregate interests in which the interests at issue are those of individual persons. Hence, a utilitarian government will be concerned with accurately representing these interests. Second, we might take at least part of the task of utilitarian government to be to enhance individuals' understanding of their interests, to make them more effectively autonomous. (This need not require paternalistic actions by government – the polity might agree that government should play this role in their interest. See Hardin, 1988, pp. 137–155). Let us address these two concerns in order.

Representing individual interests

Prima facie, we may suppose that accurate representation will most naturally follow from democratic procedures. Despite Mill's strong assertion of it, this is, alas, merely a claim from common sense without good theoretical or empirical analysis to back it ([1861] 1977, pp. 404–406). Public choice theory leaves the claim without much support and the damning criticism that all extant and theoretically designed democratic procedures often reach random results and that they often reach profoundly biased results. Aristotle – arguing from common sense rather than theory – asserted that an agrarian society was, of all societies, best suited to democracy (*Politics*, 1984, p. 2093). Why? Because farmers would be too busy to participate very much in government. We might suppose participation could be harmful to individual participants' interests in various ways other than taking time from their work in their fields. For example, heavy participation might lead to a perverse mob psychology detrimental to individual interests. Or perhaps a relatively high degree of specialization in governance produces better results than amateurish participation could produce.

At best we might conclude that the *prima facie* claim in favor of democracy seems plausible in many contexts, such as in modern societies with relatively high levels of education and political communication. It may be better suited than other practical forms of government to the task of eliciting and acting on individuals' interests despite the force of Aristotle's and the public choice theorists' criticisms. This may not be a very strong or far-reaching claim. Democracy need not do a very good job to be better than most forms of government we have known. If it also did a good job of helping citizens develop autonomy, we might finally think it a very good form of government simply on grounds of autonomy.

Developing autonomy

Mill's normative theory of government is sometimes taken to be directed more at autonomy than at welfare, although his utilitarianism would seem to require the latter (Pateman, 1970, pp. 28–29). As noted above, Elster criticizes both Pateman and Mill for emphasizing the role of participation in character development. Elster supposes that they think participation is beneficial even independently of its effect on policy. Thomas Christiano (1990, pp. 151–181) argues that Elster's criticism misses its mark because Pateman, Carol Gould (1988), and other advocates of participation generally assume that citizens take political decisions seriously. Given that we want to make good political decisions, however, we may then consider the side advantages of participation in judging alternative decision making institutions.[3]

---

3. Christiano goes on to argue that the case for participation has been overstated by its advocates. 1990, pp. 156–157.

Insofar as this debate was started by Mill, it seems to have taken a wrong turn. Let us go back to Mill for his views in his own words. The merit of a set of political institutions, he writes,

> consists partly of the degree in which they promote the general mental advancement of the community, including under that phrase advancement in intellect, in virtue, and in practical activity and efficiency; and partly of the degree of perfection with which they organize the moral, intellectual, and active worth already existing, so as to operate with the greatest effect on public affairs ([1861] 1977, p. 392).

To reverse Mill's order, government should take what human material there is to produce best policies but it also should work to improve that material.

The move Mill makes here is institutionalist. He does not simply say we ought to participate because that will be good for our characters. He says we ought to design government in ways that draw people into participating. To draw people in takes incentives, and the only plausible incentive is some kind of effect on outcomes. Hence the business of government and participation come together. Indeed, we ought even to organize the workplace to draw people into participating in collective management (Pateman, 1970, pp. 33–35). E. P. Thompson or another political activist might say, somewhat foolishly, that the whole point of their participating is the participation and not the goal for which they were contesting.[4] But we could hardly motivate general political participation with such claims. And Mill does not seem to think we will or should.

Mill notes that a benevolent dictator who could do the best possible job of aggregating and fulfilling our interests, as these are already determined, would be unable to develop in us the capacities that some degree of participatory government would develop. This is an unfortunate argument about a phony and implausible issue, posed, Mill says, by the common British saying that "if a good despot could be ensured, despotic monarchy would be the best form of government" ([1861] 1977, p. 399). Until someone genuinely believes the goodness of a despotism could be guaranteed, political philosophers can sensibly rebuff this question. All we need say is that a participatory regime that failed dismally at fulfilling our interests might be worse than a far less participatory regime. But between two regimes that are equally competent at the business of gov-

---

4. Thompson and others are quoted to their embarrassment by Elster, "States That Are Essentially By-Products," 1983, p. 100 and passim.

erning and administering, the one that encourages greater participation may be better for us.

One might think Mill's argument in the passage quoted above is strictly from virtue theory – or one might think it is eminently welfarist, as I think it is. But in either case, it is institutionalist. And it is richly institutionalist in taking into account the dynamic or incentive effects of the institution on further behavior as well as the immediate effects on aggregating from individual to public interests. To be successful, the institution cannot merely address given behaviors, it must also address the behaviors that will be stimulated by its effort to address them. And, positively, it can take into account how best to influence behaviors in the interests of all concerned.

So where does Mill stand on autonomy? He does not discuss it in the terms of the debate in our time and we cannot be sure how he would stretch it to fit into the debate. But for him autonomy is fairly clearly an institutional creation, not merely a property of the self unvarnished. If this is so, he is forced to take his institutionalist view of the value of encouraging participation. In a society more than an order of magnitude larger than his own, which was already too large for his views on participation, he might be inclined, however, to find other avenues for developing citizens' autonomy than merely in political participation, which cannot finally be a major part of the lives of most of us. Mill recognized this problem but did not draw out its consequences for his apparent concern with participation for the sake of one's autonomy.[5] In any case, the autonomy Mill sought is the autonomy of his *Utilitarianism*, the capacity for appreciating and benefiting from rich experiences ([1856] 1957, ch. 2). Again, not very much of that will come from politics in our time.

Incidentally, the utilitarian liberal would deal with cases such as the Dutch property law by looking to the institutional level of their resolution and choosing the resolution that seemed to work best on the whole for welfare somehow measured or compared in the aggregate. The utilitarian might simply commend democratic choices, perhaps even simple majoritarian choices for many such cases. Indeed, for areas in which interpersonal comparisons of welfare seem dubious, utilitarianism may entail democratic choice (Riley, 1990, pp. 335–348). For some cases, which would likely have to be substantively specified, the utilitarian might suppose, however, that interpersonal comparisons can be made

---

5. After stating the problem, Mill merely changed the subject: "But since all cannot, in a community exceeding a single small town, participate personally in any but some very minor portions of the public business, it follows that the ideal type of a perfect government must be representative." [1861] 1977, Ch. 3 (final sentence), p. 412.

and, hence, that there should be more stringent conditions before a majority could have its way. For example, super-majorities might be required in certain realms and only independent, constitutionally protected judicial proceedings might be allowed in other realms.

Institutionalizing autonomy

Many arguments in political philosophy get their moral force from consideration of small-scale interactions, such as that in which two people choose to live together or negotiate over the exchange of labor for property, or that in which one person is coerced by another. Political philosophy, however, is generally about large-scale collective resolutions. Those resolutions may contingently affect the content of the small-scale principles they are intended to uphold.

Autonomy theorists, including Mill and many contemporary writers, including the rationalist contractarians and utilitarians, seem generally to think democracy, constrained by a panoply of civil liberties, is the form of government that naturally flows from concern with autonomy. But democratic institutions do not merely defend our autonomy in making the choices we would have faced otherwise, they also determine what are the small-scale interactions we face. Our collective resolution helps create the problems it is to resolve. If our concern with autonomy is consequentialist, this may not be problematic (for example, see Raz, 1988, p. 408). We can enhance the quantity of autonomous choosing by creating opportunities for it. But if our concern is deontological or procedural, it is quite puzzling to suppose that, out of a prior concern with individual autonomy, we should massively manipulate individual-level choices.

Political choice is collective, not individual. We choose in the face of necessity of collective, not merely individual, resolution. This is a constitutive, not merely a contingent, claim. Democracy must therefore be justified, if at all, systematically, not individually, although our justification of it may include reference to its effects on individuals. Democracy is good not because it instantiates autonomy but because it may help support or even produce it. But that makes commitment to democracy contingent, not deontological.

There have surely been times and places in which democracy could not be morally defended as superior to monarchy or other forms of government. Democracy serves individual interests only if individual political participants know enough to relate government action to their interests. But none of us involved in these discussions is so omnicompetent in knowing our interests, even in our highly public and democratic society, not to be glad to be second-guessed on occasion. Indeed, most of us are willing, because we are so ignorant of how to serve our interests, to defer to experts on manifold issues throughout our lives. We all suffer from the rational ignorance that Anthony Downs says keeps individual citizens from knowing enough to vote their interests (1957, p. 236). That is to say, virtually all of us can expect to benefit more from investing our time and energy in knowing and mastering other things in lieu of knowing and mastering public policy.

It may be rational for us to be so ignorant, but is it wrong? On any plausible positive account of government and politics, it cannot be wrong in principle. There are clear limits to how much I can know about all of the many things that it might, if cost-free, be in my interest to know. I must choose, implicitly or explicitly, to be more ignorant of some things in order to know more about others. There is nothing special about politics that elevates it to priority in its demands on my limited knowledge. Knowing very much more about politics would eventually get in the way of my doing other things in which I could have a bigger impact on the welfare of myself and others. Hence, it could even be bad for me to know so much instead of remaining ignorant.

Yet, in some moments, it seems wrong to be politically ignorant. For example, if my nation is at war and is wreaking havoc on third world peasants, should I not become better informed and then take a more intelligent part in affecting my nation's policies? Perhaps then I should, in part because I might no longer be rationally ignorant in the face of overwhelming news coverage. At this point, my participation might still be very unlikely to matter. However, if my motivation is concern for others in addition to myself, as it would be for a utilitarian, I should not further discount the value of my participation according to the self-interested logic of collective action (Olson, 1965; Hardin 1982). Still, there might be no expected value from my taking action. A slogan of the 1960s in the United States was, "If you're not part of the solution, you're part of the problem." That was clever rhetoric but dismal logic. If democracy entails such a slogan, it is an offense to autonomy and to contemporary moral theories of all stripes.

If democracy is associated with autonomy in large modern societies, the relationship is not for many of us the by-product that Mill and Elster note, namely, the generation of autonomy as a by-product of participation for the sake of affecting outcomes. Through some complex causal chain, democratic institutions may make it more likely that various group interests will be taken into account in public policymaking even though few people will have participated to inject their interests into debate. The results will surely be messy and inegalitarian, so that many will justifiably be able to claim that their own or their group's autonomy is sacrificed or dishonored. But insofar as many groups are benefited, their members may be better placed to develop their characters and to enjoy greater autonomy. This causal chain makes autonomy a relatively direct product of democratic politics and not merely a by-product of participation.

Apart from such a causal chain, however, is there no conceptual connection between autonomy and democracy? Contrary to Althusius's theoretical view of democracy, there is not – or, rather, not much. We may claim that merely having the opportunity *in principle* of participation open to us enhances autonomy. Practical democracy does at least provide us that opportunity in principle. For those who wish to ground political philosophy in autonomy, this must be inadequate. But it might be enough to select democracy from possible forms of government, because democracy offers at least as much possibility of exercising one's citizenship to affect one's fate through politics and as much possibility of developing one's autonomy through political participation as any system could offer everyone. Democracy offers very little to the play of autonomy or its development in a modern, large-scale society such as the United States. Perhaps the best an autonomy theorist can claim for democracy is that it may reduce the threat of government to autonomy more than – or at least as much as – any other system could.

References

Althusius, Johannes. [1603/1614] 1991. *Politica Methodice Digesta, in The Politics of Johannes Althusius*, trans. Frederick S. Carney, trans., Eyre & Spottiswoode, London.

Aristotle. [c.335–34 B.C.E.] 1984. *Politics*, trans. B. Jowett in *The Complete Works of Aristotle* Vol. 2, Jonathan Barnes, (ed.) Princeton University Press, Princeton.

Beitz, Charles. 1989. *Political Equality*, Princeton University Press, Princeton.

Christiano, Thomas. 1990. "Freedom, Consensus, and Equality in Collective Decision Making," *Ethics* I Vol. 101, October.

Downs, Anthony. 1957. *An Economic Theory of Democracy*, Harper, New York.

Elster, Jon. 1983. "States That Are Essentially By-Products" in Elster, *Sour Grapes: Studies in the Subversion of Rationality*, Cambridge University Press, Cambridge.

Gould, Carol. 1988. *Rethinking Democracy*, Cambridge University Press, Cambridge.

Hardin, Russell. 1982. *Collective Action*, Johns Hopkins University Press for Resources for the Future, Baltimore.

______ 1988. *Morality Within the Limits of Reason*, University of Chicago Press, Chicago.

______1990a. "Contractarianism: Wistful Thinking," *Constitutional Political Economy*, Vol. 1.

______1990b. "Public Choice vs. Democracy" in *Nomos 32: Majorities and Minorities*, John W. Chapman (ed.) New York University Press, New York.

Kant, Immanuel. [1793] 1983. "On the Proverb: That May Be True in Theory, but Is of No Practical Use," *Perpetual Peace and Other Essays*, trans. Ted Humphrey, Hackett, Indianapolis.

Mansbridge, Jane J. 1983. *Beyond Adversary Democracy*, University of Chicago Press, Chicago.

Mill, John Stuart. [1861] 1977. *Considerations on Representative Government* in Mill, *Essays on Politics and Society*, J.M. Robson and Alexander Brady (eds.), University of Toronto Press, Toronto.

______[1861] 1957. *Utilitarianism*, Oskar Piest (ed.) Bobbs-Merrill Company, Indianapolis.

______[1859] 1956. *On Liberty*, Currin Shields (ed.) Bobbs-Merrill Company, Indianapolis.

Olson, Mancur, Jr. 1965. *The Logic of Collective Action*, Harvard University Press, Cambridge, MA.

Nozick, Robert. 1974. *Anarchy, State, and Utopia*, Basic Books, New York.

Pateman, Carole. 1970. *Participation and Democratic Theory*, Cambridge University Press, Cambridge.

Rawls, John. 1971. *A Theory of Justice*, Harvard University Press, Cambridge, MA.

Raz, Joseph. 1988. *The Morality of Freedom*, Oxford University Press, Oxford.

Riley, Jonathan. 1990. "Utilitarian Ethics and Democratic Government," *Ethics*, Vol. 100, No. 2, January.

Sandel, Michael J. 1982. *Liberalism and the Limits of Justice*, Cambridge University Press, Cambridge.

Weber, Max [1922] 1978. *Economics and Society*, Guenther Roth and Claus Wittich (eds.) University of California Press, Berkeley.

3
False Stability and Defensive Justification in Rawlsian Liberalism: A Feminist Critique

David Anderson

Introduction

American society suffers from the problem of false stability. Despite egalitarian ideals, the society perpetuates the systematic exploitation of some members by others. This means that citizens do not share moral and psychological sensibilities that make them equally willing to uphold the social order. Labor and business collude in order to maintain the welfare state against the socialist alternative, and males and females collude in order to maintain the asymmetrical organization of parenting against a system of shared parenting as well as living arrangements alternative to the standard husband-wife-child situation. By the asymmetrical organization of parenting, I mean the system of parenting in which women, as a rule, are the primary caretakers of children, especially when they are infants. In both processes of collusion one party is really dominated even though they cooperate to maintain the stability of the system: labor is therefore dominated by capital in the economic system and women are dominated by men in the domestic system. These two processes of collusion are of course going on at the same time. The paradigm case of the collusive process is the American family in which the husband is the primary economic provider and the wife is the primary caretaker. If it is a working class or a middle class family, then he is dominated at work by management and she is dominated at home by him. If she works, then she is also dominated at work by management. And since most managers are men, she will be dominated in virtue of being a worker and a woman at the same time.

What exactly is meant by the notion of "false stability?" Let us say that a society suffers from the problem of false stability, or is not truly stable, when the following two conditions are met: (i) the society is politically stable; and (ii) significant numbers of persons within the society (for example many of its females) are dominated, either physically, emotionally, or economically. Consider a striking case: a woman may be beaten by her husband three times a week, but she may not associate herself with a political party that opposes the whole society. Indeed, the woman would probably have great difficulty opposing her husband, let alone joining with other dominated women in order to oppose the male dominant society. The major political and economic institutions are therefore not under any form of serious criticism. Thus we say that it is possible for a society to be stable and inhumane at the same time.[1]

If it is true that American society suffers from the problem of false stability, then a political philosopher must explain how the theory of justice he defends would overcome this problem of injustice. The famous political philosopher John Rawls does not recognize a problem of false stability in American society or any society. Rather, in defending his principles of justice, the equal liberty principle, and the equal opportunity and difference principle, he argues that a society governed by these principles would be stable. In fact, he has presented two arguments for stability that differ significantly, one in *A Theory of Justice* (1971) and one in the later essays published in the 1980s.

In this paper, I examine Rawls's arguments for stability and I argue that they fail. In section two I outline the main features of both of Rawls's arguments. In sections three and four I explain why false stability exists in the United States and how this understanding of domination should alter our understanding of autonomy. Given this background, I argue in section five that the theory of stability, or what Rawls also calls a "stable social unity," would not overcome the problem of false stability plaguing American society. Finally I consider briefly two Rawlsian objections and make concluding remarks in sections six and seven.

While I will be satisfied if the paper attains its limited objectives, I regard it as part of a more general critique of Rawlsian liberalism. Indeed, the project of this paper could be said to be a broader feminist critique of Rawlsian liberalism in which the problem of stability is singled out for special attention. Moreover, my argument has a conditional form, since I will be assuming that a particular feminist account of the problem of false stability in American society is true or at least highly plausible. The feminist account is, strictly speaking, my own, but I have essentially tried to combine the ideas of various sociologists, psychologists, and philoso-

---

1. I am in debt to John Jost (1990) for his criticism of Rawls's notion of stability and also for suggesting the parallel to the standard Marxist claim that capitalist societies are stable and inhumane at the same time. The main line of argument of this paper is also in debt to Peter Railton (1984).

48

phers. I follow Alison Jaggar (1983) and others in endorsing a "socialist feminist" point of view, namely, a feminist standpoint which maintains that there are two interlocking systems of domination in American society: the capitalist economic system and the asymmetrical organization of parenting. The central thesis is that the capitalist system reproduces the problem of class domination and the system of parenting reproduces the problem of gender domination. Each system, moreover, serves to support the other. In addition, the class domination/gender domination distinction cuts across the public/private distinction since one can see the effects of both forms of domination in both spheres of society.[2]

Now my primary focus in this paper will be on the system of parenting. And my account of the problem of gender domination which stems from the asymmetrical organization of parenting is based largely on the work of Nancy Chodorow (1978, 1989).[3] I also draw on the work of Jessica Benjamin (1988), Carol Gilligan (1982, 1986), Jane Flax (1983), and Dorothy Dinnerstein (1976), as well as a number of philosophers who have been influenced by one or more of these theorists.[4] Since my primary concern is the problem of gender domination, it may be best just to grant the assumption that a Rawlsian society would have no problem of class domination at all. Thus let us assume that a market socialist economy would be needed to apply the difference principle, namely the principle which says that social and economic inequalities are to be arranged so that they are to the greatest benefit of the least advantaged members of society.[5]

---

2. Alison Jaggar (1983) critically discusses, and defends, socialist feminism. She discusses Marxism and radical feminism as versions of monistic theories of domination, since Marxists reduce all forms of domination, including the domination of women, to the problem of class domination; while radical feminists reduce all forms of domination, including class domination, to forms of gender or sexual domination. Socialist feminism therefore has a dualistic theory of domination. A proponent of socialist feminism is Zillah Eisenstein (1990). I have also benefited from Iris Young's standard essay (1990a). I should also note here that I am trying to revive a version of dual systems theory, even though this approach to socialist feminism is no longer in fashion. My more developed argument would also treat the topic of racism.

3. I also have benefited from many discussions of Chodorow's work, including Isaac Balbus (1982), Lillian Rubin (1983) and Iris Young (1990b).

4. I draw freely from many feminist sources, including Sheila Mullet (1987), Annette Baier (1985, 1986a, 1986b), Virginia Held (1987), Jean Bethke Elshtain (1981), Seyla Benhabib (1987), Jean Grimshaw (1986), Nancy Hartsock (1983), Naomi Scheman (1983), Marilyn Friedman (1987, 1989), Nel Noddings (1984), and Carole Pateman (1989). I am also in debt to Richard Rorty (1991), Jürgen Habermas (1971), and Bernard Williams (1985).

5. Alec Nove (1985) and John Roemer (1991), among others, are contemporary proponents of market socialism which, in brief, represents a middle position between the capitalist welfare state and command economies. The market socialist view, then, aims to retain the idea of a competitive market, like capitalist societies, but it rejects the idea of the private ownership of the means of production.

In *A Theory of Justice* Rawls is eminently clear that it is an empirical question how best to apply this principle (1971, p. 258). Although he devoted the second part of his book to illustrating how this principle, and the rest of the substantive doctrine, could be applied with an essentially mixed economic system, he said that it was still an open question how legislators in a well-ordered society would apply the substantive doctrine. Thus let us suppose that a "liberal socialist regime" (1971, p. 280), as Rawls calls it, would be in place.

My argument, then, is that, if feminist views of moral and political psychology and sociology are true, then a Rawlsian society would not eliminate the problem of sexism, even though it might eliminate the problem of classism by implementing socialist economic institutions. I will also indicate ways in which a Rawlsian society would not eliminate the problem of heterosexism, although unfortunately I will not be able to address the vital problem of racism in this paper.

Two Arguments for Stability

Rawls has presented two arguments for stability and these arguments plainly differ. In *A Theory of Justice* (1971) Rawls devotes chapter seven and especially chapters eight and nine to the task of showing that the principles of justice provisionally justified in chapters one through six are congruent with our good. Chapters seven and eight are devoted to the task of showing that a society governed by these principles would be stable, and this argument is a heavily psychological argument. Thus Rawls relies on "the facts of moral psychology" (e.g., p. 462) to confirm the provisional justification of the two principles. In particular, he sketches a theory of how children in a well-ordered society would develop the requisite sense of justice. He regards this as a sketch of a theory of moral development that is indebted to the writings of many psychologists, but the main structural features of the theory are most similar to those of Jean Piaget (1948) and Lawrence Kohlberg (1984), the two leading proponents of cognitive developmental theories of moral development.

According to Rawls, children would move through three stages of development: a morality of authority, a morality of association, and a morality of principles. He shows how children would gradually develop a capacity to make impartial judgments from a standpoint that would lead to mutual benefits for all. Though each stage is not exclusively about developing cognitive rational capacities (the second is about a capacity for empathetic identification from an impartial standpoint), the basic orientation of the view is manifestly about developing a capacity to reason as an autonomous being from an impartial point of view. Moreover, it is obvious that Rawls is saying that boys and girls should be raised in the same way.

Finally, it cannot be overemphasized that a constant refrain of *A Theory of Justice* is that moral philosophers must rely on facts and theories from the social sciences in order to make moral theories relevant to human life. "Moral philosophy," Rawls writes, "must be free to use contingent assumptions and general facts as it pleases (p. 51)." Rawls is a fierce opponent of the kind of analytic moral philosophy associated with the writings of R.M. Hare (1981) and it is certainly a dominant theme of his work that he has tried to naturalize Kant to the point that we can value the ideas of autonomy and respect for persons without the "misguided" metaphysics. Rawls tells us (1975, pp. 94–99) that he has tried to present the Kantian program within "the canons of a reasonable empiricism," and of course his substantive view departs from Kant's political philosophy in a fairly important sense. It is these broad commitments that led Rawls to say the following: "It is evident that stability is a desirable feature of a moral conception. . . . However attractive a conception of justice might be on other grounds, it is seriously defective if the principles of moral psychology are such that it fails to engender in human beings the requisite desire to act upon it" (1971, p. 455).

In the last decade, Rawlsian liberalism has undergone a series of changes.[6] A major change concerns the scope of the theory of justice. Rawls now says that he is only talking to persons living in liberal societies (and I will focus on American society). He grounds or motivates the original position with a set of contingent commitments which, he says, citizens of liberal states have experienced for over two hundred years. Thus Rawls refers to "the fact of pluralism" in order to motivate the idea of a procedure of impartial justification animated by an ideal of moral persons conceived as free and equal. Moreover, he discusses the fact of pluralism with explicit reference to the idea of stability, or a stable social unity.

Rawls calls the fact of pluralism "a permanent feature" of liberal societies; it designates the existence of "a plurality of conflicting, and indeed

---

6. There have been two major changes in the last thirteen years. The first is best represented by "Kantian Constructivism in Moral Theory," The Dewey Lectures, (1980). The second is best represented by "Justice as Fairness: Political not Metaphysical" (1985). In short, in the Dewey Lectures Rawls brought out the Kantian components of his moral methodology and in later essays he made it clear that he was only speaking to citizens in liberal democracies. I discuss these matters in chapters two and three of my dissertation (1990). My overall account of Rawls is in debt to Darwall (1980), Sandel (1982), Scanlon (1982), Buchanan (1980, 1982), and Daniels (1975).

incommensurable, conceptions of the meaning, value and purpose of human life. . . " (1987,p. 4). Persons have different views of the good life (or what Rawls calls "conceptions of the good") and they hold different religious, moral, and personal ideals. An adequate theory of justice, Rawls now says, would seek to achieve an "overlapping consensus" among persons who have opposing views of the good life. And Rawls adds that the original position can be used to represent this commitment. Liberal pluralism and liberal toleration are therefore manifestly in the main structural features of the original position itself. He does not deny that objective truths about justice and goodness may exist; instead, he says that reason directs us to put aside this epistemological question in order to develop a practicable moral conception for a society racked by conflicts over efforts to reconcile the values of freedom and equality. In particular, Rawls now invokes what he calls "the method of avoidance" to put aside controversial disputes in the philosophy of mind, metaphysics, and religion in order to focus on what he calls the "surface" facts or commitments we do have (see, e.g., 1985, pp. 230–231). What is striking about this second line of argument is that it articulates a general theory of social stability before the argument from the original position for principles of justice ever takes place. In *A Theory of Justice* the argument for stability takes place *after* the principles have been provisionally justified from the original position.

Moreover, Rawls says that the "only alternative to a principle of toleration is the autocratic use of state power" (1985, p. 230). Thus we must reject philosophical doctrines that breed intolerance by laying down comprehensive theories of the good life, such as perfectionism and utilitarianism, and reject actual social orders which center around some comprehensive theory of the good life. Indeed, Rawls echoes old liberal fears and anxieties about fascism and communism. His papers now invite comparison to the writings of Popper, von Hayek, and Berlin when the targets in the world were fascism, communism, and creeping socialism. His targets therefore include both philosophical moral conceptions, like Bentham's, and actual social orders, like Nazi Germany.

There is irony in Rawls's defense of liberal autonomy and liberal pluralism against these target views, because Rawls's substantive doctrine was criticized in the seventies for diluting liberalism of its force. Robert Nozick (1974), among others, said that Rawlsian liberalism did not take seriously the autonomy of persons, even as Rawls made the same charge against the utilitarians. Political practices that required as extensive a redistribution of wealth and power as advocated by Rawlsian doctrine would ultimately undermine the autonomy of the individual, or so the critics said. Rawls, of course, still holds to the same substantive principles, even though now he rarely discusses the second principle (equal opportunity and difference principle). That his complete view may still require socialism even though Rawls talks about liberal toleration as though he were Locke, or Nozick, is more than ironic. It is not only confusing to readers sensitive to the Rawlsian corpus, but very misleading to the readers of the later essays who do not know *A Theory of Justice*.

Finally, notice that on Rawls's first version persons (i.e., readers) still needed to engage in reflective equilibrium in order to determine if the premises of the argument from the original position, the principles chosen, and the stability argument itself cohered with their considered moral judgments. Thus even though the first line of argument took place inside of the original position, it still was related to what persons in the reading audience had to decide. Today, readers must still engage in reflective equilibrium, only now the audience to whom the theory is directed has changed markedly, and they are also instructed to consider their ideals of a person and their ideal of a well-ordered society, as well as their considered moral judgments.

False Stability in American Society

In this section I want to explain the problem of false stability in American society. What follows is more of an account of the problem than an argument about the dimension of the problem. My main thesis is as follows: a problem of false stability plagues many American marriages and families. A marriage suffers from the problem of false stability when the partners in the marriage collude in maintaining a pattern of domination in order to maintain the marriage, indeed, in order to prevent the marriage from collapsing. A family suffers from a problem of false stability when the children are involved in the process of collusion. And a society suffers from a problem of false stability when most of its people live in situations of false stability.

I will focus on a dominant kind of collusive marriage, namely the marriage in which a husband and wife are engaged in a sadomasochistic drama: he dominates her and she submits to the domination.[7] In a common case, the husband will not only fail to be emotionally intimate with his wife but he will emotionally manipulate her; in some marriages he

---

7. My account of collusion draws also on Herbert Marcuse (1964), Maggie Scarf (1987), Henry Dicks (1967), and Adrienne Rich (1980).

will beat her or even rape her. She will try to make the marriage work because she is emotionally and economically dependent on him. Yet she will be stuck because she will be incapable of extricating herself from the relationship. A house divided against itself can stand.

Chodorow (1978, 1989) and her followers maintain that men dominate their wives because men have been socialized to dominate their wives and wives submit to the domination because they have been socialized to submit to the domination.[8] The problem is rooted in the social construction of gender identity, masculine gender identity and feminine gender identity. According to Chodorow (1978, 1989), the masculinity/femininity distinction should be separated from the male/female distinction. Male and female are sex types that refer to anatomy; masculine and feminine are gender orientations that refer to cognitive and emotional capacities, attitudes, and needs. She believes that all persons have a potential to develop masculine and feminine aspects of their personalities; it is just a contingent fact that males have been socialized to develop masculine gender identities and females have been socialized to develop feminine gender identities.

When women are the primary caretakers, girls typically grow up to be like their mothers and boys typically grow up to be like their fathers. Girls develop relational capacities for empathy, listening, touching, and nurturing in the context of their intense relationships with their mothers. Although the mother-daughter relationship is fraught with conflict, mothers and daughters will tend to become enmeshed in one another's lives, especially when the daughter herself becomes a mother. Boys, on the other hand, because they are male, are forced to separate from their mothers in order to identify with their fathers. Whereas girls affirm feminine capacities and needs, boys deny feminine capacities and needs. The idea is that the boy consciously and

---

8. Chodorow feminizes a major tradition of psychoanalytic theory, namely, the object relations tradition associated with the work of Donald Winnicott (1958), Ronald Fairbairn (1952), and John Bowlby (1973). Object relations theorists focus on the preoedipal years of human development between birth and age three. Moreover, object relations theorists give preeminent emphasis to themes of the innate need individuals have to form emotive bonds with others, individuation, identity formation, and separation anxiety, as opposed to neo-Freudian themes about innate drives for sex and aggression and sexual rivalries. Chodorow departs from the object relations tradition in rejecting their theory of psychopathology. Whereas they typically reduce problems (such as narcissistic personality disorders) to a problematic mother-infant relationship, she indicts the social system that keeps women in their roles as primary caretakers. The object relations theorists call for a more focused mother-infant relationship, whereas Chodorow calls for new relationships between the infant and both its mother and its father. I discuss Chodorow's views and related matters in chapters four, five, and six of Anderson (1990).

unconsciously denies the value (indeed the existence) of these capacities and needs in himself in the process of denying the value of these capacities and needs in his mother.

Moreover, boys come to fear the feminine, because being feminine would threaten their masculine image as beings who can make rational decisions, control emotions, especially ones that would make them feel vulnerable, and adopt a competitive stance toward others generally. Fear of the feminine is also related to fear of homosexuality, since acting in feminine ways is associated by boys and males generally not only with females but with homosexuals. A feminist can maintain that actual homosexual impulses, in the standard case, serve to construct defensive masculinity along with denied feminine impulses, but fear of homosexuality is sufficient to explain why many men are driven to affirm their masculinity. It is clear, in any case, that denial is built into masculine development, and this denial often leads husbands to project their own needs for emotional expression onto their wives. In a common case, a husband will cause pain and frustration in his wife rather than express his own threatening emotions, be they about fear of failure, fear of death, inadequacies at work or at home, or even plain sadness. Denial of the feminine in men thus leads them also to devalue the feminine in females through various forms of domination.

Husbands and wives engaged in a collusive marriage will each fear the prospect of a failed marriage. In addition, they will each experience anxiety over the whole subject of marital stability. Moreover, the fear and anxiety that motivate husbands and wives to maintain the stability of their marriages differs. In short, husbands fear forms of emotional connection and wives fear forms of emotional separation, but both fear the idea of a dissolution of the relationship itself. It should also be noted that many men will be channeled into situations that are not in their interests either; that is to say, even though these men will have more power in their marriage than their wives, they would still benefit more from a relationship in which they did not suffer from feminophobia and homophobia. Also notice that many marriages that suffer from the problem of false stability will have some, even many, good components. Children will certainly provide a great source of satisfaction for many couples.

Finally, in families in which the couple are in collusion, children can, in a variety of ways, be dominated as well. Children of parents who are in collusion can be triangulated into the struggle. Daughters of collusive parents may develop eating disorders as they become the identified patients in families that suffer from the problem of false stability.[9] Sensitive sons may be used as sponges to absorb the parental struggle.[10] Moreover, sons and daughters will be discouraged from growing up to be adults who adopt alternative living arrangements. Because parents will try to support the status quo even though they are stuck in a collusive situation, gay and lesbian children will be alienated from the family system, children of uncertain gender or sexual direction will probably grow up thoroughly confused, and children will be denied the opportunity to grow up to be adults who, should they marry, would share equally with the child care and housework.

Understanding the Problem about Autonomy

The complete positive and feminist view that I endorse would include a new theory of autonomy, namely a theory about self-determination. Without the right public social institutions, persons will be incapable of being autonomous. The view of autonomy I endorse will require a system of parenting in which both mothers and fathers are primary caretakers. Both sons and daughters will be capable of developing a sense of autonomy, and indeed they will also be capable of developing relational capacities for empathy, caring and the like. Yet the old notions of masculine autonomy and feminine relationality must be transcended because they are each currently generated in the context of the asymmetrical organization of parenting. Male autonomy is defined largely in terms of the denial of the feminine and female relationality is defined largely in terms of the relationship to mother without adequate attention to the daughter herself.

Consider the case of raising sons in a new way. If sons were raised by both of their parents, then they would not be forced to separate from their mothers in order to identify with their largely absent fathers. Instead, they could use both parents as role models. Of crucial importance is the idea that males would not be threatened by femininity if they could develop masculine traits in a positive rather than in a defensive way.[11] Nor would

9. On eating disorders see Kim Chernin (1985), Susan Bordo (1990), and Luise Eichenbaum & Susie Orbach (1982).

10. A general treatment of problems currently facing American sons can be found in Samuel Osherson (1986). Also see the discussion about triangulation in Maggie Scarf (1987), and the various case studies in David Scharff and Jill Savege Scharff (1983). Dinnerstein (1976) takes up issues of male sexuality, especially with reference to denial of death. I discuss these matters in "Denial in the Original Position" (unpublished).

11. I am much in debt to Stephen Darwall for pointing this out to me. He also indicated numerous ways this notion is related to the whole project of criticizing our current gender relations and of proposing a new system of gender relations.

fear of homosexuality be bound up with fear of femininity. Males generally would not associate intimacy and vulnerability with weakness. Of course, these "masculine traits" will not be masculine in the old sense, and it may be best not to call them "masculine" at all. My own ideal does embrace a general theory of androgyny, since persons can, if they choose, aim to combine capacities for independence and dependence in their characters. For our purposes, though, we can identify the motivations for this new notion of autonomy without showing how it would be united with a new notion of relational characteristics. Suffice it to say that the process of union requires more than combining traits, since the connection between relationality and domination must be broken before relationality can be united with autonomy. Explaining how females would develop capacities for autonomy as they become extricated from their mothers is another topic altogether and must be left for future consideration.

But it is crucial to understand that this new approach to parenting must be made possible at the national level. What is needed is a family policy that would provide maternity and paternity leaves for parents with newborns as well as some system of nationally funded daycare. Many Western European societies have such policies now; therefore, calling for a family policy along these lines is hardly a utopian speculation. If a society had both a serious family policy and market socialist economic institutions, or at least a much stronger welfare state than we have in America today, then it could go a long way toward eliminating gender domination in the home and at the workplace at the same time that it helped to eliminate problems of class domination in the workplace and in the home.

I should also say that in my view a humane society is not a utopian society free of balancing acts or a static society free of competition, nor is it a society free of fear, anxiety, and doubt. As John Roemer (1991) and Alec Nove (1985) have pointed out, one of the virtues of the market socialist ideal is that it preserves a notion of healthy competition. And I agree with the poet John Keats that a capacity for negative capability, which he said Shakespeare possessed so enormously, is needed to live with the inevitable uncertainties of life. A capacity for negative capability enables one to live with uncertainties, mysteries, and doubts without any irritable reaching after fact and reason. The trick is to create a society that eliminates doubts and pains generated by pernicious social structures. A humane society would provide all persons with conditions they require to dance the balancing act of their uncoerced free choice.

A Criticism of Rawllsian Liberalism

I now turn to the criticism of Rawlsian liberalism. Let me begin by distinguishing the following three senses of autonomy that appear in Rawls's view: (i) a theory of autonomy that characterizes persons in the reading audience; (ii) a theory of autonomy that animates the original position; and (iii) a theory of autonomy that, Rawls claims, would animate a well-ordered society. (There is a fourth notion of autonomy that is based on the theory of moral development that is sketched in chapter eight.) Notion (i) we have already discussed. Notion (ii) refers to the ideal of a person that is employed in the original position. The parties are represented as having two highest order interests that correspond to their two moral capacities, namely a capacity to understand, uphold and apply principles of justice and a capacity to formulate, to revise and rationally to pursue a conception of the good. The principles of both instrumental and deliberative rationality are available to the parties in the original position. Thus the parties know that in an actual society they will be provided with conditions to make decisions about ends and means from a standpoint of relevant information (1971, p. 422).[12] This theory articulates the sound idea of making "well-informed" decisions, and Rawls uses it, among other reasons, because it is not esoteric, but rather commonplace in its intuitive appeal. Last, notion (iii) refers to the ideal of a just citizen. Unlike the parties in the original position, these citizens are not motivated solely by self-interest. Of course, the original parties reason from within a deliberative framework that articulates norms of fairness (for example, the veil of ignorance), but it is still the case that they are not motivated by the idea of impartial regard or mutual respect.

Rawls's three notions of autonomy are used to develop a notion of a just citizen and not a notion of a complete moral person. He gives great emphasis to this point in his recent writings. Yet let me make it clear that my strategy of argument is to deny that Rawlsian liberalism, like American liberalism, can effectively make this distinction. The major point of the false stability argument is to show that morally offensive practices in the private domain would reproduce structures in the public sphere, which would serve to reinforce the morally offensive practices in the private sphere. As I see it, the moral personality of women and children would be undermined in the private sphere by men. Therefore, though the theory of justice is intended to provide the conditions for all persons to pursue their own conceptions of the good, it will turn out, I

12. See Stephen Darwall (1980, pp. 323–327).

argue, that women and children will not be in position to pursue their interests. My criticism will focus on conception (i) and conception (iii), namely the conceptions of autonomy that characterize persons in the reading audience and persons who would live in a Rawlsian society. I essentially want to say that since conception (i) is an inadequate description of our commitments to autonomy, the aim to create persons who would be autonomous in sense (iii) will never succeed. A more systematic argument would show why exactly conception (ii) is incompatible with conception (i).

Step 1: Fear and anxiety motivate the original position

The first step of my argument is as follows: I maintain that, as a rule, American husbands (and men more generally) are committed to Rawls's first conception of autonomy. In this respect, I agree with Rawls. But I think that a central reason that American husbands are committed to this conception of autonomy is that they have been raised to deny their own feminine capacities and needs. In addition, fear of femininity is driven by fear of homosexuality. Thus these unconscious causes explain why men value autonomy. Rawls claims that men (and women) are committed to autonomy because they value freedom and because they fear totalitarian regimes. What I am suggesting is that these commitments are the surfaces of unconscious causes. And although these men are committed to avoiding feminine behavior, it would be misleading to say that they have "commitments" to avoiding feminine behavior. Rather, they are being driven to support ideals of agency for reasons of which they are unaware.

Moreover, since each party in the original position is characterized in the same way, husbands will say that they aim to regard their wives and females generally on an equal footing. And such claims will often be sincere. But even when the claims are sincere many of these men will currently be dominating their wives, especially by using subtle forms of emotional manipulation. Thus with one stroke a husband will approve of the procedure of impartial justification, welcome women into the procedure, and deny his own feminine side even as he dominates his wife.

I am not suggesting that American husbands, as a rule, are self-interested beings who have no commitments to others. Certainly some men are self-centered and suffer from feminophobia and homophobia to such a degree that they beat and rape women as a way of affirming their masculinity. My target, though, is a common kind of man, namely the husband who fails to be intimate with his wife, rarely shows his own vulnerabilities, emotionally manipulates her rather than expresses his own feelings, and dominates females in the workplace in various ways. In other words, I am indicting the average husband because he does dominate his wife and females generally, but I am not denying that he pays his taxes and gives economic and some forms of emotional support to his wife and his family. Fear of femininity and fear of homosexuality are not only compatible with certain forms of impartial behavior, they actually support it. Persons who fear emotional connection may be inspired to support forms of political or economic connection.

While I have identified some unconscious considerations that explain why many American husbands would be motivated to support the original position, I do not think that these are the only considerations that explain why they would be so motivated. Male commitments to autonomy must surely be overdetermined. Which causes or reasons are most important? I do not know the answer to that question. No doubt the capitalist system, the Protestant work ethic, and American Horatio Alger and frontier themes are also responsible for the fierce notion of independence that exists in America. But I do think that gender domination plays a major role and until it can be shown that the matter of gender domination is really of minor importance, I think we must question our commitment to a view of autonomy that now leads to human hardship.

Many American wives, I submit, would also affirm the reasonability of the original position, especially middle class wives, for middle class wives want to be regarded as equal to men, especially in the public sphere. Thus many American wives might scorn the idea of a distinctive feminine ethic, either one that centered around traditional maternal norms or one that centered around a new theory of women's consciousness. The first alternative might be despised as a reactionary view, namely a morality that put women back in their roles as primary caretakers.[13] The second alternative might be despised as a radical view, namely a morality that puts women together with women and called for a lesbian revolu-

---

13. Some people, feminists and nonfeminists, have associated Carol Gilligan's work with this point of view, notably Catharine MacKinnon (1989). While MacKinnon makes the instructive point that Gilligan's view of female relational values builds in the offensive idea that women's characteristics have been defined in relation to men, it would be an overstatement to attribute a straightforward reactionary view to Gilligan. After all, she explicitly says that she favors a view of persons in which males and females would both develop the feminine relational capacities. More to the point, Gilligan's own work, and much feminist-inspired moral philosophy, has valorized traditional feminine capacities without treating the problem of domination that feminists like MacKinnon have identified. In this respect, I think that MacKinnon is correct that much of the new feminist philosophy builds in stereotypical accounts of females. My treatment of the Chodorowian viewpoint is intended to steer between Gilliganesque inspired moral philosophy and the radical standpoint of thinkers such as MacKinnon.

tion.[14] Most American women, then, would probably prefer a procedure like the original position, namely an approach to moral theory that puts aside matters like mothering and sexuality and focuses on the equal capacities possessed by all persons of an age of justification.

Yet many of these women, I claim, are currently being dominated by their husbands. They are emotionally manipulated and some are even physically and sexually abused. They do most of the housework, they do most of the primary childcare, and they are sexually harassed at work and in public places. Still, if these women did engage in moral reasoning, they would be much more likely to support the original position than take either the reactionary or the radical turn identified above. In both cases, I think American women would be forced to suppress their commitments to their feminine capacities and needs (even to repress these commitments, that is, deny them unconsciously rather than consciously) in order to conform to an overall approach to moral reflection and morality that expresses essentially masculine values. This is plainly wrong. Here again women would be silenced by men. Now they would remain silent themselves.

Denial of the feminine is built into the original position itself

I now want to suggest that denial of the feminine itself is manifested in the original position, in particular with respect to the structure of argument itself. First, notice that a common feature of contractualist moral theories (Scanlon, 1982) is that they center around a procedure of justification. This means that the correctness of moral principles is not to be determined by substantive criteria, but by the correctness of the process by which they are selected. Thus the selection process must satisfy conditions of justification, such as rationality, fairness and impartiality. As I see it, a main objective of moral perspectives that center on justification is their focus on the future; they exist to help us arrive at norms to guide actions and practices. Procedures of justification, however, are not ideally suited to arriving at a set of norms for the future because they alienate us from both the past and the present. Thus one of the main reasons men in particular value the idea of impartial justification is that it focuses on an ideal future rather than the actual present or the actual past. The past, in

14. See, for example, Adrienne Rich (1980), Janice Raymond (1986), Catharine MacKinnon, and Victoria M. Davion (1991). Also see the discussions of radical feminism in Alison Jaggar (1983), Jean Bethke Elshtain (1981) and Elizabeth Spelman (1983), who criticizes Chodorow's approach to feminist theory from a point of view deeply informed by radical feminism and black feminism.

particular, is packed with fear and anxiety, fear and anxiety that affect the present in ways that men are unaware of. But if your method for thinking about the future builds in features that prevent you from understanding yourself and others, then the method should be rejected. A moral conception is therefore defective if it tries to justify a plan for the future before it provides a critical explanation of the past and the present. While it is tautological to say that in defending a moral conception we are trying to chart out a course to change the future, it is highly controversial whether the basic structure of a moral conception should focus on changing the future or understanding the past. This general charge has been made against the Kantian program since Hegel and Marx said that Kantianism was too abstracted from human history.

A justificatory approach to morality is, then, a defensive response to the denial of the past, in particular, the denial of the feminine in male development and the related fears about homosexuality that accompany this denial. The procedure is thus not so much a method used to defend a set of norms for the future as it is a mechanism of defense used to protect us, and men in particular, from the past (Bordo, 1987; Flax, 1983). Therefore, justification is *ad hoc* because it occurs after the facts. Moreover, since Rawls motivates the procedure by relying on surface facts about pluralism, autonomy, and fears of totalitarian societies, he evades the underlying fears that serve to construct the surface commitments. In fact, it would appear that justification is really about stability, indeed false stability, since maintaining an old system of parenting and sex roles more broadly is one of the main motivations of the procedure of justification itself. Justification is about false stability.

A Tension in Rawlsian Liberalism

How does the feminist critique of Rawls's *Theory of Justice* affect the ethical position Rawls developed in his more recent essays? One upshot of my feminist critique of Rawls is that it exposes very sharply the tension between the two arguments for stability within Rawlsian liberalism. Rawls's writings have shifted away from the moral methodology in *A Theory of Justice*, which aimed to include the social sciences and which sought to fashion a social order centered around the idea of helping those who had lost out. Rawls has not given up the difference principle, but the emphasis in recent years centers around the equal liberty principle and surface facts about liberal societies. The basic impulses of this philosopher have changed; the value of peace is now more important to Rawls than the value of justice itself – or he is at least more concerned to solve the kinds of conflicts that create havoc in the social order than he is to solve the kinds of problems that perpetuate human hardship.

Nevertheless, the new Rawls wants to believe that his social order would provide the conditions for all, including those who have lost out, to live with freedom and dignity. In addition, Rawls believes that his procedure for justifying the moral principles chosen for society has not changed. The principles that the parties would choose, as well as the procedure in which they would reason, are grounded in considered moral judgments as well as the ideals of moral personhood and social order embedded in the common sense of adult liberals. Indeed, Rawls is at pains to say that the theory of justice he constructs is a reflection of what we now believe and value, or at least what our unorganized beliefs and commitments suggest.

But the feminist critique illuminates the tension between Rawls's original and recent positions. If facts of social science are supposed to confirm the provisional justification of the two principles chosen in the original position, how are these facts doing any work now that surface facts from liberal society are being used to ground the original position and even argue for the principles themselves? The new argument for stability renders the old argument, and the role of social science, virtually superfluous. Worse yet, if the feminist account of false stability is correct, then the new argument for stability, turning away as it does from social science, conceals even more the problems of male domination and false stability that motivate both men and women to support the principles chosen by common sense liberals.

Two Rawlsian Objections

I now want to consider two objections a Rawlsian might make to my argument. My replies, though, will have to be quite brief. The first objection is as follows: even if it is true that the procedure of impartial justification is motivated by denial of the feminine in males, is it not possible that the principles that would be justified would lead to a society in which males did not have this problem and in which they did not dominate females? Thus even if actual persons are motivated to support the procedure for defensive reasons, is it not possible that the principles the parties would choose would lead these persons to change their practices? Rawls is not committed to the claim that our current considered moral judgments and ideals of personhood and society will be literally reproduced in the original position or in a new society. Rather, he wants to say that these commitments shape our approach to moral reflection but leave open a number of possibilities.

I would reply that it is indeed true that the principles may call for substantive changes in our current social order and I suspect that some changes for the good would take place. Indeed, I granted Rawls at the outset that a market socialist economy would be needed to apply the difference principle; I said that no problem of classism would exist in his society. Yet I maintain that sexist assumptions that are built into the original position would not be eliminated from the new socialist society. Why would they? If the parties, and American citizens, never consider facts about fear and anxiety, male domination and false stability, why think that the new society would eliminate these things? Possibly socialist institutions would eliminate cases of gender domination caused primarily by poverty, but my main line of argument is not about gender domination in the working class. My target was the ordinary middle class husband. It just seems to be overly charitable to Rawls to grant him that the problem of false stability would simply disappear when he never discusses these issues, and furthermore, explicitly puts aside controversial topics about political psychology.

The second objection is related to the first. If it is indeed the case that a family policy providing paid maternity and paternity leaves and nationally run day care centers would help to eliminate the problem of male domination, then why can't the Rawlsian endorse this kind of policy? Thus we may suppose that if the feminists are right about the need for a family policy, then Rawlsian legislators would be sympathetic to the policy. (This issue, like the issue about market socialism, arises at the level of applying the two principles.) Moreover, since the two principles of justice manifestly try to create conditions for males and females to be autonomous members of a democratic society, one may argue that a family policy would be needed as much to provide women with fair opportunities in the workplace as to eliminate the kinds of problems the asymmetrical organization of parenting produces.

I would reply as follows. It is likely that legislators would call for a family policy, and it is also likely that the policy would do some good. The problem is that the policy comes too late. Like impartial justification itself, the family policy is *ad hoc*. It comes after the fact that persons have affirmed the value of a method of moral reflection which builds in the problems of the previous generation. Even if the legislation passed, I doubt that it would have the plethora of effects the feminists say are necessary. For one, it is doubtful that legislators would call for the policy for the kinds of reasons the feminists identify. Would they really use feminist social science? Would they make reference to denial of the feminine, fear of homosexuality, new theories of masculinity and femininity, and the like? These notions are really foreign to the shape, substance, style, and sensibilities of Rawlsian liberalism. Why think that the persons who became these new Rawlsian citizens would understand the hard issues and make necessary changes to accommodate them?

A whole other set of issues concerns the question of whether the feminist facts could be used in the original position itself. I can note only one here. Could the parties refer to these facts rather than the facts from mainstream social science? The problem with this move is that the feminist facts are not facts in the Rawlsian sense of facts, since they are part of a critical theory of society that rejects the distinction between facts and values and moral justification and empirical confirmation. Since he uses facts to provide an empirical confirmation of a moral argument, Rawls is probably working with a notion of value-free social science, whereas the feminist social science views all facts as value laden. If Rawls wanted to say that he denies a sharp fact/value distinction, say along broadly Quinean lines (1969), then I would argue that the Quinean move builds in gender domination as well. But these are clearly matters for another time. Likewise Rawls can argue that since his theory of deliberative rationality is fundamentally different from the theory of autonomy that characterizes the populace, the old problems of defensive masculinity would not appear in the new society. Here I would ask why we have good reason to think this when the theory of deliberative rationality is housed within the same general cognitivistic framework as the theory of moral development.

Concluding Remarks

In this paper I have criticized Rawlsian liberalism from a feminist point of view. The criticism rests on controversial views about gender development and false stability in American society today. I did not defend the truth of these views in this paper, but I did try to indicate a number of implications these views would have for Rawlsian liberalism as well as the more general project of creating a humane society. In addition, while it is not a fully developed theory, my account of false stability in American marriages and families is more than a plausible scenario. Any adequate explanation of the state of affairs in American marriages and families would have to account for some obvious facts – the fact that many men do fear intimacy, many men are homophobic, many women do give priority to home life over work life, and many children do get manipulated by their parents – and my account does account for these facts.

If there is a moral to this paper, then it is that moral conceptions that center around the idea of impartial justification obstruct our ability to understand the hard issues about human social and personal life. The justificatory procedures force us to focus on an ideal future before we have achieved a satisfactory understanding of the past and its bearing on the present. We need a critical theory of society, and the family in particular, in order to approach the problem of creating a humane society.[15] Social institutions and social practices need to be criticized directly before we think about how things might be if we were not living within a system which is conditioned by these social institutions. Moreover, we are not required to give up our commitment to liberalism because there remains an untried way of reshaping liberalism. Liberalism can be joined with a modest theory of market socialism, it can be disabused of a theory of autonomy modeled on defensive masculinity, and it can adopt a family policy that will be to the advantage of parents and children alike. The task before us is to use feminist arguments and themes to update Dewey's idea of a public philosophy.[16]

References

Anderson, David. 1990. *Reconstructing the Justice Dispute in America*, University of Michigan, Ann Arbor.

Anderson, David. (unpublished). "Denial in the Original Position."

Baier, Annette. 1985. "What Do Women Want in a Moral Theory?" *Nous*, March.

Balbus, Isaac. 1982. *Marxism and Domination: A Neo-Hegalian, Feminist, Psychoanalytic Theory of Sexual, Political,* and *Technological Liberation*, Princeton University Press, Princeton, NJ.

15. Two feminist philosophers who work within the tradition of critical theory are Iris Marion Young (1990c) and Nancy Fraser (1989).

16. I have received a great deal of help in developing the arguments of this paper. I would like to thank Sherry Anderson, Alison Bailey, Gregory Beabout, James Bohman, Jane Braaten, Angela Curran, Stephen Downes, Richard Dees, Andreas Eshete, James Fishkin, Eric Gambel, Christopher Gauker, Jeff Gauthier, Donald Gustafson, Melinda Hogan, Michael Howard, Lisa Hogeland, Lawrence Jost, Alison Jaggar, Thelma Lavine, Glenn Lesses, Thomas Long, Harvey Mullane, John McEvoy, Lee Medovoi, Ted Morris, Connie Rosati, Martin Perlmutter, Michael Preston, Peter Railton, Paul Ray, Lynn Sanders, Justin Schwartz, David Velleman, Hugh Wilder, and Linda Weiner. I have also benefited from editorial advice of Paul Churchill and suggestions from an anonymous reviewer. I would especially like to thank James Cain, Don Loeb, Allan Gibbard, David Jackson, Don Herzog, Stephen Darwall, Elizabeth Anderson, and David Hills.

66

______1986a. "Trust and Antitrust," *Ethics*, Vol. 96.

______1986b. "The Moral Perils of Intimacy," *Pragmatism's Freud*, Joseph H. Smith and William Kerrigan (eds.) The Johns Hopkins University Press, Baltimore.

Benhabib, Seyla. 1987. "The Generalized and the Concrete Other: The Kohlberg-Gilligan Controversy and Moral Theory," *Women and Moral Theory*, Eva Feder Kittay and Diana T. Meyers (eds.) Rowman and Littlefield, Totowa, NJ.

Benjamin, Jessica. 1988. *The Bonds of Love: Psychoanalysis, Feminism and the Problem of Domination*, Pantheon, New York.

Blocker, H. Gene and Elizabeth Smith (eds.). 1980. *John Rawls's Theory of Social Justice*, Ohio University Press, Athens, OH.

Blum, Lawrence. 1980. *Friendship, Altruism, and Morality*, Routledge and Kegan Paul, London.

Bordo, Susan. 1987. *The Flight to Objectivity*, State University of New York Press, Albany.

______1990. "Reading the Slender Body," *Body/Politics: Women and the Discourse of Science*, Mary Jacobus, Evelyn Fox Keller, and Sally Shuttleworth (eds.) Routledge, Chapman, and Hall, Inc. New York.

Bowlby, John. 1973. *Separation and Anxiety*, Basic Books, New York.

Buchanan, Allen. 1980. "A Critical Introduction to Rawls's Theory of Justice," Blocker and Smith (eds.) *John Rawls's Theory of Social Justice*, Ohio University Press, Athens, OH.

______1982. *Marx and Justice*, Rowman and Allanheld.

Chernin, Kim. 1985. *The Hungry Self: Women, Eating, and Identity*, Harper and Row, New York.

Chodorow, Nancy. 1978. *The Reproduction of Mothering: Psychoanalysis and the Sociology of Gender*, University of California Press, Berkeley.

______1989. *Feminism and Psychoanalytic Theory*, Yale University Press, New Haven.

Daniels, Norman. 1975. *Reading Rawls*, Basic Books, New York.

Darwall, Stephen. 1980. "Is There a Kantian Foundation for Rawlsian Justice?" Blocker and Smith (eds.) *John Rawls's Theory of Social Justice*.

Davion, Victoria. M. 1991. "Integrity and Radical Change," *Feminist Ethics*, Claudia Card (ed.) University of Kansas Press, Lawrence, KS.

Dicks, Henry. 1967. *Marital Tensions: Clinical Studies Toward a Psychological Theory of Interaction*, Routledge and Kegan Paul, London.

Dinnerstein, Dorothy. 1976. *The Mermaid and the Minotaur: Sexual Arrangements and Human Malaise*, Harper and Row, New York.

Eichenbaum, Luise and Orbach, Susie. 1982. *Understanding Women*, Basic Books, New York.

Eisenstein, Zillah. 1990. "Constructing a Theory of Capitalist Patriarchy," *Women, Class, and the Feminist Imagination: A Socialist Feminist Reader*, Karen V. Hansen and Ilene J. Philipson, (eds.) Temple University Press, Philadelphia.

Elshtain, Jean Bethke. 1981. *Public Man, Private Woman: Women in Social and Political Thought*, Princeton University Press, Princeton.

Fairbairn, Ronald. 1952. *An Object-Relations Theory of Personality*, Basic Books, New York.

Flax, Jane. 1980. "Mother–Daughter Relationships: Psychodynamics, Politics, and Philosophy," *The Future of Difference*, H. Eisenstein and A. Jardine (eds.) G.K. Hall, Boston,

______1982. "The Family in Contemporary Feminist Thought," *The Family in Political Thought*, Jean Bethke Elshtain (ed.) University of Massachusetts Press, Boston.

______1983. "Political Philosophy and the Patriarchal Unconscious: A Psychoanalytic Perspective on Epistemology and Metaphysics," *Discovering Reality*, Sandra Harding and Merrill Hintikka (eds.) D. Reidel Publishing Company, Dordecht.

Fraser, Nancy. 1989. *Unruly Practices*, University of Minnesota Press, Minneapolis.

Friedman, Marilyn. 1987. "Beyond Caring: The De-Moralization of Gender," Marsha Hanen and Kai Nielsen (eds.) *Science, Morality & Feminist Theory, Canadian Journal of Philosophy*, Supplementary Volume 13.

______1989. "Feminism and Modern Friendship: Dislocating the Community," *Ethics*, Vol. 99.

Gilligan, Carol. 1982. *In a Different Voice*. Harvard University Press, Cambridge, MA.

______1986. "Remapping the Moral Domain: New Images of Self in Relationship," *Reconstructing Individualism*, Thomas Heller, Morton Sosna, and David Wellbery (eds.) Stanford University Press, Stanford.

Grimshaw, Jean. 1986. *Philosophy and Feminist Thought*, University of Minnesota Press, Minneapolis.

Habermas, Jürgen. 1971. "The Idea of the Theory of Knowledge as Social Theory," *Knowledge and Human Interests*, Beacon Press, Boston.

Hanen, Marsha, and Kai Nielsen. 1987. *Science, Morality & Feminist Theory, Canadian Journal of Philosophy*, Supplementary Volume 13.

Hare, R.M. 1981. *Moral Thinking*, Clarendon Press, Oxford.

Harding, Sandra and Hintikka, Merrill B. (eds.) *Discovering Reality*, D. Reidel Publishing Company, Dordrecht.

Hartsock, Nancy. 1983. *Money, Sex, and Power*, Longman, New York.

Held, Virginia. 1987. "Non-Contractual Society," *Science, Morality & Feminist Theory*, Hanen and Nielsen (eds.) *Canadian Journal of Philosophy*, Supplementary Volume 13.

Jaggar, Alison. 1983. *Feminist Politics and Human Nature*, Rowman and Allanheld, Totowa, NJ.

Jost, John. (unpublished). "The Marxian Critique of Abstract Psychology and Rawls's Theory of Justice."

Kohlberg, Lawrence. 1984. *The Psychology of Moral Development*, Vol. II, Harper and Row, New York.

MacKinnon, Catharine. 1989. *Toward a Feminist Theory of the State*, Harvard University Press, Cambridge, MA.

Marcuse, Herbert. 1964. *One-Dimensional Man*, Beacon Press, Boston.

Mullet, Sheila. 1987. "Only Connect: The Place of Self-Knowledge in Ethics," Hanen and Nielsen (eds.) *Science, Morality & Feminist Theory, Canadian Journal of Philosophy*, Supplementary Volume 13.

Noddings, Nel. 1984. *Caring: A Feminine Approach to Ethics and Moral Education*, University of California Press, Berkeley.

Nove, Alec. 1985. "Feasible Socialism," *Dissent*, Vol. 32.

Nozick, Robert. 1974. *Anarchy, State, and Utopia*, Basic Books, Oxford.

Osherson, Samuel. 1986. *Finding Our Fathers*, Free Press, New York.

Pateman, Carole. 1989. "Feminist Critiques of the Public/Private Dichotomy," *The Disorder of Women*, Stanford University Press, Stanford.

Piaget, Jean. 1948. *The Moral Judgment of the Child*, Free Press, Glencoe, IL.

Quine, W.V. 1969. "Ontological Relativity," *Ontological Relativity and Other Essays*, Columbia University Press, New York.

Railton, Peter. 1984. "Alienation, Consequentialism, and the Demands of Morality," *Philosophy and Public Affairs*, Spring.

Rawls, John. 1971. *A Theory of Justice*, Harvard University Press, Cambridge, MA.

______1975. "A Kantian Conception of Equality," *Cambridge Review*, March.

______1980. "Kantian Constructivism in Moral Theory," The Dewey Lectures, *Journal of Philosophy*, Vol. 77.

1985. "Justice as Fairness: Political not Metaphysical," *Philosophy and Public Affairs*, Summer.

______1987. "The Idea of an Overlapping Consensus," *Oxford Journal of Legal Studies*, vol. 7.

Raymond, Janice. 1986. "Female Friendship: Contra Chodorow and Dinnerstein," *Hypathia*, Fall.

Rich, Adrienne. 1980. "Compulsory Heterosexuality and Lesbian Existence," *Signs*, Vol. 5.

Roemer, John. 1991. "Market Socialism: A Blueprint," *Dissent*, Vol. 38.

Rorty, Richard. 1991. *Objectivity, Relativism, and Truth*, Cambridge University Press, Cambridge.

Rubin, Lillian. 1983. *Intimate Strangers*, Harper and Row Publishers, New York.

Sandel, Michael. 1982. *Liberalism and the Limits of Justice*, Cambridge University Press, Cambridge.

Scanlon, T.M. 1982. "Contractualism and Utilitarianism," *Utilitarianism and Beyond*, Amartya Sen and Bernard Williams (ed.) Cambridge University Press, Cambridge.

Scarf, Maggie. 1987. *Intimate Partners*, Free Press, New York.

Scharff, David and Scharff, Jill Savege. 1983. *Object Relations Family Therapy*, Jason Aronson, Northdale, NJ.

Scheman, Naomi. 1983. "Individualism and the Objects of Psychology," *Discovering Reality*, Harding and Hintikka (eds.).

Spelman, Elizabeth. 1983. *Inessential Woman*, Beacon Press, Boston.

Williams, Bernard. 1985. *Ethics and the Limits of Philosophy*, Harvard University Press, Cambridge, MA.

Winnicott, Donald. 1958. *Through Paediatrics to Psycho-analysis*, Hogarth Press, London.

Young, Iris. 1990a. "Socialist Feminism and the Limits of Dual Systems Theory," *Throwing Like a Girl and Other Essays in Feminist Philosophy & Social Theory*, Indiana University Press, Bloomington, IN.

______ 1990b. "Is Male Gender Identity the Cause of Male Domination?," *Throwing Like a Girl*.

______ 1990c. *Justice and the Politics of Difference*, Princeton University Press, Princeton.

4

The Self, Difference and Democratic Theory

Michael W. Howard

This paper is about the relationship between the self – that is, that conception, or those conceptions, of who we are that define what is most fundamentally important – and democratic theory, the theory of how we ought to govern ourselves.

It might seem at the outset that the problem is fairly straightforward. Since at least part of what a self is, as I have defined it, involves a specification of what is most fundamentally important – what counts as "the good" – it would seem to follow that the ideal of self-government will be one that best promotes the interests of the self – whether individual or collective – as defined by the good. Thus, for example, Aristotle could define the ideal *polis* as that most likely to promote virtue in its citizens, the exercise of which constituted their good.

However this straightforward approach runs up against the fact of pluralism, of difference, about which postmodernists and postmodern feminists are perhaps the clearest exponents.[1] I will say more in a moment about the extent and kinds of difference that can lead to alternative and sometimes competing conceptions of the good. At the outset I want simply to note that, although many postmodernists would not accept it, it seems a plausible step to move from the fact of pluralism to a familiar kind of liberalism in which the concept of justice is central. A defining characteristic of this liberalism is its insistence on abstracting from any particular conception of the good. The plurality and incommensurability of conceptions of the good is after all the starting point, in Rawls's later writings (1985, 1987, 1988), for his "political" conception of justice. And unless one is going to remain mute about the political implications of difference, one would seem to be pushed toward some kind of toler-

---

1. A couple of self-proclaimed postmodernists are Richard Rorty (1989) and Jean-Francois Lyotard (1984). Some postmodern feminists include Nancy Fraser (1989) and Linda J. Nicholson (1990), along with other authors in *Feminism/Postmodernism*, edited by Nicholson (1990); Iris Young (1990, 1989, 1986), and Jana Sawicki (1991).

ance, some kind of principle of respect for (if not celebration of) difference, which when fleshed out will begin to resemble liberalism. The idea that the standpoint of justice is itself a partial standpoint – that it is masculinist, for example – is a well-taken objection, but one that the theory itself can accommodate, for example by bringing the family out of the shadows and under the gaze of the standpoint of justice, as Susan Okin (1987, 1989) has suggested. In the process, the parties to that standpoint are reconceived, and the gaze itself is refocussed.

There is another kind of objection, associated with some postmodernists like Rorty (1989), but more commonly with communitarians, to the effect that it is the very abstractness and impartiality of justice that is the problem: that "thicker" ethical conceptions, such as friendship, or patriotism, or solidarity, are more powerful, and more authoritative, and that we ought to frame discourse in political theory in such terms.[2] The communitarian point seems particularly compelling with a view to developing the theory of democracy. From the standpoint of justice, what one can say about desirable forms of democracy is rather vague: that there should be a rule of law along with the canonical liberal political freedoms such as the right to vote, freedom of speech and the like. On the more controversial questions facing political theory today, such as whether there should be democratic rights in the workplace or over investment decisions, or equal rights of access to media, and who are the proper bearers of such rights – about these questions the theory of justice has little to say, precisely because it has abstracted from the concrete problems, and specific conceptions of community and the good life, that are at stake in struggles over the extension of democracy. (Whether, for example, we want to be essentially consumers of media products, or self-governing agents for whom the media is a common resource.)

Also, from the standpoint of justice, the insights of more particularistic traditions are unavailable. Consider two examples. First, from the point of view of civic republicanism, it is part of the citizen's good to be not only justly governed, but to be an active participant in government, and not only by voting for representatives, but by taking part in deliberation and administration. There are problems about how to interpret what this might mean for a modern nation-state, but some, such as Carole Pateman (1970), have suggested that worker self-management might be seen as a realizable extension of this tradition of democratic theory. From the standpoint of the theory of justice, such arguments are

---

2. Some communitarians include Michael Sandel (1982), Charles Taylor (1989b), and Alasdair MacIntyre (1984). Although dissociating himself from communitarians, Bernard Williams criticizes the abstractness of justice (1985).

irrelevant, or are relevant only in a very indirect way: as Quentin Skinner (1990) has suggested, policies instilling civic republican virtue, and requiring its exercise, might be justified from the standpoint of justice, if it could be shown that such participation was necessary for the preservation of liberty and justice as construed in the more austere and abstract theory of justice. Or, consider as a second example, Marxist humanism.[3] Marxist humanism considers the good of a human being to be self-creation, through interaction with nature and other human beings. Production is central to human self-creation, and for human beings to realize their good, it is necessary for alienation of work to be overcome. While the implications of Marxism for the transformation of state power have fallen into disrepute, there is still much to be learned from the Marxist tradition concerning the democratization of "civil society," particularly work, that might have wide, if not universal, appeal. Yet such insight is screened out from the standpoint of justice.[4]

So it is worth examining whether the seemingly natural step from the fact of pluralism to the standpoint of justice, to political liberalism, is the only one available. I shall argue that there are several alternatives available, the most attractive of which takes seriously both difference and the grounding of political theory in ethics, in an account of what it is to live well. For reasons to be explained later, I shall call this "ontological liberalism."

First, I want to say a little more about what I mean by pluralism. I have in mind two things, pluralism of group identity, and pluralism of conceptions of the good.[5] As for pluralism of group identity, we find ourselves in groups which are not of our own choosing, which are partially defined by how others view us, and which are inescapably part of our own self-conceptions. Thus we find ourselves to be male or female, worker or capitalist or professional, black or white, the member of a particular ethnic group. (These are not meant to be exhaustive of the possibilities.) About group differences I have two claims. First, a negative claim: no account of self or identity that considers only these "structural" aspects of the self can come to grips with the normative questions I have posed above, about how we should govern ourselves. While we can't (or can't always) escape these identities, they leave too much room for conflicting values within their parameters, too much room for interpretation of their significance and even of boundaries defining them, to allow us to

---

3. One recent exemplar is Mihailo Markovic (1982).
4. See my "A Contradiction in the Egalitarian Theory of Justice" (1985).
5. Iris Young (1986, 1989, 1990) has written extensively about the former, and I am indebted to her work on this, although I may depart somewhat from her formulations.

read a person's interests off of his or her class position, or gender, or any combination of such structural features.

Second, nonetheless, serious attention to such differences should lead us to be wary of claims of "common interest" that cut across all differences. (Just how wary we need to be I hope to clarify later.) The message of much postmodern criticism is the discovery of exclusion, and of the promotion of particular interests lying behind the masks of universal citizenship, universal rights, the common good, or the interest of the proletariat as a universal class – or within feminist theory, the idea of what is in the interest of all women. It would be too quick to conclude that all universalizing theories are to be condemned. But one cannot theorize in such a mode any longer without at the same time wondering reflexively about the excluded differences that any such common identity will be premised on.

The second kind of pluralism is that of conceptions of the good. Within the space defined by structures of class, gender, race, etc., there is much space for self-definition or self-discovery. It hardly needs to be argued at this point that we discover here a plurality of conceptions of the good. I am not advocating relativism. It is quite possible that among the many competing conceptions, one is right, and it is quite plausible that some are better than others. All I am saying is that in contemporary liberal societies – and anything likely to emerge out of them – people can be expected to disagree reasonably over conceptions of the good.

Given these facts of pluralism, how are we to proceed in political theory? There are broadly four strategies available to us, which I shall refer to as relativism, Hobbesian contractarianism, political liberalism, and ontological liberalism. The hard choice is between the last two, but I want to say a few words about the others, before setting out what is at stake in the choice between these.

Given a plurality of conceptions of the good, it does not follow that there is no normative basis for political theory, for a conception of justice. However, it could be the case that in reality the differences of self-conception are so great that we can only ask "whose justice?" Some will draw the relativistic conclusion that no shared conception of justice is possible; that people of different groups, or in different traditions, have irreconcilable interests, incommensurable ends; that we live in a state of (covert or overt) civil war, of which politics is the pursuit by other means, and all moral distinctions are flattened down onto the plain of power.[6] That these

6. These phrases are a sort of catalogue of characterizations of contemporary society and/or objections to relativism found in recent writings of such communitarians as Alasdair MacIntyre (1984) and Charles Taylor (1989a).

divisions may coexist within persons as well as between them only sharpens the problem.

While this line of thinking can sometimes produce startling insights by unmasking the pretensions of this or that particular moralizing discourse, I find the general conclusions sketched intolerable, especially if arrived at from the speculative premises with which we began. Moreover, these conclusions are, (as Steven Lukes has put it in conversation) impossible to hold in the first person. In all the familiar projects of unmasking – of the carceral society,[7] of sexism, of heterosexism – there is at least a covert taking of sides, an implicit notion of a less dominated, more liberated, or in some way, better state of affairs than those criticized. One cannot consistently regard that condition as nothing more than another configuration of power, no better than that criticized. So relativism seems to me an untenable position.

A slightly less pessimistic picture emerges from Hobbesian contractarianism. By this I mean a view that shares with relativism the belief that along with a plurality of conceptions of the good there is also a plurality of conceptions of justice. Thus, for practical purposes, getting along in society may be as problematic as it would be if everyone were following self-interest of a kind that clashed with the self-interest of others. "Justice" in such an approach is not a moral conception, but a mere *modus vivendi*, an agreement to disagree, in such a way as to maintain social peace.[8] In its contemporary forms, inspired by game theory, the strategy for theorizing is to suppose that agents have nothing in common but the most emaciated instrumental rationality, and that on this basis, with a view to their self-interest, a deal can be struck. I have only three comments on this view, which I will not argue for at any length here. First, the idea that something like a consensus could be generated on such a thin basis seems hopelessly implausible. Second, any consensus that might be produced would be highly unstable, the gap between justice and self-interest always threatening to open. And third, the conception of rationality employed may itself be more parochial, less shared than some plausible candidates for shared ethical conceptions.

We are left then with two positions both of which try to move from pluralism to a shared conception of justice. One of these, "ontological liberalism", I will take up shortly. The other, political liberalism, exemplified in Rawls' later work, argues for the necessity of developing a dis-

7. "Carceral" is a term Foucault (1970) uses to describe a society in which the disciplinary techniques of prisons have been generalized throughout the society, constituting forms of power different from those based on law and authority.

8. Rawls (1985) distinguishes his approach from a mere *modus vivendi*.

tinctly "political," not metaphysical, conception of justice, abstracting from any ethical conception, and drawing only on elements of a shared political culture, the elements of an "overlapping consensus." The result, as we have noticed, is austere and abstract, but it must be, so its advocates will say, to give full respect to difference, without resigning oneself to civil war, or to a mere *modus vivendi* that rests on the brink of civil war.

This conception of justice as grounded in reflective equilibrium with the prevailing political culture runs into a problem encountered by consensus theories of truth: different theories may both be congruent with the political culture and tradition. As Dworkin (1990) has argued, both utilitarianism and justice as fairness can make sense of core features of our political tradition, and yet do so in different ways, with different implications for the more controversial questions such as how to distribute the wealth. How do we decide, within the austere strictures of overlapping consensus, which theory is best?

A more profound problem arises if the political tradition is itself characterized by deep injustices, so that congruence with the tradition justifies, or could justify, an unjust status quo. When Rorty (1989) wishes to reduce moral principles to "we-intentions," he fails to come to terms with the possibility that the "we" of American liberal culture is not only concerned with equal opportunity, but also with unprincipled domination and exploitation of the lower half of the hemisphere, consistently throughout its history.[9]

The contract device, as Dworkin (1990) has shown, does not lever us out of this problem, for what then is at issue is the status of the hypothetical contract. And a hypothetical contract, unlike a real contract, does not oblige at all. There are a variety of attempts to show how hypothetical contracts could generate obligations. But the way Rawls has attempted to show this – as articulating the overlapping consensus of our political culture – runs precisely into the problem I just mentioned.

Thus if there is to be a shared conception of justice, we might do better to explore the fourth approach, which I have dubbed "ontological liberalism." By this I mean an approach that does not abstract from all conceptions of the good but, instead, seeks to make the right continuous with, and based upon, the good. I call this "ontological" because the strategy is to provide an account of the self, of the kind of being a self is, and of the goods that are real for it. This account of the self is not likely to be derived from Platonic realities that transcend human existence and history. More plausibly, it will develop from our efforts to respond to the

9. I owe this example to Maurice Glassman.

question – given where we are and in the context of our attempts to make sense of ourselves and the world around us – what conceptions are we hermeneutically unable to do without?[10]

I can only gesture at the end here toward the ways ontological liberalism might be developed. Let me suggest two paths, and some considerations for pursuing one rather than another. I will refer to them as formal and substantive. The first is exemplified by Ronald Dworkin's (1990) recent attempt to articulate a "liberal ethics" which can serve as a basis for liberal political theory. This ethic must be one that can plausibly be said to be held by most people, despite their substantive differences about what is good, and hence will be rather abstract or formal. Nonetheless, what Dworkin has in mind is a particular conception of what it is to lead a life that is worthwhile and specific enough to yield some conclusions about what justice is. There isn't space to review his argument here. For those familiar with it, I can only say that it seems to me to fail at the crucial point, where he attempts to show that a good life, conceived as living up to a challenge one sets for oneself, must include justice among its parameters. The "challenge model" is sufficiently abstract to encompass other more substantive conceptions of a good life, but for that very reason cannot be said to imply justice without begging the question. As in Plato's discussion of the good of justice, there is a fatal ambiguity between "justice" understood as a pattern of rules that give structure and point to one's activity, and "justice" understood as moral rules of the community. The former may be necessary for a self-governing soul or a good life, but it need not take the shape of morality.

Hence, if there is hope for a theory of justice grounded in ethics, rather than discontinuous with it, it is more likely to be found in the plurality of more substantive ethical conceptions available to us in contemporary culture, and in our history. One could try to defend one or another of these as the right conception. But for political purposes and given, as I have maintained, that we are likely always to reasonably disagree about such conceptions, it seems to me more fruitful to try to arrive at a shared conception of justice from a variety of distinct, substantive ethical positions. Such an approach takes ethics seriously, recognizing the priority of the good, and the deep claims that conceptions of the good have variously on each of us. It also takes difference seriously, recognizing that there is a plurality of conceptions of the good, a plurality of communities; and furthermore that these may conflict and that we may find ourselves members of several communities. Taking both difference

10. For an elaboration of this formula, see Taylor (1989a).

and ethics seriously, we have no choice but to try to find our way out of the woods with all the baggage we are carrying. The political theorist has a two-fold obligation: on the one hand to the project of a shared conception of justice; on the other hand to the diverse communities he or she belongs to or addresses in putting forward proposals for political consensus. Political theory should itself reflect this two-sided character.

My argument ends at this point. But as an afterthought, I cannot help but note the irony of arguing so abstractly for a more substantive or particularistic mode of theorizing. What troubles me about the position I have put forward is an inability to come up with "thicker" ethical conceptions that seem to do the job required. My only consolation is that I have not found others arguing in a similar vein – Charles Taylor (1989b), for example, or Bernard Williams (1991)-able to be any more specific.[11] My hunch is that if we were to pay a little more attention to what I earlier called group differences, and not attend so exclusively to the history of ideas and the differences emerging therefrom, we might make a little more headway in articulating a political theory addressed to distinct audiences. I do not mean to disparage the importance of the history of ideas for identifying diverse moral sources. But such moral sources must find their roots in the distinct contexts provided by group differences.

11. Charles Taylor (1989b) has suggested that something of the civic republican tradition can be resuscitated, but given that the conditions civic republicans held to be necessary for republics to survive – smallness, rough equality, and the like – are not to be found in contemporary capitalist democracies, this seems a non-starter. Williams (1991) would agree with this assessment, but offers no other political theory grounded in "thick" ethical conceptions.

References

Dworkin, Ronald. 1990. "Foundations of Liberal Equality," *The Tanner Lectures on Human Values*, Vol. XI, University of Utah Press, Salt Lake City.

Foucault, Michel. 1977. *Discipline and Punish*, Pantheon, New York.

Fraser, Nancy. 1989. *Unruly Practices: Power, Discourse and Gender in Contemporary Social Theory*, Minnesota University Press, Minneapolis.

______and Linda J. Nicholson. 1990. "Social Criticism without Philosophy: An Encounter between Feminism and Postmodernism," *Feminism/Postmodernism*, Linda J. Nicholson (ed.) Routledge, Chapman and Hall, New York, pp. 19–38.

Howard, Michael. 1985. "A Contradiction in the Egalitarian Theory of Justice," *Philosophy Research Archives*, Vol. X.

Lyotard, Jean-Francois. 1984. *The Post-Modern Condition*, Minnesota University Press, Minneapolis.

MacIntyre, Alasdair. 1984. *After Virtue*, University of Notre Dame Press, Notre Dame, IN.

Markovic, Mihailo. 1982. *Democratic Socialism: Theory and Practice*, St. Martin's Press, New York.

Nicholson, Linda J. (ed.) 1990. *Feminism/Postmodernism*, Routledge, Chapman and Hall, New York.

Okin, Susan. 1987. "Justice as Gender," *Philosophy and Public Affairs*, Vol. 16.

______1989. "Reason and Feeling in Thinking about Justice," *Ethics*, Vol. 99 No. 2.

Pateman, Carole. 1970. *Participation and Democratic Theory*, Cambridge University Press, Cambridge.

Rawls, John. 1985. "Justice as Fairness: Political not Metaphysical," *Philosophy and Public Affairs*, Vol. 14.

______1987. "The Idea of an Overlapping Consensus," *Oxford Journal of Legal Studies*, Vol. 7.

______1988. "The Priority of Right and Ideas of the Good," *Philosophy and Public Affairs*, Vol. 17.

Rorty, Richard. 1989. *Contingency, Irony, Solidarity*, Cambridge University Press, Cambridge.

Sandel, Michael. 1982. *Liberalism and the Limits of Justice*, Cambridge University Press, Cambridge.

Sawicki, Jana. 1991. "Foucault and Feminism: Toward a Politics of Difference" in *Disciplining Foucault*, Routledge, Chapman and Hall, New York.

Skinner, Quentin. 1990. "The Republican Ideal of Political Liberty," *Machiavelli and Republicanism*, Gisela Bock, Quentin Skinner and Maurizio Viroli (eds.) Cambridge University Press, Cambridge.

Taylor, Charles. 1989a. *Sources of the Self*, Harvard University Press, Cambridge, MA.

______1989b. "Cross-Purposes: The Liberal-Communitarian Debate," *Liberalism and the Moral Life*, Nancy L. Rosenblum (ed.) Harvard University Press, Cambridge, MA.

Williams, Bernard. 1985. *Ethics and the Limits of Philosophy*, Harvard University Press, Cambridge, MA.

______1991. "Enlightenment and Community." Lecture Presented May 17 to the European University Institute, Fiesole, Italy. Unpublished.

Young, Iris. 1986. "The Ideal of Community and the Politics of Difference," *Social Theory and Practice*, Vol. 12 No. 1.

______1989. "Polity and Group Difference: A Critique of the Ideal of Universal Citizenship," *Ethics*, Vol. 99, No. 2.

______1990. *Justice and the Politics of Difference*, Princeton University Press, Princeton.

5
A (Somewhat) Communitarian (Partial) Reformulation of Liberalism

Maurice L. Wade

Introduction

According to the prevailing economistic approach to public policy, the fundamental task of government is to serve and supplement the functioning of the market. On this view, public policy should be limited to providing the background necessary for the market's proper functioning as well as to identifying and providing those opportunities, if any, for maximizing aggregate preference satisfaction that cannot be provided by the market. Is this the view of public policy that should prevail in a democracy that is consistent with the definitive moral commitments of deontological liberalism? This paper argues that it is not, if certain strands of communitarianism are correct.

Two communitarian positions are important here: 1) the claim that, in spite of its celebrated neutrality, the liberal social ideal itself presupposes a substantive theory of the good and; 2) the claim that the link between the individual and society is, at least partly, constitutive in nature. Together these claims mean that deontological liberals have misidentified the social ideal that follows from their basic commitments and that the correct liberal ideal argues against the economistic outlook.

The argument is presented in four stages. The first sketches the economistic outlook, the social ideal it implies, and the conception of democracy that best coheres with that ideal. The second discusses the social ideal currently favored by deontological liberals. In section three, the relevant communitarian claims are discussed and liberalism's social ideal is reformulated to successfully capture its foundational moral commitments. Section four explains why this corrected liberal ideal provides compelling reasons against the economistic outlook and discusses some of its implications for public policy and democracy.

The aim of this paper is extremely limited. It does nothing to show that liberalism's moral commitments are correct or that the social ideal that best captures them is plausible. It only shows that, when this ideal is correctly delineated, it supports a conception of democracy that is ill-served by economistic public policy. And, it does this on the assumption that certain elements of the communitarian critique of liberalism are correct.

–I–

The economistic conception of sound public policy is rooted in the depiction of the individual as *homo economicus* and the notion of efficiency provided by contemporary neoclassical economics. On this conception the individual's good is constituted by her preferences and she is rational to the degree that she aims to maximize their satisfaction. She alone determines her preferences and they are most reliably revealed in how she uses her resources, particularly her willingness to pay. Rational individuals will undertake social cooperation only to maximize personal satisfaction. Accordingly, social life is purely instrumental and society has no substance or standing beyond its individual members, their interactions, and the consequences of their efforts at preference satisfaction. The appropriate organization of social life is thus whatever results from these choices of satisfaction-maximizing individuals.

The economistic perspective maintains that the free operations of the market embody this social ideal. Here rational individuals interact, cooperate, and exchange goods and services when doing so maximizes personal satisfaction, and the various institutions and policies generated thereby are simply the aggregate consequences of these choices.

When the market functions properly, the social status quo is voluntarily altered only when someone can thereby increase his satisfaction and no one else's is thereby decreased. Typically, this is what is meant when the market is said to be efficient. It alters the social status quo only when doing so produces preference satisfaction winners and no losers.

What roles do government and public policy play on this view? Most economistic theorists agree that the market itself depends upon a background of institutions, such as property and enforcement of contracts, which the market alone cannot supply. Government and public policy are apt instruments for the creation and maintenance of this background and, in so doing, serve the market (see, for example, Stokey and Zeckhauser 1978, Feldman 1980, Gramlich 1981, and Friedman 1984). Many economistic theorists also recognize opportunities for increases in total preference satisfaction which, for various reasons, are not accessible by means of the market alone (see, for example, Leonard and Zeckhauser

1986 and Lindbloom 1977). These theorists also give the task of realizing these opportunities to government and public policy.

What conception of democracy best coheres with this economistic outlook? Briefly, one in which individuals support political parties and vote for candidates for the same reason they expend resources in the market, i.e., to maximize personal satisfaction. Parties and candidates receive majority support on this basis and the mandate provided by victory in a democratic election is a mandate to support and supplement the functioning of the market. On this view of democracy, the overriding public responsibilities of winners of democratic elections are to provide both the background necessary for the market's operations and efficient social outcomes that the market itself cannot provide.

–II–

An apt place to begin in understanding the nature of liberalism is with its commitment to the view that the fundamental rules and institutions that regulate social life, what Rawls (1971) refers to as principles of justice and the basic structure of society, respectively, must be neutral between different conceptions of the good, different ways of life. If this general characterization of liberalism is correct, then clarity about the sort of neutrality to which liberals are committed is crucial to understanding liberalism. Simon Caney (1992, p.458) has elaborated a useful distinction in this regard, the distinction between justificatory neutrality and consequential neutrality. Although Rawls (1988, p. 262) finds the term "neutrality" highly suspect, he has noted much the same distinction in terms of the difference between neutrality of aim and neutrality of effect.

A form of social organization attains consequential neutrality or neutrality of effect to the degree that its fundamental rules and institutions have equal impact upon different ways of life. Here the neutrality of a society is a matter of the consequences those rules and institutions have for various conceptions of the good. As many critics who take liberalism to be committed to consequential neutrality have persuasively argued, no plausible form of social organization could have equal effects upon all ways of life (see for example, MacIntyre 1988, Salkever 1990, and Shapiro 1986). No matter how the fundamental rules and institutions regulating social life operate, some ways of life will thereby fare better than others.

Fortunately, liberals need not be committed to this kind of leveling egalitarianism. The neutrality required by liberalism is justificatory neu-

trality or neutrality of aim. A society achieves this whenever its fundamental rules and institutions are not premised upon any conception of
the good. To assess a society's neutrality of aim, we look not to how various ways of life fare within it but rather to the kinds of reasons that are
offered as bases for the decisions it takes. As Caney correctly notes (1992,
p. 459), to achieve justificatory neutrality, a society need only refrain
from invoking certain kinds of reasons to justify its decisions, i.e., reasons
that are rooted in preferences for and against differing conceptions of the
good. Insofar as its fundamental rules and institutions operate independently of such reasons, a society embodies the form of neutrality required
by liberalism. In Ronald Dworkin's words:

> Political decisions must be, so far as is possible, independent of any particular
> conception of the good life, or of what gives value to life. Since the citizens of
> a society differ in their conceptions, the government does not treat them as
> equals if it prefers one conception to another. . . .(1978, p. 127)

Commitment to this sort of neutrality more than anything else distinguishes liberalism from other political moralities. How this commitment
is defended, in turn, distinguishes deontological forms of liberalism from
teleological forms. Teleological liberals defend neutrality of aim on the
grounds that its consequences are superior to all alternative conceptions
of proper governmental decision-making. In other words, teleologists
who favor justificatory neutrality do so because they believe that when
society's principles of justice and basic structure are neutral between
competing conceptions of the good life the balance of good over bad
effects is always superior to that produced in the absence of such neutrality. Hence the teleologist's commitment to neutrality of aim and thereby
to liberalism is contingent in nature. It depends entirely upon assessment
of the effects produced by such neutrality. The organization of social life
is but a means to maximizing good outcomes. When a neutral organization best achieves this the teleologist will be a liberal but when it does
not he must renounce liberalism. From the standpoint of deontological
liberals, to reduce the merits of neutrality of aim to its consequences is to
misunderstand those merits. In their view, justificatory neutrality has
compelling grounds that are utterly independent of its consequences.
The nature of those grounds will become clear in section III below.

Why might deontological liberals find the economistic outlook,
sketched in section I above, especially attractive? Michael Oakeshott's
(1975, pp. 199–206) distinction between a *societas* and a *universitas* provides a useful way to get at this. In a *universitas*, social life is organized
around a substantive conception of the common interest. The funda-

mental rules that regulate social life direct the efforts and resources of individuals and their associations toward pursuit of that communal purpose. Accordingly a *universitas* will not be neutral toward particular conceptions of the good. Its principles of justice will be systematically biased against conceptions that do not serve its communal goal and in favor of those that do.

This intolerance, this non-neutrality, is precisely why deontological liberals reject the model of society as a *universitas*. The social ideal they favor instead is what Oakeshott designates a *societas*. Here the bond that forms a community is not some overriding social end but allegiance to a fair framework of fundamental social rules that enable individuals to pursue their own self-determined values and ends. The common good is not a substantive end in its own right, which can override the goods of individuals, but is itself constituted by those individual values and ends.

Consequently, the principles of justice appropriate to a *societas* are designed to facilitate individuals' life plans and to fairly adjudicate conflicts between them. I take it that this is what theorists such as Rawls (1971, pp. 30–33) mean by saying that the right is distinct from and prior to the good in liberal society. The principles of justice appropriate to a *societas* are not based on a conception of the good and so comprise a neutral framework, a neutral basic structure, which coordinates and structures pursuit of particular life plans without imposing a preferred way of life on anyone.

While deontological liberals disagree over how to discover correct principles of justice as well as over the correct content of such principles, they tend to agree that liberal principles will specify a set of individual rights that serve as trumps in social decision- making. These rights ensure that the definition and realization of their conceptions of the good are left up to individuals themselves. As Robert Nozick (1974, pp. 30–35) notes, such rights serve as inviolable side-constraints on how people, individually and collectively, can legitimately treat each other. They establish for each a private sphere into which the purposes of others cannot legitimately intrude.

Commitment to liberal democracy is then commitment to government by the governed themselves, but where the collective will cannot override individual rights. Even the collective will, on the liberal conception of democracy, must tolerate ways of life of which it disapproves. Such tolerance, for the liberal, is the essential difference between a free society and a tyranny. In a nontyrannical democracy, the will of the people rules but only outside that private sphere established by individual rights.

The economistic conception of public policy and democracy coheres nicely with this ideal of social life organized as a *societas* and so might be particularly appealing to deontological liberals. As with the liberal social ideal, on the economistic conception the common good is fully reducible to the various goods of individuals. Like the liberal ideal, it views society as properly organized to facilitate the purposes of its individual members and recognizes no fundamental communal ties between them beyond this end. Like the liberal ideal, it is therefore neutral toward different individual values and ends. It leaves each free to pursue what she sees fit, subject only to the constraint that others have the same freedom.

Yet deontological liberals should reject the economistic outlook. The liberal social ideal with which it so nicely coheres does not adequately capture liberalism's definitive moral commitments. Indeed, the social ideal that does so successfully gives liberals good reason to reject this prevailing philosophy of public policy.

–III–

Is the liberal social ideal genuinely neutral toward individual conceptions of the good? That the answer to this question is "no" can be seen by attending to a common but inept defense of liberal neutrality. As Michael Sandel notes, liberals constantly "distinguish between permission and praise, between allowing a practice and endorsing it. It is one thing to allow pornography, they argue, something else to affirm it" (Sandel, 1990, p. 110). Individuals must be allowed to pursue conceptions of the good that are morally bankrupt so long as they do not violate the rights of others. A common defense of this tolerance "implies some version of moral relativism, the idea that it is wrong to 'legislate morality' because all morality is merely subjective. 'Who is to say what is literature and what is filth? That is a value judgment and whose values should decide?'" (Sandel, 1990, pp. 110–111).

As Sandel (p.111) notes, this defense of liberal neutrality is equivalent to no defense. The commitment to allowing individuals to determine and pursue their own conceptions of the good, of course, is itself a moral commitment. To hold, as liberals do, that society must not impose any favored way of life upon its members is, of course, to make a value judgment. If this sort of relativism is correct, then this liberal value judgment is not susceptible to defense. It is no more or less valid than the contrary commitment or judgment. Therefore, the deontological liberal's position that social life should be organized on the model of a *societas* has no more validity than the nonliberal's claim that it should be organized on the model of a *universitas*. This kind of relativism reduces the difference between advocating the liberal social ideal over a nonliberal counterpart to the difference between preferring chocolate ice cream over peach sorbet. In either case, the position taken is but a matter of taste, neither susceptible to nor in need of defense.

Surely this misrepresents deontological liberalism. These liberals are not offering bare assertion of a shared taste when they offer their social ideal. They are taking a position that they believe can be defended in a manner compelling to rational people. That deontological liberalism itself depends upon a definite theory of the good is clear when that defense is examined. Why must principles of justice accord to individuals rights of the kind that ensure tolerance of diverse conceptions of the good? Deontological liberals broadly agree that this is because individuals are endowed with a capacity of unique moral significance, the capacity for rational self- determination. In other words, such rights are necessary in order to protect that which most merits protection, individual autonomy. Deontological liberals are not of one mind about the exact contours of this capacity, about why it has special moral significance, or about what schedule of rights best protects it. But for purposes of this discussion, these differences are irrelevant. All that needs to be seen here is that this commitment to the special moral status of the capacity for rational self-determination is, for deontological liberals, the definitive commitment underlying liberalism's social ideal. (Thus unlike the teleological liberal, the deontological liberal's defense of liberal neutrality is independent of its consequences and is grounded instead in respect for individual autonomy. This respect constitutes the merits of liberal neutrality for the deontological liberal.)

Why is this commitment inconsistent with liberalism's claim to take a live-and-let-live attitude toward particular conceptions of the good? Why does it fail to ground the very neutrality it is taken to require? Well, because it is a theory of the good itself. To hold protection of the capacity for rational self-determination to be the foundational value of social life is, as Gerald Doppelt notes, to treat autonomy as a meta-value, as "a universal precondition or ground of all value, that in virtue of which any particular conception of the good or way of life has value" (1988, p. 420). It is to say that the "goodness" of living in accordance with one's own particular conception of the good derives "from the more basic good of its being freely chosen and pursued: its being an embodiment of persons' uniquely valuable capacity for rational self-determination" (Doppelt, 1988, p. 417).

Another way of putting this is in terms of Martha Nussbaum's notion of a vague theory of the good. A theory of the good is vague if "[i]t admits . . . of many concrete specifications; and yet it draws, as Aristotle puts it, an 'outline sketch' of the good life. It draws the general outlines of the target, so to speak. And yet, in the vague guidance it offers to thought, it does real work" (Nussbaum, 1990, p. 217). The liberal theory of the good is vague in just this sense. It admits of indefinitely many particular articulations, yet makes clear what must be true for any given conception of the good to be an articulation of the liberal theory. It must be freely chosen and pursued.

Why do deontological liberals mischaracterize their position as not involving any substantive conception of the good? Using Nussbaum's formulation again, they do so because of the vagueness of the liberal conception of the good, because this conception is susceptible to indefinitely many particular articulations. In Doppelt's conceptualization of the liberal good as a meta-value, they commit this error because it is a good that "can only be realized indirectly through the mediation or choice of some particular conception of the good" and because "the content of any particular conception of the good which satisfies the meta-value cannot be inferred from the meta-value and is not evaluated as a means for realizing or maximizing the meta-value" (1988, p. 421).

Deontological liberals fail to distinguish between having a theory of the good and having a maximizing theory of the good, one according to which identifying something as the good is tantamount to holding that all individual and collective efforts and resources should be directed to maximizing it. But a theory of the good that is vague in Nussbaum's sense, and which functions as a meta-value in Doppelt's sense, does not equate the good with that which is to be maximized. Instead, it specifies the conditions that any particular life plan must meet in order to have value and to merit respect by others, and, it does so in a fashion compatible with indefinitely many particular ways of life. This is the kind of theory of the good that deontological liberals should recognize as the core commitment of their political morality. Deontological liberalism should hold that a particular conception of the good is itself good only if it is freely determined and pursued; if it is grounded in the individual's capacity for rational self-determination. In terms of the language of the right and the good, this means that "while the right is prior to legitimately pluralistic, 'particular' conceptions of the good, it is not prior to, but dependent on . . . a . . . conception of the supreme good as Kantian self-determination understood as a meta-value. . . ." (Doppelt, 1988, p. 428).

If the preceding considerations are correct, are deontological liberals mistaken in holding the model of a *societas* as the social ideal that captures their essential moral commitments? Yes and no! At one level, these commitments do require a conception of society organized as a *societas* – at the level of those particular conceptions of the good that are themselves articulations of the liberal theory of the good. In other words, deontological liberals must be committed to neutrality, but only regarding conceptions of the good that are freely chosen and pursued. They must tolerate any such conception, and principles of justice specifying inviolable individual rights enforce this. But these principles are themselves determined by deontological liberalism's own theory of the good. This means that at the level of society that Rawls (1978) refers to as its basic structure, the level to which principles of justice apply, liberalism presupposes a conception of social life as a *universitas*. For liberal principles must systematically discriminate against particular conceptions of the good that are not freely chosen and pursued or whose realization undermines such autonomy. Liberal society thus has a vague but substantive communal purpose, i.e., protecting the value of all conceptions of the good that have value, all conceptions of the good that are rationally self-determined. It makes the meta-value of rational self-determination the bar before which all individual and collective endeavors must submit.

Having traced out the implications of the communitarian claim that liberalism is not neutral in the sense that it takes itself to be, we can now turn to the implications of the second communitarian position crucial to this paper. Communitarians are noted for insisting that human beings are social creatures. What does this mean? This means more than the banal and widely accepted claim that we need social intercourse in order to survive or the equally banal and widely accepted claim that we naturally find such intercourse enjoyable and fulfilling. It means that the very capacities that various political moralities, including deontological liberalism, have identified as having special and unique moral status are socially determined. It means that the relationship between society and the morally most significant features of individual identity is constitutive in nature. As Charles Taylor puts it:

> What has been argued in the different theories of the social nature of man is not just that men cannot physically survive alone, but much more that they only develop their characteristically human capacities in society. The claim is that living in society is a necessary condition of the development of rationality, in some sense of this property, or of becoming a moral agent in the full sense of the term, or of becoming a fully responsible autonomous being. These variations and other similar ones represent the different forms in which

a thesis about man as a social animal have been or could have been couched. What they have in common is the view that outside society, or in some variants outside certain kinds of society, our distinctively human capacities could not develop. From the standpoint of this thesis, too, it is irrelevant whether an organism born from a human womb would go on living in the wilderness; what is important is that this organism could not realize its specifically human potential. (1985, p. 191)

If this communitarian thesis is correct, then basing political morality on the morally unique value of some human capacity entails valuing to the same degree the social arrangements that are necessary for its development, protection, and sustenance. If one holds that the principles of justice appropriate to a liberal democracy must accord inviolable rights to individuals because of the unique moral value of their autonomy, and autonomy is itself socially determined, then one must also hold that society should be organized in whatever fashion is required in order to develop, protect, and sustain that autonomy. Individual rights that function as trumps in social decision making will protect autonomy only insofar as certain social conditions exist, the conditions that enable autonomy.

> . . . the developed capacity for this kind of autonomy . . . is something which only develops within an entire civilization. Think of the developments of art, philosophy, theology, science, of the evolving practices of politics and social organization, which have contributed to the historic birth of this aspiration to freedom, to making this ideal of autonomy a comprehensible goal men [and women] can aim at – something which is in their universe of potential aspiration (and is not yet so for all men, and may never be). But this civilization was not only necessary for the genesis of freedom. How could successive generations discover what it is to be an autonomous agent, to have one's own way of feeling, of acting, of expression, which cannot simply be derived from authoritative modes? This is an identity, a way of understanding themselves, which men [and women] are not born with. They have to acquire it. And they do not in every society; nor do they all successfully come to terms with it in ours. But how can they acquire it unless it is implicit in at least some of their common practices, in the ways that they recognize and treat each other in their common life (for instance, in the acknowledgement of certain rights), or in the manner in which they deliberate and address each other, or engage in economic exchange, or in some mode of public recognition of individuality and the worth of autonomy? (Taylor, 1985, p. 204–205)

The basic moral commitments of deontological liberals commit them not only to a set of inviolable individual rights but also to the full array of social conditions that enable individual autonomy, which is, after all, the moral ground of these rights. For instance, if a particular level of poverty inhibits or undermines autonomy, then liberal society must take elimination of that sort of poverty as a fundamental communal purpose. If, for example, some particular form of child rearing inhibits or undermines the ability of children to become autonomous adults, its elimination or mitigation must be a fundamental communal purpose of liberal society. If, for example, a particular form and/or level of education is critical to the development of autonomy, then provision of such eduction must be a communal purpose of liberal society.

–IV–

Why does all of this mean that the prevailing economistic conception of sound public policy should be rejected by deontological liberals? Critics of the economistic approach to public policy have compellingly exposed various failings that provide sufficient grounds for rejecting it from the standpoint of any political morality (see, for example, Kelman 1987, Sagoff 1988, Majone 1989, and Gillroy and Wade 1992). While these "technical" flaws are important, they are not germane here. The argument here is that even were there no such flaws, deontological liberals nonetheless ought to reject the economistic position.

Remember that from the economistic outlook, public policy is sound to the degree that it supports the market and engenders efficient social outcomes that the market will not yield by itself. The main reason deontological liberals should reject this conception of public policy is that these kinds of social outcomes, even when limited by respect for individual rights, are only contingently connected to the social conditions upon which autonomy depends. Policies that generate such outcomes may or may not provide and protect the social conditions necessary for autonomy. Indeed, such policies may actually undermine those conditions.

That current criteria for sound public policy might yield social conditions that erode individual autonomy ought to be intolerable to anyone with the moral commitments that define deontological liberalism. The individual rights upon which liberals insist are premised on the unique value of autonomy. Policies that do not protect or that might destroy the social conditions upon which autonomy depends can rob these rights of their point. Why insist that governmental action be limited by rights that protect autonomy while allowing governmental action that fails to protect autonomy's social sources? Commitment to the unique moral value of individual autonomy entails that creation, protection, and sustenance of its social sources ought to take complete priority over producing efficient social outcomes. In a liberal society, identifying and accomplishing whatever is necessary to sustain autonomy ought to be the overriding communal end of policy and policy analysis. All other policy ends must have second rank.

Consequently, winners of democratic elections who take their victories to be mandates to maximize aggregate preference satisfaction by serving and supplementing the market misidentify their primary public responsibilities. On the liberal theory, preferences have value, are themselves good, only insofar as they constitute a freely determined and pursued conception of the good, are products of such a conception, or do not subvert such a conception. These criteria will be met only by those preferences that arise in contexts in which individual rights are guaranteed *and* in which the social sources of the autonomy that grounds these rights are also guaranteed. From the deontological liberal perspective, creating and securing this context is the primary public responsibility of democratically elected parties and candidates. Maximization of preference satisfaction can come into play only after that responsibility is discharged. Only then will preferences be grounded in the meta-value of deontological liberalism; only then will they count as particular articulations of liberalism's vague theory of the good. Democratically elected parties and politicians who place supporting and supplementing the proper functioning of the market ahead of this responsibility will realize the liberal theory of the good only by happenstance and may govern in ways that tend to defeat it. Their conception of the primary ends of policy and their primary criteria for assessing policy must be deemed severely deficient by deontological liberals.

Economistic public policy and its conception of democracy are an invitation to disaster from a deontological liberal position, if my (somewhat) communitarian (partial) reformulation of it is correct.

References

Caney, Simon. 1992. "Consequentialist Defences of Liberal Neutrality," *The Philosophical Quarterly*, Vol. 41, no. 165.

Doppelt, Gerald. 1988. "Rawls' Kantian Ideal and the Viability of Modern Liberalism," *Inquiry*, Vol. 31 No. 4.

Dworkin, Ronald. 1978. "Liberalism," *Public and Private Morality*, Stuart Hampshire (ed.) Cambridge University Press, Cambridge.

Feldman, Allan M. 1980. *Welfare Economics and Social Choice Theory*, Prentice Hall, Englewood Cliffs, NJ.

Friedman, Lee S. 1984. *Microeconomic Policy Analysis*, McGraw-Hill, New York.

Gillroy, John Martin and Maurice Wade. (eds.) 1992. *The Moral Dimensions of Public Policy Choice: Beyond the Market Paradigm*, University of Pittsburgh Press, Pittsburgh.

Gramlich, Edward M. 1981. *Benefit-Cost Analyses of Government Programs*, Prentice Hall, Englewood Cliffs, NJ.

Kelman, Steven. 1987. *Making Public Policy*, Basic Books, New York.

Leonard, Herman B. and Richard Zeckhauser. 1978. "Cost–Benefit Analysis Applied to Risks: Its Philosophy and Legitimacy," *Values at Risk*, Douglas MacLean (ed.) Rowman and Allenheld, Totowa, NJ.

Lindbloom, Charles E. 1977. *Politics and Markets*, Basic Books, New York.

MacIntyre, Alasdair. 1988. *Whose Justice? Which Rationality?*, Oxford University Press, Oxford.

Majone, Giandomenico. 1989. *Evidence, Argument, and Persuasion in the Policy Process*, Yale University Press, New Haven.

Nozick, Robert. 1974. *Anarchy, State and Utopia*, Basic Books, New York.

Nussbaum, Martha. 1990. "Aristotelian Social Democracy," *Liberalism and the Good*, R. Bruce Douglass, Gerald M. Mara, and Henry S. Richardson (eds.) Routledge, Chapman and Hall, New York.

Oakeshott, Michael. 1975. *On Human Conduct*, Oxford University Press, Oxford.

Rawls, John. 1971. *A Theory of Justice*, Harvard University Press, Cambridge, MA.

______1978. "The Basic Structure as Subject," *Values and Morals*, A. Goldman and J. Kim (eds.) Reidel, Boston.

______1988. "The Priority of Right and Ideas of the Good," *Philosophy and Public Affairs*, Vol. 14, no. 3.

Sagoff, Mark. 1988. *The Economy of the Earth*, Cambridge University Press, Cambridge.

Salkever, Stephen. 1990. "'Lopp'd and Bound': How Liberal Theory Obscures the Good of Liberal Practices," *Liberalism and the Good*, Routledge, London.

Sandel, Michael L. 1990. "The Political Theory of the Procedural Republic," *The Power of Public Ideas*, Robert B. Reich (ed.) Harvard University Press, Cambridge, MA.

Shapiro, Ian. 1986. *The Evolution of Rights in Liberal Theory*, Cambridge University Press, Cambridge.

Stokey, Edith and Richard Zeckhauser. 1978. *A Primer for Policy Analysis*, Norton Publishers, New York.

Taylor, Charles. 1985. "Atomism" in Charles Taylor, *Philosophy and the Human Sciences: Philosophical Papers II*, Cambridge University Press, Cambridge.

Democracy, the Individual, and Moral Community

FOREWORD

The first essay of this part, "Bringing Deliberation to Democracy," by James Fishkin offers a natural bridge between the theoretical issues of Part I and the more practical concerns of Part II. Fishkin's essay places present difficulties of democracy in a theoretical setting; he shows how in part they are outcomes of inadequate theories of representative democracy. At the same time, Fishkin offers practical solutions that many should find persuasive. The other essays of Part II likewise engage our concerns with flaws in democracy in action and seek, or at least explore, possible solutions.

James Fishkin, in particular, is troubled by the gap between democratic ideals and the reality of representative government in mass societies. Taking the United States as the democracy in which this problem has become most acute, Fishkin argues that American politics suffers from the flawed notion that more direct and more majoritarian processes automatically mean more democracy. On the contrary, given the vast scale of America, these processes do not generate greater citizen participation or voter deliberation – the conditions necessary, on Fishkin's view, to ensure that representative systems are genuinely democratic. Fishkin presents an analytic framework that gives concrete meaning to the notion of deliberative democratic institutions and that explains why American democracy has been sliding increasingly toward the dangers of shallow "mass democracy" and a tyranny of the majority.

But the main thrust of Fishkin's essay is his argument for new forms of representation (which he is presently engaged in trying to develop). Fishkin argues that these new forms of representation will better provide for political equality and will revitalize deliberation and the "public voice," without which genuinely representative democracy is impossible.

Like James Fishkin's essay, the contribution by Lisa Heldke, "Do You Mind If I Speak Freely? Reconceptualizing Freedom of Speech," analyzes an indispensable feature of liberal democracy – in this case, freedom of speech – both in terms of its conceptual and theoretical foundations and its practical implications. No one who reads Heldke's article can doubt that her reconceptualization of free speech, if accepted, would have enormous practical implications for freedom and for the quality of life in a democracy.

Heldke admits her initial interest in justifying the claim that certain occurrences of sexist speech qualify as a form of sexual harassment. Thus Heldke seeks to characterize free speech in such a way that some constraints on sexist language cannot be automatically disqualified as violations of freedom of speech. This objective leads Heldke to a thoroughgoing critique of liberal conceptions of free speech that are dominated, Heldke believes, by an inadequate paradigm of speech as individual utterances or expressions that may be restricted in various ways, or left unrestricted. Heldke points out that because, on this paradigm, speech acts have been regarded as the products of individual speakers, our interests in protecting freedoms related to speech have been overly concerned with the effects of restraints on speakers.

But Heldke protests that the liberal conception of freedom of speech rests on an incomplete and biased definition of speech. A more adequate definition recognizes speech as an activity that is necessarily collective because it equally requires the roles of speaker and listener. While Heldke recognizes that a definition of speech as communication would claim too much, she insists that as "connecting activity," speech is relational: "the expression or utterance cannot be severed from its receipt." Thus, by denying that speech consists of singularly individualistic acts, Heldke's collective conception of speech thereby weakens claims that it can be protected by appeal to liberal conceptions of individual rights. At the same time, by defining speech as an activity that is necessarily *interpersonal*, Heldke's approach allows her to assess the effects of speech on listeners or potential listeners as well as speakers. This enables her to claim that the protection of *free speech* must be sensitive not only to the speaker whose freedom may be curtailed, but also to the listeners and potential speakers whose freedom may be limited by the affects on them of speech that is threatening, intimidating, oppressive, or degrading.

Heldke maintains that her collective conception of speaking will preserve the values of free speech advanced by liberals better than does the liberal conception of speech. This is a claim that surely will be hotly contested. And some readers may be concerned that, if the conception of speech as a collective activity were to be adopted, then freedom of speech as a distinctive freedom would melt into some vague conception of the "freedom of the community." Whatever the outcome of this debate may be, Heldke's challenge to the traditional liberal position is daunting indeed, backed up as it is by the clear vision and careful analysis of an argument that is remarkable for the originality of its purchase on familiar terrain.

In his provocative piece, "Voting Rites: A Study in Ceremonial Democracy," Ron Hirschbein examines some of the mythology common in mass democracies. Rather than treat myths as simple falsehoods or as unexamined assumptions subject to correction, Hirschbein believes that political mythology is more deeply embedded in the collective symbolism that provides a people with a sense of meaning in life. Like James Fishkin, Hirschbein is dismayed by the dilution of the effects of individual participation in a mass democracy. But Hirschbein approaches the problem in an entirely different way. Unlike Fishkin, Hirschbein does not regard the dilution of citizen participation as a problem to be remedied through better institutional design or the reform of present processes. Instead, taking a skeptical view, Hirschbein argues that voting, properly understood as a social convention, is a "civic rite" that fulfills political elites' needs for legitimacy and their "audience's needs for meaning and drama."

Drawing on an insight from Michel Foucault, Hirschbein seeks to historicize our beliefs about voting rights as a narrative about the superiority of Western reason and the civic religion of progress. By "decontextualizing" voting, this privileged narrative blinds us to the reality that the significance of a vote depends on the circumstances in which it is cast. Hirschbein believes that in the present context citizens are reduced to passive spectators and the franchise is "stripped of its classic meaning and fetishized."

Why do we accept this debasement of one of the fundamental aspects of democratic process? Hirschbein argues that voting rites provide the electorate with a false sense of participation and empowerment, make some sense of political drama, and bestow the aura of legitimacy on governing elites, while distracting us all from the "enduring problems of politics and political life." Still, very many citizens sense the fraudulence of the ritual and don't vote. This may be one additional source of the "politics of indifference" noted by many commentators.

Hirschbein's essay is incisive and incitive – a rapier's jab – rather than a sustained argument, or finished project of historization. Thus Hirschbein examines beliefs that could be dealt with on the theoretical plane: any complete justification of representative democracy must refute the claim that voting is predominately ceremonial. But Hirschbein's concern with these beliefs as *mythical* indicates the need to probe their origins and effects within "popular consciousness." After all, if the people are to be capable of self-government, then at a minimum, they must believe themselves to be so capable. It would make little effect on the *practical* chances for democratic success, if we proved that democracy is ethically the best system but people were unable or unwilling to grasp this reality. Hence the need to explore, as Hirschbein does, the formation of a collectivity's self-perceptions as a *public*; and the need to track debate over these perceptions and to check the consolidation of mythical notions into beliefs that will impair democratic functioning. Perhaps some reader will think he or she can present reasons why Hirschbein's "slant" on the problem of participant ineffectiveness has gone wrong at the outset. If not, then we must deal with his challenge on two levels: first we must consider "deconstructing" mass society, as Hirschbein suggests, into smaller units in which participation is more meaningful, or alternatively, pursue more vigorously proposals such as James Fishkin's that may enable voters – even in national elections – to penetrate prefabricated images and to debunk marketed imagery in order to make informed, and hence, effective decisions.

Hirschbein is correct in asserting that, with the casting of numerous ballots and given ordinary conditions of uncertainty, one person's vote will rarely make a difference. But, of course, it doesn't follow that the voting of large numbers will hardly make a difference. Voting is one way in which we express collective choices. Hence, if voting is to remain a viable means of participation, then citizens must not abandon the belief that their own participation, in league with like-minded citizens, will make a difference. Yet, paradoxically, if we wish to maintain the vitality of democracy, then we must respect those individuals who are willing to break rank with their fellows and resist the acceptance of a belief or a law simply because of its popularity. Whether or not Hirschbein is correct about the symbolic function of voting, there can be no doubt that acts of individual heroism – the spectacle of the lonely individual's will pitted against the power of the state – can so dramatize doubts about political legitimacy as to rock the ship of state. Indeed, ever since Sophocles's portrayal of the defiant Antigone and Plato's portrait of Socrates, acts of civil disobedience have been the cause of reflection about the morality of "law and order" in Western political thought. The subject of civil disobedience was connected more firmly with the democratic tradition following John Locke's emphasis on government by consent and his struggle to make sense of "tacit consent." What are the limits of the citizen's obligations to the state when the state requires what the citizen conscientiously believes to be wrong?

In "Is Civil Disobedience Morally Coherent?" Matt Silliman offers a refreshingly original contribution to this tradition of reflection about the justification of dissent and disobedience. The crucial issue, Silliman believes, is whether there is any inconsistency between the necessity to act in accord with one's conscience and the requirement that disobedience be "civil," that is, that one submit to punishment for breaking the law. Silliman is thus concerned with the conflict between the morality of conscience and the morality of consequence. The objective of many civil disobedients is, after all, not primarily to palliate their consciences, but to effect social change.

Silliman's view of the civil disobedient's dilemma is premised on the fact that civil disobedience is usually effective only when dissidents, in subjecting themselves to punishment, characterize it as state repression, thereby joining issue with the state's defense of the law as legitimate. If the dissident evades or resists punishment, then although her actions are morally coherent, her disobedience turns into a politically ineffective, symbolic gesture. But if the dissident accepts punishment, then while her disobedience may be politically effective, she will be acting in a morally incoherent manner. In the latter case, Silliman claims, the civil disobedient's action is flatly inconsistent with her belief that the law is morally wrong and therefore does not deserve respect.

Some traditionalists might respond that in accepting punishment the civil disobedient manifests respect for the legal system as a whole, whereas her disobedience is aimed at one unjustified law. But this "solution" does not help us understand the civil disobedience of those like Mahatma Gandhi or Martin Luther King, Jr., whose targets were the injustice of whole systems of law; moreover, it is a distinction without a difference for an outraged majority that regards the violation of any law passed "in due process" as a challenge to the principle of majority rule. For Silliman, puzzlement over this dilemma is the occasion for an invitation into a deeper exploration of the role of civil disobedience in the democratic polity. In the course of this exploration, Silliman challenges the traditional beliefs that support both horns of the dilemma. We should not always think of conscience as uncompromising because it is individualistic and absolute. At the same time, we should free our conception of law from its narrow, positivistic sense and reintegrate it into the wider normative concept of nomos. Silliman proposes that we acknowledge the need for sustained moral discourse over the socially constructed character of conscience and the failure of positive laws, even at their best, to articulate more than a partial vision of the nomoi that legitimize them. Understood in this light, the moral discourse in which the civil disobedient engages us is a political narrative that appeals dramatically to a vision of the good our collective life should attain. Viewed in this way, Silliman argues, civil disobedience represents a "deeper moral coherence than can be offered by purism of either conscience or positive law."

6
Bringing Deliberation to Democracy

James S. Fishkin

We have only imperfectly adapted democracy to the large-scale nation-state. It is worth remembering that until the latter part of the eighteenth century, democracy was thought to be a curiosity reserved for city-states. It was only the crucial innovation of representation that permitted versions of popular control to be brought to the large-scale nation-state. We need to examine strategies for how the democratic idea might be better adapted to the large scale. This essay is intended to contribute to that process.

American politics exhibits a near-fatal attraction to a too simple notion of democracy. Anything more direct and more majoritarian is thought to be more democratic. Primaries and referendums have proliferated, particularly since 1968. The performance of the president, political candidates and the Congress is measured on almost a daily basis by widely-reported public opinion polls. We have even been treated to nationally televised versions of teledemocracy, such as the "America on the Line" program on CBS after the President's State of the Union Address. Seven million people attempted to phone in their instantaneous reactions to the speech and the issues of the campaign. The technology could only handle three hundred thousand calls during the program, but future versions are likely to perfect the process. Despite the unrepresentative character of the self-selected sample, and despite the unreflective and volatile character of the instantaneous reactions, the results were presented as the voice of the people, one that, we were told on the program, did not "bode well" for the president after his speech.

The move toward mass direct democracy in the large-scale nation-state derives much of its appeal from an image of direct democracy reminiscent of the Athenian Assembly or the New England town meeting. But such an appeal commits a category mistake. The social conditions for face-to-face interaction and deliberation, present in the small-scale case, are not present in the large-scale nation-state. In primaries, referendums, opinion polls and teledemocracy, we get the isolated, atomized citizen, pulling a lever, casting a ballot or dialing an "800" number based on very little reflection or interaction. His or her vote is just one of millions that will have little effect on the outcome. The citizen has little incentive for informed debate or for investment in political knowledge. Citizen preferences are characteristically trivialized by a collective action problem. Even the most optimistic account of contemporary voter rationality, Samuel Popkin's recent book, *The Reasoning Voter* (1991), characterizes voter thinking in terms of "low information rationality": the voter's motivations can be generalized from "what have you done for me lately?" (1991, pp. 7–11). Later we will explore the possibility of new strategies of institutional design that would create incentives for what might be called "high information rationality" where, hopefully, the voter will be motivated to consider a broader range of questions and issues. It is necessary first, however, to consider how the decline in voter deliberation may be related to changes in our conceptions of democratic process.

Consider the following scheme for conceptualizing alternative forms of democracy. (See the diagram on the following page.)

The scheme fills out three dimensions: a) The north-south dimension can be thought of as Madisonian versus majoritarian. By majoritarian, I mean the degree to which majorities get their way, and by Madisonian I mean the degree to which there are impediments to majorities getting their way – impediments that are usually motivated by efforts to prevent tyranny of the majority. As Robert Dahl noted in his *A Preface to Democratic Theory* (1956), majority rule can be invoked as a guiding principle in a system, such as the American one, in which the operative decision rule is actually "minorities rule." Intense minorities tend to prevail on issues of greatest concern to them. While this pattern is clearest in the United States, it occurs to some considerable degree elsewhere as well. Hence, it becomes an interesting empirical issue how, precisely, to place a given system on the north-south dimension. Some systems, such as the American one, will appear more Madisonian in the formal structure of their political institutions than they actually are, because of the role of informal factors, such as the influence of opinion polls and the mass media.

b) The east-west dimension can be thought of as representative versus direct. It expresses the degree to which a mass public has the opportunity to participate in decision making directly, or the degree to which selected officials act on their behalf. The selection of political leaders will also vary in degree along this dimension. For example, the change in the United States from indirect election (via state legislatures) to direct election of senators was a notable move in the western direction along this dimension. A similar point can be made about the proliferation of direct primaries in the presidential nomination system.

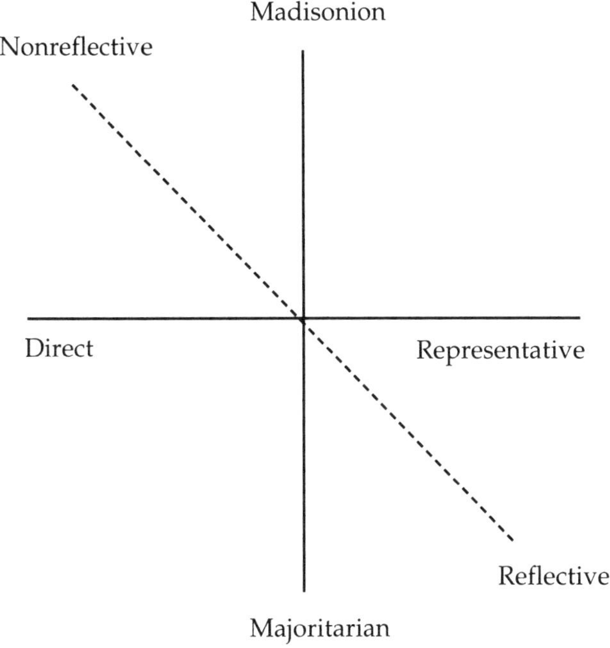

CHART 1

c) The near-far dimension can be thought of as deliberative versus nondeliberative with respect to the decision-making arena considered. (For further definition of all three of these dimensions, as well as a more detailed discussion of deliberative opinion polls, see Fishkin 1991.)

A significant strand of democratic theory would make distinctions among forms of public opinion. In one of the most famous examples, Madison argued in *Federalist* 10 that an extended republic was not to take public opinion in its raw form. Rather it was "to refine and enlarge the public views by passing them through the medium of a chosen body of citizens." The "public voice" arrived at by such representatives "will be more consonant to the public good than if pronounced by the people themselves, convened for the purpose" ([1787] 1961, p. 82). Similarly, Hamilton, in *Federalist* 71, clearly distinguished the "temporary delusion" of "inclination" or "transient impulse" from the public's consideration of its interests when there was "opportunity for more cool and sedate reflection." According to Hamilton, "the deliberate sense of the community should govern." His republican principle "does not require an unqualified complaisance to every sudden breeze of passion or to every transient impulse which the public may receive from the arts of men who flatter their prejudices to betray their interests" ([1788] 1961, p. 432).

This distinction between the inclinations of the moment and those public opinions that are refined by deliberative reflection is an essential part of any adequate theory of democracy. Democratic institutions can be considered deliberative or nondeliberative to the degree that the effective decision making is informed by the full diversity of alternative arguments any participant believes to be relevant. My colleague David Braybrooke has articulated an ideal that he calls "logically complete debate" (forthcoming). Jürgen Habermas has, of course, voiced the famous ideal of the "ideal speech situation." (For a good summary with some criticisms see Geuss 1981, Ch. 3 and Habermas's reply to critics: 1982, pp. 219–283.) Such ideals may be utopian or hypothetical. Yet as the ideal end point, a notion in which all the rival arguments get a full hearing available to all of the relevant participants may serve as an aspiration defining the outer limits of the deliberative dimension.

I will stipulate that institutions and situations are closer to the nondeliberative end when they exhibit various forms of incompleteness: incompleteness in the arguments (thought to be relevant by one participant or another) that have not been expressed so that others can be aware of them, incompleteness in the opportunities for the proponents of a position to answer the arguments expressed on behalf of rival positions, incompleteness in the knowledge or capacities of participants that would permit them to understand the arguments expressed on behalf of one position or another. We can consider situations that are more and more extreme in their incompleteness in one or another of these ways so that, at some point, we arrive at an end point of nondeliberation, an end point where an alternative is not contrasted effectively with its rivals, where arguments are not answered and where the decision makers have little competence or factual background to evaluate the proposals offered to them. Given these two endpoints, our discussion of the deliberative dimension will, obviously, always be a matter of degree. I will sometimes speak of an institutional innovation serving deliberation when it falls far short of the ideal but when it represents, nevertheless, a significant improvement over the lack of deliberation that we routinely encounter at present.

The basic direction of American democracy has increasingly been in the nondeliberative, south-western direction. In my book, *Democracy and Deliberation* (1991), I chart how a variety of formal and informal changes have contributed to a basic movement in the far south-western direction (from a point clearly in the north-eastern portion of the diagram).

With this scheme in mind, I will offer a general diagnosis for what I think ails the American political system and then I will offer a prescription that is not, by itself, a cure, but that would, I believe, exemplify a strategy for a useful program of treatment.

My general diagnosis is that in moving in the south-western direction, we have also been moving in the far or nondeliberative direction. In other words, we have brought power to the people under conditions in which the people have little opportunity and motivation to think about the power they exercise. The result is a shallow form of mass democracy, shallow because it offers us democracy without deliberation.

Three factors are particularly notable in bringing us this result: first, the entirely laudable impulse to bring the people directly into the process; second, the development of television as the major arena for political campaigning; and third, the use of public opinion polling as an ever-present mechanism for giving expression to the people's views. Together, these factors have yielded us a system that is far more plebiscitary, far closer to a "teledemocracy," than a focus on our formal political institutions would suggest. Later, I will propose how these same three factors can be turned to a constructive purpose to give us a deeper, more deliberative version of democracy.

Beginning with the impulse to bring the people directly into the process, recall that when Hubert Humphrey got the Democratic nomination in 1968, he did not enter a single primary. The McGovern-Fraser commission, which sparked a series of reforms in the democratic party, reforms that were basically paralleled on the Republican side, announced that "the cure for the ills of democracy" was "more democracy" (Commission, 1970, esp. pp. 10 and 11). From 1968 to 1988, the number of primaries went from 17 to 37 on the Democratic side and from 17 to 38 on the Republican side. While less than half of the delegates to each party's convention were selected in primaries in 1968, the number in both parties reached about 81 percent by 1988.

More importantly, the primaries have acquired great legitimacy and visibility. They attract enormous media coverage, particularly at the beginning. They are treated with the solemnity due the voice of the people. This attribution of legitimacy has reached such a point that even if the conventions had a heavier representation than they do now of "super delegates," of party elites capable of peer review, there would be a heavy onus on them to defer to any candidate who was perceived as having won the marathon of primaries.

Referendums, particularly in the western states, have also proliferated. In 1990, for example, there were at least sixty-seven proposals on statewide ballots, the largest number since 1932 (Pear 1990, p. A11). Both referendums and primaries exemplify a vision of mass democracy that is both direct and majoritarian.

The proliferation of primaries and referendums is symptomatic of a conceptual defect in our political culture: increases or improvements in democracy have been equated with movement in the south-western direction in our scheme. The possibility that democracy might be improved in any meaningful way by any change other than movement south-west has been discounted. Yet the experience with movement south-west has been that it trivializes the preferences and the opportunities for deliberation, the public voice, that is supposed to be in control of the system. Because the incentives for mass deliberation are so minimal, my focus will be on possibilities for achieving democratic values through new ways of filling out the northeast quadrant – new forms of representation that might achieve political equality along with deliberation.

Public opinion polling has given us a kind of "plebiscitary" democracy, where immediate reports of the public's surface impressions are given legitimacy as the voice of the people. The public gets only surface impressions on most issues because the sound bites have shrunk, candidate's appearances are orchestrated, and the techniques of advertising have become a primary filter through which our political discourse must pass. If all the minutes devoted to the issues (rather than to the horse race) on the CBS Evening News in a recent presidential campaign from January to June (covering the entire primary process) were put back to back, they would add up to a little less than two hours.[1] By contrast, the pregame show in this year's Super Bowl was two and a half hours long. Sound-bites of presidential candidates averaged about nine seconds in 1988 (Adato 1990, p. 4). Our political discourse is getting reduced to messages worthy of fortune cookies. Under these conditions, why should we pay so much attention to the unreflective first impressions of ordinary citizens?

Polls, primaries and referendums bring power to the people, but they bring it under conditions where the people have difficulty thinking about the power they exercise. Efforts at democratic reform appear enmeshed in a dilemma. It appears we must choose between politically equal but relatively incompetent masses and politically unequal but relatively more

---

1. I calculate this from tables in Robinson and Sheehan (1983, p. 149). Bruce Buchanan's study (1991) of the 1988 campaign supports a similar picture.

competent elites. In the area of presidential selection, the smoke-filled rooms of the prereform days at least had the benefit of providing for "peer review" of candidates. On the other hand, primaries have brought the people into the process, but in a manner that gives them little opportunity for deliberation.

Consider a way out of this dilemma, one that reconfigures the northeast quadrant with a different kind of representation, one that embodies both political equality and deliberation. By political equality, I mean the property any institution achieves when it gives every citizen a statistically equal chance of being the decisive voter. This form of political equality is achieved by primaries, referendums and other forms of mass democracy. It is also achieved by the proposal I will ask you to consider.

Imagine a new beginning to our season of presidential selection. Suppose we took a national random sample of the citizen voting age population and we transported them to a single site. We invite the major presidential candidates for several days of face-to-face questioning in small group sessions. We provide the citizens with briefing materials beforehand on the major issues facing the country. At the end of these deliberations, we poll the citizens on their views of both the candidates and the issues.

Such an event would constitute what I have called a "deliberative opinion poll." An ordinary poll models what the public thinks, given how little it knows and how little it pays attention. A deliberative poll models what the public would think, if it had a more adequate chance to think about the questions at issue. The point of an ordinary poll is descriptive. It provides a snapshot of the state of mass unreflective preferences in the public at large. The point of a deliberative poll is prescriptive. It gives voice to the people under special conditions in which the people would have a voice worth listening to. The poll can be thought of as a sample of what would be the public judgments of the entire society in a hypothetical version of our actual society – a hypothetical version where everyone had been given the same opportunity for thoughtful deliberation and interaction that the members of this sample would have been given.

In order to make this more concrete, imagine our experiment done over and over with innumerable versions, until every member of the society had participated. Clearly, such a supposition is only appropriate to a philosopher's thought experiment. However, unlike most such thought experiments, we could actually realize it by exposing a representative sample to the required stimulus of face to face interactions with ordinary candidates. Unlike the Rawlsian "original position" or Habermasian "ideal speech situation," we can concretize and actually poll the citizen preferences in a deliberative opinion poll. These preferences can be thought of as an actual sample of the hypothetical version of our society that would have achieved a superior form of democracy – one based on thoughtful, face-to-face questioning of the candidates and deliberation on the issues. No one would doubt that a poll of all the preferences in such a society would be a poll of the voice of the people when the people had collectively achieved a voice worth listening to. Our deliberative opinion poll of a national random sample exposed to these special opportunities and incentives for deliberation would be similarly thoughtful and representative of what the entire mass public would come to under such hypothetical conditions.

Just as we customarily make do with the opinions of a sample for plebiscitary democracy, we should make do with the opinions of a sample for deliberative democracy. The difference is that the opinions represented by the sample are actually shared by the mass of citizens out there in the case of ordinary opinion polls, while in the case of the deliberative poll, they are not. Rather, they rest on a morally relevant hypothetical. This is the public voice the country would come to, if it had better conditions for considering the problem at issue – if it had better opportunities for debating the issues and for questioning the candidates in face-to-face democracy. Just as we do not have to actually implement Rawls's original position to see its moral relevance (indeed, we could not actually do so), I submit that we do not have to actually achieve a fully deliberative society to see the moral relevance of this hypothetical world from which we can achieve an actual sample. Both the original position and the deliberative opinion poll depend on a morally relevant hypothetical that is held to offer a superior vantage point for making decisions. In the Rawlsian case, the vantage point is purely hypothetical. In the case of the deliberative opinion poll, the decision situation is real, but its moral relevance comes from the fact that it is taken to represent a purely hypothetical condition – the condition in which our entire society had achieved a superior form of deliberative democracy.

I and colleagues proposed to demonstrate this notion on national television (on the Public Broadcasting Service) in 1992. After the event was announced by WETA (the Washington PBS station), full funding was not, unfortunately, achieved and the event was cancelled for this presidential season. However, the event has now been adopted by all ten of the nation's presidential libraries and we propose to start early for 1996. Note that a successful demonstration of the idea could transform the presidential selection system by turning the "invisible primary" into a deliberative event. The invisible primary is the period before the first official events when candidates jockey for position, for credibility with the media and potential donors.[2] Given the role of momentum in the invisible primary, a change in the way candidacies are launched could determine the results. Instead of an event like the Florida straw poll, which is both unrepresentative of the country and undeliberative, we would have an event that is both representative of the entire country in all its diversity and deliberative on the issues.

The Florida straw poll, which represents party activists in one Southern state, played a major role this year in Clinton's rise to the front, just as it played a major role in Jimmy Carter's emergence before the Iowa caucuses in the 1976 campaign. Instead of candidates repeating standard stump speeches, we might imagine a process whereby they are forced to respond in depth on the issues, with sustained follow-ups. The premium that applies to unrehearsed political discourse was dramatized by the incident in December in which President Bush, in a teleconference to a teacher's convention in California, complained that he was asked the questions in the wrong order. An apparently spontaneous event was actually one that was carefully scripted.

New innovations are necessary if we are to create a public voice for the expression of the will of the people. The recommending force of a deliberative opinion poll at the beginning of the process could have a major effect on all that follows. It would represent a constructive use of the same three factors that have facilitated the rise of plebiscitary democracy – the impulse to bring the people into the process, the rise of television and the development of public opinion polling.

Thus far, the impulse toward political equality has pushed our system in the south-western-far direction, leading to a trivial form of mass democracy. Proposals to counteract this trend – bringing in super delegates, giving more power to party elites – have been perceived as undemocratic precisely because any movement north-east has been thought to undermine political equality, to undermine power to the people. Rethinking how to fill out the north-eastern portion of the scheme opens up the possibility of representative institutions that overcome this false dilemma, that bring the deliberation that used to be the province of elites and smoke-filled rooms to institutions that also embody political equality.

2. I take the term "invisible primary" from Arthur T. Hadley (1976).

References

Adato, Kiku. 1990. "The Incredible Shrinking Sound Bite," Joan Shorenstein Barone Center of the John F. Kennedy School of Government, Research Paper no. 2, June.

Braybrooke, David. "Changes of Rules, Circumspection and Issue Processing," [Forthcoming].

Buchanan, David. 1991. *Electing a President*, University of Texas Press, Austin.

Commission on Party Structure and Delegate Selection, Mandate for Reform. 1970. Democratic National Committee, Washington, DC.

Dahl, Robert A. 1956. *A Preface to Democratic Theory*, University of Chicago Press, Chicago.

Fishkin, James S. 1991. *Democracy and Deliberation: New Directions for Democratic Reform*, Yale University Press, New Haven.

Geuss, Raymond. 1981. *The Idea of a Critical Theory*, Cambridge University Press, Cambridge.

Habermas, Jürgen. 1982. "A Reply to My Critics," *Habermas: Critical Debates*, John B. Thompson and David Held (eds.) Massachusetts Institute of Technology Press, Cambridge, MA.

Hadley, Arthur T. 1976. *The Invisible Primary*, Prentice Hall, Englewood Cliffs, NJ.

Hamilton, Alexander. [1788] 1961. "Federalist No. 71," *The Federalist*, Clinton Rossiter (ed.) New American Library, New York.

Madison, James. [1787] 1961. "Federalist No. 10," *The Federalist*, Clinton Rossiter (ed.) New American Library, New York.

Pear, Robert. 1990. "Number of Ballot Initiatives Is the Greatest Since 1932," *The New York Times*, November 5.

Robinson, Michael and Margaret Sheehan. 1983. *Over the Wire and on TV*, Russell Sage Foundation, New York.

Popkin, Samuel L. 1991. *The Reasoning Voter*, University of Chicago Press, Chicago.

7

Do You Mind if I Speak Freely?
Reconceptualizing Freedom of Speech

*Lisa M. Heldke**

Introduction

In this paper, I develop a way to conceive of free speech that begins by redefining speech.[1] My definition affirms the fact that speaking is an activity that goes on *among* people in a community. Speaking, I will suggest, is an activity that involves not only the present speaker, but also others who act as listeners and potential speakers.

I contend that liberal conceptions of free speech have often proven ill-equipped to address certain free speech issues, precisely because they have tended to conceive of speech not as a collective activity in which participation involves both speaking and listening, but as an individualized activity in which only speakers and their utterances are relevant.[2]

The conception I develop defines speaking as collective, thereby illuminating the role played in it by listeners/potential speakers. In the bulk

* © 1992 *Social Theory and Practice*. Reprinted with permission.

1 Earlier versions of this paper were presented at the Fall, 1989 Midwest Society for Women in Philosophy Conference in Evanston, Illinois, and the New Feminist Scholarship Conference at SUNY, Buffalo, March, 1990. I would also like to thank the members of a political philosophy reading group – Jeremy Iggers, Tamara Root, Corinne Bedecarré, Tom Atchison, and Nancy Potter – for an extremely helpful discussion of the paper; Peter Dalton and the anonymous reviewers from *Social Theory and Practice*, for their written comments; and Stephen Kellert, for many challenging conversations about the issues involved.

2. Of course not all liberal notions of speech are radically individualistic; a useful distinction might be made between "solipsistic" liberal models, and "two-or-more-person" models. The latter sort do ascribe some sort of role to those who hear and respond to speech. John Stuart Mill's arguments for the value of free speech, for example, display a significant emphasis on the role of the community. Mill's model emphasizes the importance of free debate and discussion as a means by which to improve one's ideas. One of his chief arguments in support of free speech is that collecting others' responses to one's speech enables one to develop clearer, stronger ideas. But such a view only addresses others' roles as speakers – as producers of ideas. My position recognizes an even broader role for these others; I shall suggest that listening/potential speaking are themselves aspects of speaking. Thus, others' interests do not become relevant (and eligible for protection) only when others themselves become speakers; the interests of listeners (and even "ignorers") as listeners must be taken into account in evaluating whether speech in a particular situation is free.

of activities that go under the name "speech," a community of "others" (listeners, potential listeners, "ignorers") plays some sort of role. Those instances of speaking in which there are no relevant others may be defined in terms of their relation to speech-with-listeners. That is, they are exceptions to the general cases, and their presence in the category "speaking" can be understood by reference to one of these general cases.

My original motivation for developing this conception of speech was to provide a way to illuminate those forms of sexual harassment that consist of sexist speech. I intend for the conception to characterize free speech in such a way that preventing someone from using sexist language does not (at least automatically) constitute a violation of their free speech rights, but in fact may increase the level of freedom of the community.

I develop my account by first providing a critical outline of one version of a liberal conception of free speech.[3] In the course of this outline, I examine two central liberal justifications for protecting speech; the argument from individual rights and the argument from utility. I conclude this section by making explicit my criticisms of this liberal conception.

Following this, I turn to develop an alternative collective conception of speaking and of free speaking. I argue that this conception is preferable for two reasons; first, because speaking is a collective activity, and to treat it otherwise is to mask its powers and disguise the benefit or harm it may bring to users. Second, a collective conception of speaking preserves the values of free speech advanced in liberal views better than does a liberal conception.

–I–

A. To begin with a definition that will require some unpacking, I'll describe a liberal notion of free speech as speech that is unconstrained. Obviously two components of this definition require particular attention: what is meant by speech? and what does it mean to be unconstrained?

1. The liberal conception tends to focus on speech (as opposed to *speaking*), and treats speech as the utterances of an individual.[4] Indeed, the word "utterance" crops up in discussions of freedom of speech with

---

3. Obviously, there is more than one liberal model of free speech, and what I will say about this model is not true of every liberal model.

4. I think it not insignificant that discussions of the First Amendment tend to refer to "freedom of speech," and not "free speaking." The former construction draws our attention to the product, while the latter focuses on the activity of speaking.

some regularity. (Francis Canavan, for example, describes speech in the broadest sense to "include every kind of utterance and publication" (1984, p.2). The word "utterance" – a noun – conveys the notion that speaking is an activity that creates some "thing" that may be shared or traded with others.[5]

An essential feature of such speech is that it is the product of an individual. Speaking, on a liberal conception, is done by a single person. Only derivatively is it understood as conversing, corresponding, communicating *among* individuals. The community into which utterances are issued is relevant only secondarily.

This liberal conception of speech depends for its legitimacy and cogency upon a particular conception of the nature of the individual and of the relationship between the individual and society. The individual on this conception is unattached to others; it is not formed out of relations to others. Rather, it is an independently-created self that, for a variety of reasons, chooses or is constrained to enter into relations with others. At its core, this self is discrete, detached.

Emerging from this understanding of the individual is a conception of speech as the utterances of such an individual. Of course the liberal conception recognizes that speech may have an effect upon the individuals who hear it (just as it acknowledges that our development as individuals will be shaped by outside influences such as speech), but it regards that effect as extraneous to the speech itself. Speech is the act of discrete, independent individuals, and it too is discrete, independent and individual.

2. This notion of the individual as detached, and of speech as the discrete utterances of that individual, motivates and supports a description of free speech as speech that is unconstrained. This, recall, was the second component of the liberal definition I proposed that required some examination. "Unconstrained" here means that the individual speaker is in no way actively prevented, or coerced into refraining, from speaking.

On this view, assessing the freedom of any "piece" of speech requires determining who the speaker is, and whether their speech is being allowed to flow unrestrictedly. (The image that comes to mind is that of a river; free speech is a river that is allowed to flow from its mouth unimpeded by debris, dams or diversionary measures.) No other concerns

---

5. Plato could have told us that this was a bad way to think about speaking. In the *Protagoras*, he suggests that knowledge is not a substance you can take home in a bottle and inspect to see if it's safe. Knowledge goes directly into you (1961, 314a–b). Although he is talking about knowledge here, his remarks are also relevant for the speech through which learning takes place.

enter into the assessment at this stage; the only real consideration is whether the individual who would speak has been impeded in any way.

If individuals are restricted – if they're forced to cut out parts of their speech, or call off a planned rally – then their speech is no longer unconstrained. Of course most people (though not everyone)[6] would argue that there are times when restrictions on freedom are appropriate or even necessary; that the unconstrained speech of individuals is not something always to be protected. But, whether the restriction be justified or unjustified, on this conception, to restrict someone's speech is to limit their freedom. That is, while you might agree that those who would yell "fire" in a crowded theater ought to be restricted from doing so – or prosecuted for doing so – you are thereby agreeing that speech ought not be entirely unconstrained, that its freedom ought not be unconditional.

On the liberal view as it is realized in United States Supreme Court decisions, free speech issues have tended to arise in the form of questions about whether or not the utterances of particular individuals ought to be limited in particular situations – whether, that is, our freedom to speak ought to have limitations. The history of free speech decisions by the Supreme Court is a history of stipulating if and when restriction is justified; when my freedom may legitimately be curbed, and when such a curb is an illegitimate constraint. Making these decisions, the Court suggests, generally requires looking beyond speech itself.[7] When speech is defined as utterance, any decision to restrict it because of its effect on others is a decision that requires taking into account issues that are not relevant to the concerns of free speech alone. (I shall say more about this later.)

As a result of the Supreme Court's decisions, an individual may not utter "fighting words" to another individual face-to-face, but a group of Nazis may hold a rally in a predominantly Jewish community, in which they vilify Jews.[8] Calling a police officer a "God-damned racketeer" (the "fighting words" case) raises certain concerns that take precedence over an individual's right to speak – namely, concerns about the breach of peace likely to result when the insulted party retaliates. The white supremacist rally does not involve such issues; in the case in question, the

6. Canavan cites U.S. Supreme Court Justices Hugo Black and William O. Douglas as two examples of those who regard freedom of speech to be a freedom that must never be abridged in any way (1984, p.7).

7. "Looking beyond speech itself" often involves claiming that speech is not just speech, but is also action – illegal action at that. MacKinnon, in discussing this issue, says, "Consider for example that First Amendment bog, the distinction between speech and conduct. Most conduct is expressive as well as active; words are as often tantamount to acts as they are vehicles for removed cerebration" (1987, p.208). She points to laws against treason, bribery and blackmail as illustrations of this fact.

8. *Chaplinsky v. New Hampshire* 315 U.S. 568 (1942); and *Smith v. Collin*, 439 U.S. 916, 918 (1968).

114

Court ruled that the presence in Skokie of many Jewish survivors of the Holocaust did not in itself constitute a compelling reason to restrict the free-speech rights of Nazi demonstrators. No ordinance forbidding their demonstrating there has been allowed to stand. Of course this conception of freedom of speech recognizes that to protect an individual's utterances is to incur certain costs; it is understood that people may in fact be damaged either directly or indirectly by the speech of another. However, advocates of this conception argue that the benefits of protecting such speech generally outweigh the costs incurred in protecting it. Therefore, unless extenuating circumstances are sufficiently extreme, the utterances of the individual must be protected.[9]

B.   A liberal defense of freedom of speech frequently focuses on two types of values or aims that it claims are best protected and promoted in an atmosphere of unconstrained utterances. They are: individual self-fulfillment, and the attainment of truth. In other language, they're the arguments from individual rights and utility; freedom of speech must be protected in order to safeguard/promote the rights of individuals, and in order to arrive at truths. I'll consider each claim briefly.

1.   Thomas Emerson argues that:

> The right to freedom of expression is justified first of all as the right of an individual purely in his capacity as an individual. It derives from the widely accepted premise of Western thought that the proper end of man is the realization of his character and potentialities as a human being (1966, p.4).

Free speech figures in here because:

> every man – in the development of his own personality – has the right to form his own beliefs and opinions. And it also follows that he has the right to express these beliefs and opinions. . . For expression is an integral part of the development of ideas, of mental exploration and of the affirmation of self (1966, p.4).

Emerson's rights-based defense of freedom of speech rests upon two notions that I've described as being part of a liberal conception of the indi-

---

9. Of course the question is, "what constitute sufficiently extreme circumstances?" and this is one of the questions the Court has been answering. It is not my project to summarize its answer here. In raising this discussion, I wish only to emphasize the way that the issue is formulated in the first place; to highlight the fact that, for the Court, any conditions that warrant restricting someone's speech are themselves regarded as extraneous to the (free) speech itself. (This is a particular illustration of my more general claim about a liberal conception of free speech – namely, that the roles of listeners, etc., are not regarded as being parts of the activity of speaking itself.)

vidual and of speech. There is the idea that human (intellectual) development is a solitary project – one in which others' ideas can be of assistance to the individual, but which ultimately is a highly individual enterprise. And there is the emphasis on speech as a thing – an utterance or, for Emerson, an "expression." Emerson suggests that expressing our ideas – that is, speaking – is essential if they are to have any significance. Note that Emerson doesn't suggest that expression is necessary because humans and their ideas are social, and must have contact with other ideas in order to develop. Indeed, he seems to reject the idea that human intellectual development is inherently social. Instead, he argues that humans must express ideas as a way of developing/asserting independence, autonomy, and maturity. It is the act of issuing them to others that develops maturity in us. To suppress speech is to negate "man's essential nature" (1966, p.5).

There is something slightly dizzying about such a defense of freedom of speech. On one level, it seems like a defense I would want to support – one that it would be almost blasphemous to reject – but on another level, I am left wondering just what is being defended. It is not the right to talk with others. It appears to be the right to express. Emerson defends the right to produce just what a liberal conception defines as speech; individual utterances or expressions.

But it isn't clear just how speech defined this way can contribute to our growth as individuals. What is it about expressing ideas that promotes our intellectual growth? In my discussion of an alternate conception of free speech, I'll show that this argument implicitly assumes that speaking goes on in a community. It's because we're talking *with* others who *respond* (or might) that expressing our ideas helps us mature.

2. For a characterization of the utilitarian defense of free speech, consider Mill: "[T]he peculiar evil of silencing the expression of an opinion is that it is robbing the human race [of a potentially correct opinion] . . ." (1978, p.16). Mill's defense of freedom here assumes that speech is an activity through which we attempt to arrive at the truth, an assumption that quite clearly does not encompass all of the uses to which speech is put. But, setting that complication aside, what is Mill's defense?

Mill is arguing that the best way for us to arrive at the truth is for the community to be jammed with as many ideas as possible, and for all these ideas to challenge and confront each other. Only if all possible views get articulated can we be reasonably sure that we haven't eliminated any *true* ones; and only if we perpetually subject our roughly-true ones to the criticisms posed by other positions can we be sure that our most-valued ideas *legitimately* retain their status.

116

It seems to me that Mill's conception (even more than the individual rights notion) is collective at heart, for it recognizes the centrality of exchange and interchange.[10] Thus, this utilitarian defense of free speech implicitly acknowledges the collective nature of speech. Utilitarian values also would better be realized by a collective conception of speech.

C. I've been suggesting that liberal conceptions of free speech tend to be problematic because they treat speech as the utterances of an individual. This treatment obscures the fact that speaking is something we do with (or to) each other, that we are not solitary utterers of statements so much as participants in a collective activity. Because of this, a liberal notion of free speech is ill-equipped to analyze situations in which listeners are silenced or otherwise harmed by another's speech. For instance, it cannot analyze situations in which an utterance itself illegitimately restricts another's speech – in which speech restricts speech.

1. In the first place, a liberal conception of freedom of speech (which focuses on the present speaker) often makes it difficult even to articulate the fact that a listener may also become a speaker, thus obscuring the right that is violated when that person is prevented from speaking.[11] For example, in almost none of the cases in which the Supreme Court has ruled to restrict someone's right to speak has the restriction been applied because someone else was being kept silent. In the few cases in which the courts have seen fit to limit someone's speech in order to protect someone else's,[12] the fact that this liberal conception was in force meant that

10. As Tom Atchison suggests, Mill's model may be described as a "two-or-more-person" liberal model of free speech, for Mill does indeed acknowledge the role played by others in the community. It is through conversation that we improve our ideas. So it might be said that Mill is more immune to my criticisms than someone like Emerson, because he adopts a kind of community-based model. This is true, but as Corinne Bedecarré points out, Mill only recognizes part of the social context of speech. He still ends up focussing attention exclusively on the speaking part of speech – on what other speakers can add to my thought/speech. The receiving of speech is irrelevant to him. Thus, as I've already suggested, my position is not reducible to his. This fact will become more clear when I turn to explicate my position directly.

11. I would suggest that this is a rather conservative criticism, one that addresses the liberal conception on its own turf. That is, it criticizes the liberal conception for being less than thoroughgoing in its protection of speech, because it fails to recognize that some speech is suppressed even before it is started. As such, it is a criticism to which Mill's position is certainly less susceptible than some others'.

12. MacKinnon refers to such cases as "guarantees of access to speech" (1987, p.208). One case MacKinnon points to as an example of an affirmative guarantee of access to speech is the *Red Lion* decision (*Red Lion Broadcasting Co. v. F.C.C.*, 395 U.S. 367 [1969]). "Because certain avenues of speech are inherently restricted – for instance, there are only so many broadcast frequencies...some people's access has to be restricted in the interest of providing access to all. In other words, the speech of those who could buy up all the speech there is, is restricted" (1987, p.208).

117

such a ruling – which seems so commonsensical – could be reached only after some rather gymnastic thinking.

On a liberal conception, the most straightforward way I can see to understand such a guarantee-of-access case is as two separate freedom of speech cases. One involves the speaker, whose freedom is going to be curtailed if it is decided that their speaking prevents someone else's. The other case involves the party prevented from speaking, a party who tends to be invisible (a fact that partly explains why so few cases of guarantees of access come before the courts).[13] The speech-as-utterance notion involves interpreting such a situation as one in which one party's speech is freed at the expense of the other's. The notion sets up a situation consisting of two parties with separate and competing interests. In this setting, (at least) one party must "lose."

2. Furthermore, a liberal conception makes no genuine acknowledgement of the fact that speech is an activity generally involving listeners; on this conception, evaluating the freedom of an individual's speech does not include evaluating the effects upon the community in which the speaking is done. Appealing to community concerns is something one *might* do – and perhaps even routinely does in certain kinds of cases. (Treason, bribery and conspiracy laws are examples of this.) But on a liberal conception, the moment you take such considerations into account, you go beyond the concerns or requirements of free speech proper. You assert that other concerns take precedence over the protection of speech. For example, in this country, the law that makes it a crime to advocate the violent overthrow of the government acknowledges that there are situations in which speech ought not be protected.[14]

13. MacKinnon: "By contrast with those who wrote the First Amendment so they could keep what they had, those who didn't have it didn't get it. Those whose speech was silenced prior to law, prior to any operation of the state's prohibition of it, were not secured freedom of speech" (1987, p.207). MacKinnon's analysis points to the fact that there are several levels at which one's speech may be restricted, and that it is important to focus an eye on each of those levels, to see the relations between them. My claim is a particular application of the more general claim that it's necessary for individuals to see their experience in the context of the larger social structures that shape their experience. In the case of speech, it is important for a woman who is denied access to speech to recognize her exclusion in relation to the historical denial of access to women.

14. An anonymous reviewer of this paper asks why this is an objection to the liberal model. "It is one thing to state what *constitutes* free speech; another to determine what value should be attached to it. . . . The liberal approach can take account of any and all effects of free speech when it comes to this evaluative question. The alternative account offered by the author seems to want to build the evaluation into the very conception of free speech itself. . . ." In response to this reviewer, I would agree that my account builds an evaluation into the conception of free speech – but so does the liberal conception. The difference between the two views is a difference over which aspects ("effects") of speaking one takes into account in determining its freedom – not between an account that builds evaluation into it and one that does not. My account calls into question the very legitimacy of calling someone's speech "free" when it perpetuates the silence of another.

In Part II, I will attempt to show that if we conceive of speech as an activity that takes place among – and often with – other people, we can address such problems as access to speech and harm to listeners directly. We can do so because the larger situation isn't divided into separate, speaker-specific situations with competing concerns; and because speech, on this conception, is defined as an activity that involves listeners/potential speakers.

On such a conception, it is true that certain things we've come to regard as *prima facie* examples of restricted speech may not turn out to be such. This may well be a cause for a certain amount of consternation. It is not my project here to suggest that certain views or certain people ought to be silenced, period. Rather, I am attempting to show that a liberal conception of speech already enables such silencing to go on, along with other kinds of harm as well – and it does so *in the service of protecting speech*. The fact that a liberal conception actually facilitates certain kinds of silencing (to say nothing of other harm to listeners) provides a serious argument for reconceptualizing speech.[15]

–II–

A. The conception of free speech set forth here is predicated upon the view that we are constituted as persons in part through our connections with others.[16] This is no accidental fact about us – although our relations with any particular "others" may be accidental.[17] This conception of per-

---

15. It has frequently been asked whether my reconceptualization here is legal or moral. Although I illustrate my position with reference to Supreme Court decisions, and use the position of Catharine MacKinnon, a legal theorist, my project is primarily a moral or social one. This is because I have little confidence in the power of legislation to effect changes in the ways people think and act – and I have considerable suspicion about the ways such legislation would be enforced.

I therefore regard my reconceptualization of speech as a tool for groups of people interested in rethinking/reshaping their ways of talking together – and for making policy decisions within that community. I think a college establishing policy against sexist or racist speech might exemplify its use – although showing whether and how this is so must be the project of another paper.

16. My conception of individuals as relational has been shaped by Deane Curtin, Sarah Lucia Hoagland, Suzanne LaGrande, Maria Lugones, and Susan Heineman, among others.

17. In support of this claim, I would suggest, for example, that we really can't imagine what a human who grew up and lived entirely outside human culture would be like. Our difficulty in imagining this is not confined to our worry over how an infant could survive without a human parent. It extends to a genuine confusion about how such a being would behave, and what they would "be." To paraphrase Wittgenstein, even if "humans raised by lions" could speak, we wouldn't know what they were saying (1958, p.223). And if they weren't raised by *anyone*, we couldn't imagine them talking.

sons as partially constituted by relations with others motivates a conception of speaking which understands it as an activity that takes place *among* people and involves their participation as both speakers and listeners.

1. For many of us, talking with other people is the kind of speaking in which we engage most often. Our days are filled with conversations with other people; intimate conversations, casual conversations, exchanges of information or pleasantries.[18] In all these cases, there is interaction among participants – individuals who are sometimes talkers, sometimes listeners.

Not all speech situations consist of actual exchanges among individuals; often someone speaks, but others don't or can't respond. By defining speaking only as an activity that takes place among people – rather than as communication *per se* – I mean to include situations in which actual conversation cannot or does not take place. For even if the listener has no opportunity to respond to a speaker, they are connected to that speaker because they are or may be affected by that speech. Such an effect is not some accidental or secondary by-product of speech; speaking always holds at least the potential to affect those who receive it. (Indeed, conversation is one of the chief means by which we become the particular relational selves that we are.) I would argue that a definition of speech – and, consequently, of free speech – must recognize this. Unless you always talk only to yourself, whenever you speak you are entering into a relation with someone who stands to be affected by what you say.[19]

What happens if I apply this definition of speech, which emphasizes relationality, to a "hard case" like television, in which case I'm physically prevented from responding to the speaker in person? Even this speech is relational, I'd argue, because as the viewer I am clearly affected by what is said; I'm angered or pleased or offended or enlightened or bored. The same is true if I'm part of a crowd listening to a speech. In this case, there is only a small chance that I will actually have an exchange with the speaker. But even if that doesn't happen, their talking affects me, and this effect is not extraneous to the speech itself. (To import the liberal vocabulary, the expression or utterance cannot be severed from its receipt; speaking involves both.) These examples serve to show that, while to define speech as communication makes too strong an assertion, we can

---

18. This description highlights another difference between the model I'm developing and the liberal model. Liberal theorists – one thinks especially of Mill here – consider speech only insofar as it is aimed at the acquisition of knowledge. But clearly that is not what all talking aims at; some of it aims at having fun with words, killing time, even preventing the acquisition of knowledge (as when I talk while you're trying to study).

19. Of course this is not to deny that your speech may have a very small (verging on nonexistent) effect on someone.

claim that speech is relational, if we recognize that relations vary in intensity and aren't always reciprocal.

Another qualification of the definition is required to address cases in which no listening goes on, for in many situations, the speaker intends to be listened to, but isn't. The "non-listening" may be passive (as when the listener's mind is elsewhere and they just aren't paying attention) or it may be active (as when an audience shouts down a speaker). The important thing to note in most all such cases, though, is that despite their failure to be heard, the speaker did intend to be. Cases of failed hearing, I'd argue, still are best understood in relation to cases where speaking and hearing both go on.

To sum up, this conception of speaking views it as a connecting activity in which the role of listener/potential listener/ignorer is not derivative but partially constitutive of the activity. The situations I've outlined support and expand the claim that it is more useful as well as more accurate to understand speaking as a collective activity rather than to define speech as the product of an individual utterer. Ultimately, it is unhelpful and distorting to separate the "receiving" of speech from the "issuing" of it.[20]

2. Given a conception of individuals as constitutively relational and of speaking as an activity involving both speakers and listeners, it is also necessary to redefine *free* speech. This definition should acknowledge that it is not only the current speaker whose freedom may be curtailed; listeners/potential speakers may also suffer limitations on their freedom.[21] And, because their activity is part of speaking as defined here, limitations on

---

20 However, there is nothing in my definition that prevents treating certain acts of speech as genuine utterances. A liberal definition of speech may be more descriptive of some speech. But I would argue that such instances are the exceptions, and not the standards they are made to be. (I'm inclined to think that the sort of situation that is best described by a liberal model is one in which the speaker is utterly ignored by all potential listeners – or in which they are only talking to themselves. And of course in such situations, the problem of censorship is not likely to arise: if no one's paying attention to you, it's unlikely that they'll try to restrict you either.)

21. An anonymous reviewer worries that my definition makes speech unfree only if those whom it harms are present in the room with the speaker. Such a definition would exclude all-male "locker room" talk, for example. The reviewer writes, "I hope for a conception of free speech that excludes sexist talk whether or not women happen to be listening. . . ." I concur with the desire for such a conception. And, though I will not develop the claim here, I would suggest that this desire could be met by understanding the notion of listener/potential listener as including persons who are not present (and perhaps never could be present) at the scene of the actual conversation, but are present for its aftermath. Women who bear the repercussions of conversations in which "men forge and strengthen their bonds with one another and their domination through misogynist talk" could then be regarded as potential listeners. This means of addressing the example uses a very broad notion of what counts as the relevant community.

such activity may also count as restrictions on freedom. Speaking in a particular situation is not free if my talking silences (or in other ways harms) another through threat, intimidation, or oppressive generalization.[22]

Free speech on this view should be attributed not to the individual (or to communities that can be reduced to individuals) but to the relevant community and to individuals only as members of that community. When I conceive of myself as a being-in-relations-with-others, and of speech as an activity that places me in relations with particular others, I must also regard my speech as a thing that may build or disrupt those relations. In other words, I cannot consider my freedom-to-speak outside of the context in which I am speaking. In fact, it is only by reference to this context that I can adequately assess the freedom of any particular speech. In shifting attention away from the individual speaker, the question changes from "Is this speaker free to say what they will?" to "Is the talk in this situation free – are all members of the group participating at a level that promotes, rather than prohibits, the speech of others?" On the view I'm constructing, the interests of listeners are a part of the very fabric of the speech. In determining whether the speech is free, their perspectives must routinely be considered.[23]

Sexist language is one pervasive variety of speech that empowers the speaker at the expense of the hearer. Such speech – conceived of as a community activity – is not free. The speech in a classroom is constrained if a professor speaks "freely" in a way that systematically debases a student or students. (The same is true for a student who debases others – student or teacher.) Thus, this conception makes it possible for some-

---

Another way to address this example is to recognize that it is not only women who are harmed by sexist speech, though the harm to women is generally greater and more direct. Thus, men telling sexist jokes together in a locker room must also be understood as harming not only women, but also themselves through such practices (and thus, as not speaking freely). Sexist talk is harmful to the men who use it, and to the men who listen to it. This is true whether or not they recognize or acknowledge the harm as such.

22. I recognize that I run the danger of being perceived as advocating that everyone "be nice" to each other and never make anyone uncomfortable. This clearly is not my aim; in fact, my model virtually guarantees that those who talk in oppressive, arrogating ways will feel very uncomfortable when others in the group silence them. Although I will not develop the claim here, I suggest there is a difference between the discomfort you feel because you are the object of sexist or racist talk and the discomfort you feel because, as the perpetrator of such talk, you are subject to the criticism of others. (This is a variation on the familiar "toleration of the intolerant" issue.) Stated another way, just because you are uncomfortable doesn't automatically mean your freedom is being violated.

23. As Nancy Potter notes, this conception of responsibility bears certain similarities to the view Claudia Card develops in her paper "Intimacy and Responsibility: What Lesbians Do" (unpublished paper). Jeremy Iggers also points out that taking into account the perspectives of hearers (or readers) could transform the notion of a "free press;" what if the perspective of newspaper readers were routinely considered in assembling a paper?

one's speaking quite literally to count as an instance of the violation of the community's free speaking. For instance, when a classics professor in his lectures consistently makes remarks that suggest that he thinks women are ill-suited to the study of classics, his remarks serve to limit the freedom of the classroom. By suggesting that women are not equipped to study classics, he is "inviting" certain members of the class not to speak.

This example may seem like it counts as a restriction on free speech even from a liberal view, however – because it denies access to some. Consider instead a case in which a professor tells suggestive jokes that focus on women's sexuality. Here, the professor is not so clearly suggesting that women are not welcome in classroom conversation, so it seems less likely that it could be understood in terms of guarantee of access. However, such joke telling would be likely to squelch women's willingness to participate in discussion (for fear it would call even more unwanted attention to them); it would move women into the "uncomfortable listeners" category. Thus, on my conception, such action would count as a violation of freedom of speech.

Furthermore, to consider an even harder case, even if this were a class in which student discussion played no role, I would still argue that the professor diminishes the freedom of speaking in this classroom, through humiliating (some of) his listeners. As you recall, my definition stipulates that the listener/potential listener is a part of the speaking situation, even in instances in which they are not able to respond.[24] For a male professor to speak in ways that humiliate women students is to lend support to systems which subordinate women, to bolster the stratification of an already-stratified system.[25]

I describe the community as "already-stratified" because clearly, a classroom in which I am forbidden to speak is already a classroom where speech is not free. In fact, it may seem beside the point, even obfuscatory, to say that the freedom *of speech* of this community is further diminished by an instructor's singling out and degrading particular people or

---

24. Again in response to the anonymous reviewer, I would suggest that even if women are not able to respond because they are not *present* (the locker room again, or a classroom in a men's college), this still constitutes a harm to women as potential listeners, and to men as actual listeners, whether they acknowledge it or not.

25. Again, I rush to emphasize that I do not intend to advocate everyone "tolerating" everyone else, or being nice to everyone else. I begin from the assumption that oppression, objectification, arrogation, are real features of classroom discussion, and that their presence ought to be addressed and dealt with just as routinely as would be an error in using *modus ponens*. (The fact that this attitude sounds to many like a violation of academic freedom is, to me, an indication that there are some problems with this latter concept.) The question to be asked always is, "in what sense does this way of talking contribute to the freedom of the community?"

groups. Doesn't such a claim mask the significant suppression of free speech that is already present in a classroom where students aren't allowed to speak? And while we certainly should recognize the damage done to one who is forced to listen to sexist or racist talk, do we really want to call that a diminishment of the community's *freedom of speech?*[26]

Indeed I do. It is important to recognize not only the speaking from which students are prohibited, but also the potential speaking, and active, engaged listening that is blocked in an atmosphere which dehumanizes them. With respect to potential speaking, consider that these students leave the classroom and enter other classes where talking is expected, perhaps even required. The experience of being harassed through sexist speech may make them reluctant to talk even when given the opportunity; as Tamara Root suggests, their "entitlement to speak" is curtailed.[27]

Furthermore, students' functioning as listeners is harmed in a context in which they are denigrated. Listening and "listening-type activities" (like ignoring) are part of speaking. Even when listeners don't have opportunity to talk, the freedom of speech of the community is further diminished when they are not treated as full humans.[28]

B. Recall my discussion of the two defenses offered of the liberal conception of freedom of speech. Here I shall attempt to make good the claim that these defenses are better served by a collective notion of speaking than by a liberal conception of speech.

1. The first defense was the argument from individual rights. I suggested that there was something slightly peculiar about such a defense, because it wasn't at all clear how speaking could promote intellectual growth when it was treated as a singularly individualistic act. I asked how uttering – as opposed to talking – could foster intellectual growth. It is my experience that it is precisely when I am uttering, rather than talking-and-listening, that I am least likely to learn anything.

In contrast, a collective conception of speaking, by recognizing its interactive nature, and by acknowledging the potential effects that speakers and listeners can have on each other, gives us a clear way to understand the role of talk in an individual's intellectual growth. Consider, for example, the way one develops as a philosopher through one's training in

26. Thanks to Jeremy Iggers for drawing this to my attention.
27. In discussion.
28. Perhaps it would be easiest to show that harm to listeners is harm to freedom of speech if I could come up with a case in which all but one person were prohibited from speaking for "purely technical" reasons. I'm not sure there is such a case, however.

graduate school.[29] One learns to formulate and understand arguments through interchange with one's graduate student peers, one's professors, the authors of one's texts, etc. Even when one is engaged in the seemingly solitary endeavor of writing a thesis, one is surrounded by other philosophers, in the form of texts, with whom one is engaged in philosophical debate and discussion. Speaking, as discussion, is central to one's mental maturation.

If we assume that our talk with others can affect their beliefs, and that their responses will in turn shape our thoughts, it follows that speaking in the community ought to be free, to enable persons to develop. It also follows that a definition of free speaking that treats objectifying, degrading, oppressive speech not as free but as destructive of freedom, is better equipped to enable free and full intellectual development than is a definition that suggests that the principles of "free speech" require us to listen to words that demoralize and silence us.[30]

2. Turning to the second liberal defense of freedom of speech, it can also be argued that this goal is best met by a collective concept of speaking as well. Recall that Mill's defense of free speech argues that we must keep our ideas circulating in public (through speech), if we are to have the best chance of developing true ideas. As our ideas are challenged, embellished, encouraged, refuted by others, they become stronger. Or they become weaker and we replace them.

Mill emphasizes the role of speech in the development of truth to the virtual exclusion of any other use it may have. Furthermore, he emphasizes that the community must allow all ideas, because we can never be sure an idea is really false. Such tenets clearly are not in keeping with the collective conception, where it is recognized that people talk and listen (or don't listen) for all sorts of reasons, and where it is suggested that certain ideas, when expressed, actually undermine the freedom of the relevant community. The utilitarian goals are not in harmony with the goals of a collective notion of speaking.

---

29. The example comes from Peter Dalton.

30. This model not only identifies such limiting speech, but also challenges the recipients of speech to work to make speech situations more free by eliminating it. That is, the model might call us to shout down someone giving a speech against civil rights for lesbians and gays, or to make lots of noise during a showing of a porn movie, in the name of free speech.

To take this notion of freedom seriously demands that we actively promote the speaking of those who are most systematically silenced – and work to eliminate speaking that silences them.

Nonetheless, those goals can be achieved better on a collective than on a liberal conception. This, again, is simply because the collective conception begins with the assumption that speaking goes on among people. It is acknowledged from the outset that when we talk about an idea, someone might well listen – that's probably the reason we are saying it out loud in the first place. And in listening, they may be prompted to respond. Thus, while I reject many of the assumptions and the tactics of the utilitarian defense, I would argue that a defense of free speech that derives from the value of exchanging ideas is, in the end, a defense better served by a collective conception of speech than by a liberal individualist conception. (In some ways I think Mill would agree; as I have already suggested, his position is more cordial to a collective conception than is a position like Emerson's.)

C. In sketching out a collective conception for free speaking, I intended to show why it is more useful for thinking about speaking than is a liberal conception of free speech. In calling for a transformation in the ways we think about free speaking, I'm also calling for a change in the ways we act, particularly in the concrete situations we find ourselves, such as the classroom and the political meeting. (As I've already suggested, however, I am suspicious about the chances that externally-imposed regulations could bring about the kind of respect for the freedom of the community that this conception intends to promote. Thus this is not a call for *enforcing* action.)

On a collective conception of free speech, issues of power become paramount in importance. Those members of the community who, because of the construction of that community, are granted illegitimate power over other members must act to understand and to transform the ways that power figures into speaking in the community. On this view, we are responsible for the ways we perpetuate the silencing of others by talking in ways that support systems of domination and subordination, and that preserve illegitimate positions of power.

References

Canavan, Francis. 1984. *Freedom of Expression*, Carolina Academic Press, Durham, NC.

Card, Claudia. [Undated]. "Intimacy and Responsibility: What Lesbians Do," unpublished paper.

Emerson, Thomas I. 1966. *Toward a General Theory of the First Amendment*, Random House, Inc., New York, NY.

MacKinnon, Catharine. 1987. *Feminism Unmodified*, Harvard University Press, Cambridge, MA.

Mill, John Stuart. [1861] 1978. *On Liberty*, Hackett Publishing Company, Indianapolis.

Plato. 1961. *Protagoras*, trans. W.K.C. Guthrie in *Plato: The Collected Dialogues*, Edith Hamilton and Huntington Cairns (eds.) Princeton University Press, Princeton, NJ.

Wittgenstein, Ludwig. 1958. *Philosophical Investigations*, trans. G.E.M. Anscombe, MacMillan Publishing Company, New York, NY.

Young, Iris. 1990. *Throwing Like a Girl and Other Essays in Feminist Philosophy and Social Theory*, Indiana University Press, Bloomington, IN.

8
Voting Rites: A Study in Ceremonial Democracy

Ron Hirschbein

> All voting is a sort of gaming . . . with a slight moral tinge to it, a playing with right and wrong, with moral questions; and betting naturally accompanies it. . . . I cast my vote, perchance, as I think right: but I am not vitally concerned that the right should prevail. . . . Even voting for the right is doing nothing for it. It is only expressing to men feebly your desire that it should prevail (Thoreau, [1849], 1971, p. 145).

This is a paper about the predicament of the individual in mass society. We have somehow grown accustomed to a feature of mass society that has profound and unsettling implications: the very size of modern nation-states precludes the possibility of an ordinary individual influencing the choice of leaders or policies. No wonder Camus's Stranger – neither a hero nor villain, but a victim of mass society – laments, "A person can get used to anything." It is not without reason that theorists from Plato to Marx have insisted that a self-conscious, efficacious polity is not possible when the population exceeds fifteen hundred. As Dewey observed:

> it seemed almost self-evident to Plato – and to Rousseau later –that a genuine state could hardly be larger than the number of persons capable of personal acquaintance with one another (1927, p. 114).[1]

To be sure, there are possibilities for economic and political reforms.[2] But no reform can obviate the intractable mathematics of our predica-

---

1. D. Ross Gandy (1979, Part IV) discusses Marx's vision of a future society of small communes and worker's palaces. Marge Piercy (1976) develops an engaging vision of an autonomous society of six hundred informed by Marxist, anarchist, and feminist theory.

2. Dewey (1927) provides a classic example. He offers a familiar crisis narration in which the eleventh hour has dawned but it is not too late. The public spiritedness of small town America has been eclipsed by a mass society characterized by alienation, apathy, and cynicism. However, attempting to revive the Enlightenment faith in reason and progress, Dewey argues that the social problems that fragment society can be resolved scientifically as the nation is galvanized into a public spirited "Great Community." More recent contributions to this genre include Philip Stern's indictment of Political Action Committees (PACs)

ment: in a society of 250 million the voice of the ordinary individual is lost.

What, then, does the leviathan offer hapless individuals involuntarily thrown into a world beyond their comprehension and control? It offers spectacles and commodities, at least to the privileged – less fortunate are neglected or governed by force.

This paper examines the centerpiece of the American political spectacle: the right to vote. I confront two questions:

1. What is the right to vote? To paraphrase Nietzsche: concepts with a history cannot be defined; they must be narrated. Therefore, I ask: what is the story about voting rights, and to what extent is it mythic? I start by rejecting natural rights theory as mystic and unintelligible, and I argue that voting is a social convention that must be understood in its economic, political, and demographic context. I conclude that in its current context voting does not empower the ordinary individual to influence the choice of leaders or policies.

2. What is the function of voting in mass society? I argue that voting is a civic rite that fulfills the political players' needs for legitimacy and their audience's need for meaning and drama.

Voting Rights

> There is scarcely a society without its major narratives which are recounted, repeated and . . . recited in well-defined circumstances; things said once and preserved because it is suspected that behind them there is a secret or treasure. (Foucault, 1984, p. 114)

The right to vote is such a narrative – a saga recounted, repeated, and recited in the ritual of American civic religion. School books and learned treatises teach that voting is a hard-won, sacred obligation. Every four years the media remind Americans of their blessing and duty; even those inattentive to television, radio, and the press cannot escape injunctions

---

in *The Best Congress Money Can Buy* (1988). The title speaks for itself; however, it should be noted that his concluding chapter is entitled, "How We Can Get Out of the Mess We're In." *In Why Americans Don't Vote* (1988), Frances Piven and Richard Cloward argue that the registration process must be reformed because it *de facto* inhibits the enfranchisement of the poor and of minorities. In my view this reform would not transform the insignificant, passive individual of mass society into an active player in the political arena; it would merely invite the less fortunate to participate in the spectacle. After offering an incisive and accessible account of this spectacle in *Amusing Ourselves to Death* (1985), Neil Postman subscribes to Dewey's faith in the redemptive power of education.

about their civic duty emblazoned on countless banners, billboards, and grocery bags. What's the story?

It is an Enlightenment narrative so sacred to conservatives and liberals alike that it seems like part of the natural order of things: it is unthought and unquestioned. It is a saga about the conquest of despotism by reason and revolution. Long ago selfish and cruel princes and prelates ruled without the consent of the governed. Sparked by such thinkers as John Locke ([1690] 1959),[3] the revolutions of the eighteenth century began the long struggle for popular enfranchisement that culminated in the United States in the Voting Rights Act of 1965: for the first time, any adult regardless of gender, race, or class could vote.[4] Other means of political participation, such as organizing, protesting, and disobedience, are excluded from popular discourse. The civic faith decrees an eleventh commandment: Thou shalt restrict thy political activity to voting – *Vox populi vox dei.*

Recent events in the Soviet Union and Eastern Europe are interpreted as a reaffirmation of the universality of Western conventions and faith in progress – the best is yet to come. Decadent dictatorships succumb to a vibrant democratic spirit as citizens elect officials in multiparty systems. The day will dawn when all of humanity recognizes its natural right to vote and acts accordingly. History seems headed for a happy ending.

This narrative reifies voting by assigning the ontological status of a mysterious natural right destined to fulfill itself in history. It fails to see voting for what it is, an occasionally useful convention of mere mortals. In the conceptual universe of American civic religion the right to vote is akin to a Newtonian law of nature. Just as the laws of Newtonian mechanics were deemed applicable at all times and places, the right to vote is exalted as the *summum bonum* of any conceivable collective life. By decontextualizing voting, this privileged narrative fails to recognize that the significance of voting depends upon circumstances: a vote cast in an Athenian assembly, Jeffersonian town meeting, or a factory seized by the workers has a meaning radically different from pulling a lever in a booth once every four years in mass society.

What is the meaning of casting a vote in the contemporary American context? Specifically, does it enable the individual to influence the choice of leaders and of policies? Concentrations of economic and political

---

3. This most conservative and perhaps least consistent of all revolutionaries merely insists that citizens must *consent* to the appointment of their rulers and the policies they enact. In the Lockean scheme, the people neither govern themselves nor participate directly in their governance.

4. G.R. Stantion provides glosses on original sources (1990, pp. 40–85).

power diminish the efficacy of an individual vote. Worse yet, no reform can mitigate the mathematics of mass society: the probability of an individual vote influencing the outcome of a national election is near zero.

The Economic Context

It takes a flair for the obvious to recognize that the rich are more influential than the poor. Economic power buys political power; yet, delusions persist about the egalitarian nature of electoral politics – one person one vote. Curiously, an ordinary citizen with one share of General Motors would not presuppose that her vote enables her to influence the Corporation. Yet this same citizen might believe that one vote influences a much larger organization – the U.S. Government.

I suspect that the rich and powerful do not labor under such delusions. Imagine that you win a state lottery. The chances are considerably better than the probability that your vote will decide an election. Emboldened, you decide to buy political influence. An advisor concerned with job security would not urge you to restrict your activity to voting. He or she would recommend strategies unavailable to ordinary folk: running for office, buying candidates through PACs (Political Action Committees), or sponsoring commercials that eschew substantive issues in favor of resonant symbols. In any case, given the role of economic power in America, one begins to suspect that the Athenian 400 have become the Fortune 500.

The Political Context

Deconstructing the right to vote leads to the columns of ancient Athens. Contrasting Solon's time with the present reveals the role of context in determining the significance of a vote. I invoke this contrast not because Athens was a golden age (it was decidedly tarnished for slaves, noncitizens, and women), but because it reveals the significance of a vote in a small, participatory – albeit elitist – democracy.

In Athens a vote was merely a means: a protocol for bringing closure to meaningful debate among full-time, empowered citizens deliberating about candidates and issues close at hand. Today, under participatory totalitarianism, individuals can say what they want as long as elites can do what they want: citizens are reduced to passive spectators, and their vote is stripped of its classic meaning and fetishized – it has become an end-in-itself. Voters neither govern nor are they conversant with candidates or issues. If the past is a foreign country, so is the present: the average voter has the same familiarity with the executive memoranda of Bush that he has with the laws of Solon.

Voters no longer select and debate over candidates. Candidates appear *ex nihilio* on the cathode screen while spin-controllers script seven-second sound-bites. As Edelman observes: "Politics is for most of us a passing parade of abstract symbols . . ." (1967, p. 5). Leaders do not merely manage symbols: mass society dissolves the classic distinction between appearance and reality. In its dramaturgic electoral ceremonies enacted at every Olympiad, mass society appears to present choices as momentous as those pondered by the Athenians. Improvising a familiar crisis narrative, candidates represent the election as a choice between redemption and catastrophe. Engels may have exaggerated when he urged that in bourgeois democracies political parties are different wings of the same bird of prey. However, as many learned in 1964 after voting for Lyndon Baines Johnson, the peace candidate, the election of a Republican or a Democrat makes little difference in foreign policy. The passing parade of candidates merely offers fanciful interpretations of our lives and the ongoing drama unfolding in the international arena.

The Demographic Context

Even if it were possible to control economic and political power, such a feat would not obviate the predicament of the individual in mass society. Edelman thinks the unthinkable:

> Everyone who grows up in our society is bound to become aware, at some level of consciousness, that an individual vote is more nearly a form of self-expression and of legitimation than of influence. . . . (1988, p. 97)

The existential truth of mass society is that the vote of an individual only matters in an election decided by one vote. Curiously, this truth is recognized by those who are unrestrained in their celebration of enfranchisement. In *Why Vote?* Mitchell urges young citizens to exercise their newly-won franchise. Yet, he observes, "few voters will ever participate in elections that are decided by one vote" (1971, p. 36). Indeed, in all probability there will never be such an election on the national level. Even if only a small fraction of the electorate vote in the next national election, the odds that your vote will influence the outcome are infinitesimal. A single vote matters only if the election results in a tie or in a candidate winning by a single vote. In these unlikely circumstances, you could tell yourself that the outcome would have been different if you had stayed home. What if everyone engaged in these ruminations: what if they gave an election and nobody came? Not to worry. The American civic religion is more influential than any iconoclasm. That tens of millions of individuals will vote in the next national election is one of the safest bets you can make.

Voting Rites

> Through participation in the [civic] rites, the citizen of the modern state identifies with larger political forces that can only be seen in symbolic form. And through political ritual, we are given a way to understand what is going on in the world, for we live in a world that must be drastically simplified if it is to be understood at all. (Kertzer, 1988, pp. 1–2)

Mass society transforms voting into a civic rite. These repetitive, symbol-laden activities channel emotion, guide cognition, and organize collective life. Rituals do not merely celebrate political reality, they construct it for players and spectators alike (Kertzer, 1988, pp. 8–9).

The Significance of Voting Rites for Governing Elites

Voting rites bestow legitimacy upon elites while distracting attention from the enduring problems of politics and personal life. Legitimation is not simply a matter of being duly elected. The electoral process itself legitimizes the status quo in more subtle ways. In order for such an abstraction as "The Government" to exact obedience and devotion, it must become incarnate in what Marx called the fantasy of everyday life. Kertzer quotes Walzer as explaining:

> The state is invisible; it must be personified before it can be seen, symbolized before it can be loved, imagined before it can be conceived. (1988, p. 6)

The Federal Government manifests itself in political campaigns, secret rites in voting booths, election night dramas, and the ceremonial spectacles that follow.

Legitimacy is also reinforced when elites orchestrate simultaneous activity among those they govern. For example, by persuading your students to take exams simultaneously you reinforce your professional legitimacy. Likewise, elites assert and reinforce their legitimacy by orchestrating elections. As Edelman explains:

> Ritual is motor activity that involves its participants symbolically in a common enterprise, calling their attention to their relatedness and joint interests in

a compelling way. It . . . promotes conformity and evokes . . . joy in conformity. (1967, p. 16)

Like other civic rituals, voting distracts attention from the connection
between personal difficulties and public problems. The spectacle focuses
attention on differently packaged candidates intent upon perpetuating
the status quo. It distracts voters from their powerlessness and vulnerability to corporations and bureaus beyond their control.

The Significance of Voting Rites for Spectators

Voting rites perpetuate the sacred illusion that the spectators live in a
democracy in which their actions are politically significant. By pulling a
lever, they offer up what Kenneth Burke calls a "secular prayer" – a peti-
tion to the remote powers to intercede in their behalf.

These rites also engulf the citizen in what Freud calls an "oceanic
experience." The first Tuesday in November millions of individuals
enact a ceremony replayed in the election-night drama. In so doing they
become part of something larger than themselves. Not only are they
immersed in the present, they experience connectedness with a collective
past and future.

Voting rites also simplify an ambiguous, anxiety-provoking world by
imposing a seamless narrative – a formulaic story with a happy ending.
The narrative enables spectators to make sense of the political drama that,
on occasion, threatens their well-being and existence. In effect, voting is
a gloss on politics that makes events intelligible by infusing them with
meaning, direction, and hope· leaders and their programs supposedly
express the will of those who must prevail in such matters – the majority. The discontent can rely upon the "free marketplace of ideas" to persuade the majority to abandon their folly in the next election. Ultimately,
the good sense of the electorate prevails, or so the story goes.

Voting rites, of course, serve more mundane ends. As Thoreau recognized, elections punctuate the monotony of everyday experience by providing suspenseful entertainment that is the subject of much gossip and
gaming.

Postscript

Recent domestic and international developments suggest that ordinary
individuals are becoming aware of their predicament in mass society. As
Edelman concludes, the widely criticized indifference of the American

electorate may be a sign of their increased awareness and newfound concern for problems within their control. He writes:

> Nonvoters constitute a larger political grouping in America than the adherents of any political party. . . . That indifference which academic political science . . . treats as an obstacle . . . to democracy is . . . a refuge against the kind of engagement that would . . . keep everyone's energies taken up with . . . political activities that displace living, loving and creative work. (1988, p. 7)

Beyond American borders the third world war has begun. Unlike the wars of modernity, it is not about constructing larger social units such as nations and empires. On the contrary, these struggles are postmodern strategies to deconstruct mass society into smaller, more manageable units: the Soviet Union is dissolving into its constituent parts; and similar dissolutions are occurring in Eastern Europe, the Middle East, Southeast Asia, and Africa. True, many of these struggles are sparked by archaic ethnic passions. But could it be that at some dim, inchoate level, this strife is also a rebellion against mass societies that individuals can neither comprehend nor control?

References

Dewey, John. 1927. *The Public and Its Problems*, Henry Holt, New York.

Edelman, Murray. 1967. *The Symbolic Uses of Politics*, University of Illinois Press, Urbana.

______ 1988. *Constructing the Political Spectacle*, University of Chicago Press, Chicago.

Foucault, Michel. 1984. "The Order of Discourse," *Language and Politics*, Michael Shapiro (ed.) New York University Press, New York.

Gandy, D. Ross. 1979. *Marx and History*, University of Texas Press, Austin.

Kertzer, David. 1988. *Ritual, Politics and Power*, Yale University Press, New Haven.

Locke, John. [1690] 1959. *Second Treatise of Civil Government*, Appleton-Century-Crofts, New York.

Mitchell, William. 1971. *Why Vote?*, Markham Publishing Co., Chicago.

Piercy, Marge. 1976. *Women on the Edge of Time*, Fawcett Books, New York.

Piven, Frances and Cloward, Richard. 1988. *Why Americans Don't Vote*, Pantheon, New York.

Postman, Neil. 1985. *Amusing Ourselves to Death*, Penguin Books, New York.

Stantion, G.R. 1990. *Athenian Politics*, Routledge, New York.

Stern, Philip. 1988. *The Best Congress Money Can Buy*, Pantheon, New York.

Thoreau, Henry David. [1849] 1971. "Civil Disobedience," *War and Christian Conscience*, Albert Marrin (ed.) Henry Regnery, Chicago.

9
Is Civil Disobedience Morally Coherent?

Matt Silliman

Both ancient and modern practice and theory of civil disobedience present many unresolved problems, among them: is civil disobedience basically a conservative or reformist activity, or can it be a tool of revolutionaries? Is it essentially a political tactic, a form of political expression, or an act of personal moral conscience, the political consequences of which are incidental? Can violence be part of an act of civil disobedience, or must it always remain nonviolent? Is there a *prima facie* obligation to obey the law, and if so how can civil disobedience be justified?

In this essay I shall examine what I take to be a more basic question, the answer to which I hope will shed light on many of these specific problems: is the necessity to act in accord with one's conscience, which is the justification and strongest defense for much civil disobedience, undermined by an implicit granting of the legitimacy of the law being broken by the actor's willingness to submit to punishment?[1] That is, how can a conscientious person agree – in order to be politically effective against the law or practice being protested – to the justness of punishment for an action which, according to her conscience, is not wrong? One *must* submit to punishment for breaking the law, if the argument that one is a conscientious citizen is to carry any weight, but the civil disobedient cannot regard action conscientiously undertaken as *deserving* of punishment.

The civil disobedient seems to be in an ambiguous position vis-à-vis the legal proceedings; some refuse to cooperate altogether, but in participating, mounting a defense, etc., the others might be variously understood as acting responsibly or as merely playing for media attention to further their educational and political purposes. The latter is not a morally unacceptable thing to do; gaining the ear of the media in order to edu-

---

1. This question arose very poignantly for me during a year in court, after I was arrested for trespass with five other people at the Yankee Atomic nuclear power station in Rowe, Massachusetts. The details of this case are fascinating, to me, but serve only as a starting-point for the present deliberations. A formulation of the problem in something like these terms was first suggested to me in the summer of 1990 by my friend and colleague Dr. Shyli Karen-Frank of the University of Tel Aviv.

cate the public about some serious but ignored problem can be both difficult and admirable. We perceive it, however, to be very different in motive from following one's conscience despite the consequences, and to the extent that effectiveness in moral and political persuasion relies on conscientiousness, any hint of a mixed motive (of overt attempts to be politically effective) seem to undermine the moral claim, and hence its effectiveness. Apparently the would-be civil disobedient must risk choosing between an ineffective, merely symbolic moral gesture and morally incoherent political effectiveness.

The dilemma arises in part because we tend to think of conscience in individualistic and absolutistic terms; we admire a "person of principle," and speak of respecting the depth of her conviction even when we disagree. Gandhi is better remembered, at least in the West, for his (admittedly striking) personal moral character than for the acuity of his political imagination, reflecting our preference for romanticizing personal moral conviction (and even martyrdom) rather than understanding a person's acts of conscience in their political context.[2]

A part of my riddle might be solved if we acknowledge the socially-constructed character (and consequent plurality) of conscience. Robbed of its special, absolutist appeal as an heroic "last stand" moral argument, unanswerable because the soul of the conscientious person is the court of final appeal, conscience becomes available as a more relevant element in public moral discourse. We can still understand conscience as arising from personal conviction, but rather than a discussion-stopping (and usually implausible) claim as to the moral purity of the individual, or an attempt to shame those who are (allegedly) impure, it can become part of a passionate and reasoned conversation about what we, collectively, ought to do.

One characteristic of civil disobedience, as opposed to disobedience *simpliciter*, is its forthrightness, its publicity. It cannot be simply a private act of conscience, but must be an act of conscience that takes place in the public eye, and for which the actor takes full public responsibility. For the civil disobedient, as opposed to the martyr, acting in public is not

---

2. Among the absurdities to which this way of thinking about conscience leads is the refusal to believe well founded reports of the moral failings and inconsistencies of Martin Luther King, Jr., on the part of those who had come to see him as a perfect, god-like leader. But to concede that he might have been guilty of plagiarism or sexual irresponsibility should in no way mitigate the strength of his arguments for social justice, or his calls for noncooperation with an oppressive system. No one is morally pure or wholly consistent, and a political act of conscience should be understood not so much as an application for sainthood as an attempt to do at least one thing right.

only a matter of putting your body where your heart is, nor of just risking public scrutiny to test the purity of your soul; it is a matter of presenting one's conscience to one's neighbors in hopes both of affecting them and effecting change. This inherent publicity suggests both that there may be something to the claim that civil disobedience functions like speech (and so might be defensible under the First Amendment), and that the moral discourse in which the civil disobedient engages is not simply a witness to some entirely private conviction but also a narrative of political vision, appealing dramatically to an idea of what our collective life should become.

In order to shift from thinking of civil disobedience as a narrow violation of law to conceiving it as dramatizing and clarifying alternative visions of citizenship, social and personal responsibility, I must detour briefly into ancient and contemporary notions of law. The "laws" that the character Socrates opted not to disobey in Plato's *Crito* were both more and less than the constitutional requirements, legislative enactments and judicial decisions for which we in the modern world use the term "law." *Nomos* encompasses positive law, but also includes customary practices and a more general notion of social order, a complexity that we need to understand if much of what Socrates says about his obligation to the *nomoi* of the Athenians (for example the analogy he draws between them and his parents), is to make sense.

It is a commonplace that ancient political theorists emphasize the primacy of the political community, while modern Enlightenment liberalism begins with the liberty of the individual. Bruce Sieverts (1989, pp. 177–179) usefully concludes from this that the Greeks understood morality and politics to be much more closely related than does liberal modernity.[3] I would argue that the difference goes even further, and that for Socrates the appeal to the *nomoi* is both personally and politically much more compelling than any modern rhetoric about the rule of law. Law in the narrow, positive sense covers a far smaller portion of Socrates' everyday concerns than it does for us, both because of the rootedness of Athenian society in a powerful and detailed poetic mythology (as opposed to our prosaic, constitutional mythology), and because of a reasonable reaction against the proverbially harsh Draconian laws (called *thesmoi*; not *nomoi*), of two centuries before. Socrates, as Plato's other dialogues attest, is hardly an indiscriminate defender of tradition as such,

---

3. I appreciate the attempt of Sieverts to reunify morality and politics, as well as his insistence that civil disobedience is irreducibly a *political* act, in the sense of "political" that contains a pre-Hobbesian moral dimension.

suggesting that his defense of the *nomoi* in the *Crito* is motivated not by formulaic devotion to what we would call "law and order," but by a genuine respect for the particular way Athenian society had come to do things, taken on the whole – not least its (qualified) tolerance for philosophy.

In light of this, I submit that civil disobedience, so far as it can consistently be both conscientious and effective, treats laws as though they were *nomoi*. By this I mean that it challenges the positivity of law, its privileged and arbitrary status, seeking to return law to the disorderly and particular world of moral choices and social relations whence it came. On this account, neither absolute purity of personal conscience (remaining free of the taint of war by paying no taxes, for example), nor cynical appeal to political necessity (adopting a moral pose for popular impact) can, by themselves, justify civil disobedience. To engage in civil disobedience one must certainly be clear about where one's conscience leads, and one must also attend to political realities and opportunities. But unless the moral claim is also an argument about the morality of public life, linked to a vision of a different social reality, and unless the political calculations that motivate it are made openly and in good faith, one's disobedience is hardly civil.

During the struggle for independence from the British Raj, Gandhi was arrested and tried for sedition before a British court in India, and he made an inspiring and curious speech. Taking the stand on his own behalf, he asserted that he would make no defense; he was guilty as charged, and if the judge believed in the system of law which he was pledged to uphold he had no choice but to sentence Gandhi to the maximum punishment permitted by law (Collins and Lapierre, 1975, p. 64). This inspiring and puzzling speech might suggest that civil disobedients might be wrong to contest in court the charges against them. Certainly doing so introduces a potential ambiguity about motive: are they playing for politically useful publicity from the trial? Do they secretly hope to evade punishment and thus responsibility for their acts?

Notwithstanding the risks of being perceived as having mixed motives, in light of the above discussions of law and conscience one should not assume that civil disobedients are wrong in every case to contest the charges. Politically useful publicity is no violation of the conscientiousness of a public act of disobedience, the purpose of which is to further political change. Moreover, we should consider the wider context of Gandhi's speech: he had laid the groundwork of political organization over many years, and the timing of this particular plea had maximum political effect; he was no naive martyr to lost causes.

Secondly, although Gandhi had made careful spiritual preparation for the ordeal of his punishment, he did not insist on serving out his sentence when the British authorities offered release in response to his ill health. There was in Gandhi's practice of civil disobedience neither a slavish obsession with positive law nor a blind devotion to private conscience at any cost, but an acute and principled moral-political sense and a powerful vision of the social harmony he was trying to articulate and build.

I would argue, therefore, that the alleged saintliness of Gandhi's personal life is a red herring for understanding the ground and effectiveness of his civil disobedience. Similarly, Socrates presents an argument that because neither death nor a fine can harm his character, he actually accepts no punishment by submitting to the court's decision. This position, which surely no one but Socrates himself would have taken seriously, is beside the point, and only ancillary to his lengthy argument in the *Crito* that disobedience to the *nomoi* in this case is a much greater, or compounding harm to his character and the social order than the worst the court can inflict on him. The uniquely principled personal morality of these characters is interesting, and even inspiring, but their status as paragons should not deter us from engaging in the kind of active citizenship that sometimes requires civil disobedience.

Briefly put, then, I suggest that the dilemma with which I began this essay becomes evidently artificial, once we reintegrate conscience into its public, social context, and law into the wider normative concept of *nomos*. Neither private moral purity nor political efficacy alone can justify an act of civil disobedience. The final judge of such an act is the collectively determined value and power of the social vision, the good story which that act instantiates, as it invites others to realize it. Civil disobedience thus emerges as an extreme or dramatic example of engagement in public moral and political discourse: a powerful (if personally risky) means of articulating the vision one has of the good society or (what is the same thing) the good life.

One interesting consequence of this way of thinking about civil disobedience is that it represents a deeper moral coherence than can be offered by purism of either conscience or positive law. This is because, as I conceive it, far from justifying the means (law-breaking) by reference to the end (integrity of conscience), civil disobedience must integrate means and ends if it is to be either moral or effective. The acts one commits in consistently and effectively realizing a vision of a just community must not only be consistent with that vision, but must *instantiate* it – must be the acts of a functioning member of the community being realized. Only the means themselves can exhibit to those still needing to be persuaded that the end at which one aims is both justifiable and beautiful.[4]

From this perspective, I will suggest a preliminary resolution of the question of civil disobedience and violence. Violence seems to many commentators inimical to the theory and practice of civil disobedience, although they seldom offer arguments in support of this view. On my contention that an act of civil disobedience functions as a living example of the vision that the actor has of a better society, an act of violence against other persons would legislate for a violent social order. One could argue that it would thus be morally ambiguous, and politically inefficacious, to pursue peace, or any other sustainable social ideal, by violent means; the story one told in this way would contain powerful seeds of its own narrative collapse.

On the other hand, the subtlety of the story and the artfulness with which it is told could conceivably overcome (at least temporarily) what looks like such a patent contradiction. Human communities have functioned for long periods of time with a distinction between members of their own group, against whom violence is unacceptable, and members of "enemy" groups, against whom violence is deemed, at times, to be necessary and even honorable. It is not my task here to determine whether this conception necessarily falls from the weight of its own internal contradiction, as I suspect it does, but to allow that, in principle, an honest argument might be made in particular social circumstances for an act of civil disobedience that contained violent elements, or (perhaps more plausibly) elements of carefully limited coercion.

Some commentators argue that because civil disobedients submit themselves for judgment and punishment, they implicitly affirm the legitimacy, in general, of legal authority, and that civil disobedience is thus an inherently reformist method, and never revolutionary (e.g. Walzer, 1970, p. 24ff.). This conclusion arises partly, I think, from a tendency to assume that revolution is inherently violent (Fortas, 1989, pp. 91–105, implicitly assumes just that), and that civil disobedience can never involve violence. It is worth noting in this regard that Gandhi's submission to law in the example above was both nonviolent and revolutionary, both in its intentions and in its consequences. In light of this, I do not think that any general claim can be made that subjecting oneself

4. It is not fair to conclude that I am talking here about a Kantian "realm of ends," except in an attenuated sense. I do not argue that all rational beings would, so far as they are rational, assent to the same vision of collective human perfection, but only that it is possible (in many ways, civil disobedience among them), to articulate visions, and tell stories, which might persuade others to pursue them.

to legal process and punishment precludes revolution. Moreover, if (as I have argued) civil disobedience treats positive laws as though they were *nomoi*, acknowledging both their power and the (often flawed) social processes that produce them, the civil disobedient can consistently acknowledge the political reality of existing social relations, and the need for some measure of social stability and continuity, without granting the general legitimacy of the particular positive laws, or even the rule of law, that happen to prevail. One can in some important sense be both a citizen and a revolutionary.

But if civil disobedience can be revolutionary, then perhaps we must grant that it can involve violence, for revolution, however benign, always risks violence. The conceptual transformations accompanying any revolution profound enough to deserve the name inevitably redefine for a society such basic concepts as violence, so that what is understood as necessary violence, or not as violence at all, according to the narrative underlying the *status quo*, might look very different in the context of a society transformed by a fundamentally different story. For example, most Americans do not regard the present automotive orientation of our society to represent the fundamentally violent assault on the habitability of the planet, which I consider it to be.[5] Yet in the course of my reform efforts I often have recourse to automobiles, absent the saner methods of transportation which I hope and intend those very efforts to eventually create. Thus it can happen that civil disobedients may do things in the course of civil disobedience which their existing culture understands as violent, or which the alternative society they strive to articulate will come to so understand. It is worthwhile to struggle in their personal lives to become consistent with their ideals, but to distance themselves so far from the culture in which they live as to be entirely free of its taint would render them totally ineffectual. Civil disobedience must employ the forms and language of its indigenous culture; otherwise its audience will not hear the story.

Finally, my analysis may suggest a way out of the dispute over *prima facie* obligation to law. Feinberg (1989, pp. 151–173) argues cogently that there may be no *prima facie* obligation to obey the law, and thus that civil disobedience is justified. Sieverts (1989) counters that if this were true, it would undermine the point of civil disobedience, for it is precisely because such an obligation exists that violating it in particular circumstances (which render it not an *actual* obligation in the instant case), is permissible or even conscientiously obligatory. I resolve this dilemma in

---

5. It was not accidental or only symbolic that I bicycled to the site of my arrest.

the following way: Feinberg is probably correct that no compelling argument can be made for a *prima facie* obligation to obey positive law, but it is hard to imagine what would be left of the concept of *prima facie* obligation, or the possibility of human community, if there were no *prima facie* obligation to *nomos* – to the settled though ever-changing cultural ground of our human associations, in the context of which dialogues about obligation take place.

I have argued that conscience and political effectiveness are enemies only in the eyes of purists, either of law or of morality, and that such purisms have limited moral or social usefulness because they fail to reach out in action to inform the public narrative. I suggest as a substitute for such purism a fluid conception of social relations in which "private" moral convictions are understood to have their meaning primarily in the context of other cultural practices, and in which law is understood as merely one contextually-conditioned component of our collective life, rather than comprising its authoritative definition. I make this case with the hope that clarity on these issues will strengthen both the political efficacy and the moral grounding of well considered acts of civil disobedience.

References

Collins, Larry, and Dominique Lapierre. 1975. *Freedom at Midnight*, Simon and Schuster, New York.

Feinberg, Joel. 1989. "Civil Disobedience in the Modern World," *Civil Disobedience,* Paul Harris (ed.) University Press of America, Boston.

Fortas, Abe. 1989. "Concerning Consent and Civil Disobedience," *Civil Disobedience*, Paul Harris (ed.) University Press of America, Boston.

Sieverts, Bruce. 1989. "Civil Disobedience in Political Theory: The Classical Model Revisited," *Civil Disobedience*, Paul Harris (ed.) University Press of America, Boston.

Walzer, Michael. 1970. *Obligations: Essays on Disobedience, War and Citizenship*, Harvard University Press, Cambridge, MA.

Ethical Issues in Democratic Public Policy

FOREWORD

Whereas all of the essays in Part III address issues and problems that connect in various but important ways with the essays in Parts I and II, they all share a common and special focus on the ways in which public policy choices are made, or ought to be made in the democratic polity.

The dominant model of policy analysis, influenced as it has been by both economistic notions of efficiency and philosophical currents of positivism and subjectivism, weights policy alternatives in terms of the degree to which they satisfy aggregates of subjective preference. On this model, the best or right public policy is the one that maximizes the subjective preferences of individual citizens. Despite widespread criticism of this model, Nancy E. Snow, the author of the first selection, assumes in "Should Drugs Be Legal?" that this *is* the appropriate policymaking model for policy choices concerning drugs, *provided that the implications of the model are understood and correctly applied to concrete problems of "substance abuse."*

Problems related to "substance abuse" in the United States certainly represent significant policy problems concerning which government regulation has been highly inconsistent and citizen preferences have been strong and sharply divided. Indeed, it might be argued that politicization of problems of "substance abuse" has undermined efforts to implement rational and just policies. Yet "substance abuse" also consists of a set of problems about which we possess considerable information as to risks of harm, costs to users and nonusers, and the strength of preferences expressed in terms of compliance or noncompliance with the law. Snow believes that, for this problem set – about which we have compelling evidence – it is possible to identify *the* best public policy. Indeed, one of the fascinating qualities of Snow's essay is the clarity with which she selects, from *eight* policy options, the one she supports as rationally superior for a liberal democracy.

As previously noted, Snow's position is that for problems of substance abuse where the costs, benefits, and preferences are relatively easy to identify and assess, liberal principles indicate that the best policymaking model is the one that maximizes the aggregate of preferences – with the added proviso that the indicated policy be one that can be applied consistently in its regulation of substances. The interesting question, then, is why it has been so difficult for policy analysts and the public to agree on the best policy. Snow's argument is that we have not been faithful to our liberal principles and, more important, we have failed to reason correctly about the implications of maximizing preference satisfaction concerning drug use. In the first place, we have not fully appreciated that liberalism's commitment to value neutrality requires that we adopt a policy that respects equally preferences for the use or nonuse of all "substances" – be they tobacco, alcohol, marijuana, or the "hard" drugs (e.g., cocaine, heroin, LSD, PCP). Second, Snow tries to show how a definite policy option can be selected if we adopt two stratagems: first, that we "conceptualize the process of policy selection as a two-party problem of rational choice in which one of the parties is a rational substance user and the other a rational nonuser"; second, that we represent the problem of choice among options as an "assurance game."

Nancy Snow's argument is a *tour de force* for the model of rational choice in policy analysis. Of course, because of its virtues of insight, clarity, and completeness, Snow's argument also makes an excellent target for those who decry the excesses of individualistic, or "atomistic" liberalism, as well as for those, like Gillroy in the concluding essay, who are concerned with the excesses and inadequacies of rational choice theory in the domain of public policymaking.

How well will "ivory tower," abstract, academic exercises in policymaking apply to the hurly-burly world of real politics? Snow argues convincingly at the end of her essay for the relevance of the policy she recommends to the hustle and bustle of daily life. But a similar question can be asked of any policy in which rational and ethical reflections must confront a plethora of obstacles or constraints, as well as human frailties and temptations.

In "Ethics, Democracy and Foreign Policy: Manipulation or Participation?", Robert J. Myers is interested in democracy as an ethical standard – not in the abstract, but as a constraint on and beacon for the formation of foreign policy. Myers asks, "[H]ow does the ideal of democratic governance translate into practice, particularly in the most complex areas of policymaking such as foreign affairs . . .?" Myers's case study for the "translation" of democratic ideals into practice involves the United States and Desert Storm – the 1991 United States-led United Nations war against the Iraqi occupation of Kuwait.

Myers notes that, even in theory, coherence and consistency – traits vital to the practice of foreign policy – are hard to attain in a democratic system buffeted by shifts in public opinion and the pressures of special interests (among other influences). Myers avers, nevertheless, that democratically made foreign policy can lay claim to firmer normative ground, just because of popular participation, which may succeed in attaining the collective moral judgment of the *demos*. But how effective can this ideal be, given the fast-breaking and nerve-wracking crises we encounter in foreign affairs?

In his case study of the gulf war, Myers doesn't distinguish between what government officials or the people *believed* to be moral reasons for the war and what were *defensibly* moral reasons according to moral standards for rational choice. But such fine distinctions may be too much to expect given the press and heat of the circumstances: constraints of time and uncertainty, the confusions of authority affecting Congress and the executive branch, the difficulty of locating boundaries between what is morally permitted (or required) and what is "politically possible," not to mention strong temptations to exploit crisis "opportunities" for political advantage. Despite all of this turmoil, Myers is encouraged by his study of the gulf war: while highly imperfect, the exposure of administration planning in the media, public responses, and congressional involvement, as well as the administration's responses to public and congressional concern, had a significant "braking" effect on the proceedings. This was reflected, for instance, in the shift in the administration's proclaimed reasons for going to war from those related to the national and geopolitical interests of the United States to those related to principles of international law and just war doctrine.

Certainly, no moral consensus emerged and the morality of the war is still highly debatable. Yet Myers calls our attention to the important "leavening effects" of democratic processes – even flawed processes – which "make vulgar realpolitik, *raison d'état*, and unmitigated consequentialism impossible for the statesman." Insofar as possible, the public will not tolerate decisions greatly at odds with its values and traditions. That is perhaps a slender basis for optimism, but it suggests that democrats can hope for and work at improving two sources for ethical policy: improving the sensitivity to ethical reflection of the institutions through which decisions are made and working to bring the values the *demos* presses its representatives to respect into greater harmony with ethical standards.

Whereas Myers discusses foreign policy and Snow focuses on "substance abuse," John Martin Gillroy draws our attention to policy problems concerning environmental risk in "When Responsive Public Policy Does not Equal Responsible Government." Gillroy rejects the view that the best public policy is always the policy that maximizes aggregate preferences. He argues therefore that the policy most *responsive* to public preferences may not be most *responsible* to the citizens it is intended to serve. The challenge Gillroy faces is thus two-fold: to disassociate the democratic policymaking process from preference satisfaction, and to articulate a moral and non-preference standard for making public choices.

Gillroy is not making global claims about policy formulation. Given significant differences between the types of policy democracies must make, it is possible that he would accept Snow's determination of policy for "substance abuse." Certainly many of the problems of environmental risk differ significantly from the problems related to drug use. Indeed, Gillroy is at pains to show why environmental risk requires policy *ex ante* – before we have suffered from the harmful effects of radioactive waste or toxic chemicals, for example. His point is that democratic procedures based on preference satisfaction produce policy only *ex post facto* – and that is wholly inadequate as a response to risks posing "resounding uncertainties," including uncertainties about possibly irreversible damage. Indeed, Gillroy notes that what consumers desire "*de facto*" sometimes turns out to be what they confess, with the benefit of greater knowledge, to be undesirable.

Gillroy advocates anticipatory regulatory policies to maintain a sound level of environmental quality and to accept only those risks that are truly in the collective interest. But such anticipatory policies will not be forthcoming as long as policy analysis is dominated by the view that policymakers must maximize aggregate preferences. This traditional view, Gillroy notes, ties policy analysis to the market paradigm and thereby to democratic principles. "Here democracy . . . take[s] up the market paradigm as the basic expression of the underlying normative assumptions of the electorate." Policymakers are relieved from decisions about the potential hazards of technology; indeed, the market gives them the imperative to allow the introduction of any technology for which there are unknown risks but known consumers.

Thus Gillroy must show that an "anticipatory" policy process is not inconsistent with the moral foundations of democracy. Drawing on the Kantian conception of a democratic republic and the principle of autonomy, Gillroy argues for a "thick" definition of liberal democracy. In evoking "ideal-regarding principles" to compete with principles of efficiency, Gillroy appeals to the intrinsic value of the individual understood as an autonomous agent and thereby moves past assumptions (of a "thin" definition of democracy) about the self-sufficiency of individuals and their preferences. In this way Gillroy reunites the topic of Part III – democratic policymaking – with the theoretical arguments of Part I over the moral principles justifying democracy as "the best" of available social and political systems.

10
Should Drugs be Legal?

Nancy E. Snow

Introduction[1]

Drug, alcohol, and tobacco use continues on a grand scale in the United States, despite a costly "War on Drugs," legal restrictions on alcohol and tobacco use, and considerable publicity about the hazards that substance use can cause.[2] If substance use had no negative consequences, there would be no need for a government regulatory policy. However, extensive use creates serious problems, both for users and for other members of society. These ills can be divided into three broad, overlapping categories: crime and physical injuries caused by users, either in efforts to obtain money to fund their habits or while under the influence of drugs

1. A few initial caveats are in order. The concern of this paper is the government regulation of alcohol, tobacco, and currently illegal drugs. Although some of the remarks made in the text could apply to the regulation of other substances, for example, prescription and nonprescription medications, I leave these issues aside. My discussion of the regulation of tobacco applies to smoke-producing tobacco products. I use the term "substances" to refer to drugs, alcohol, and tobacco, or to specific kinds of drugs and of alcohol and tobacco products. "Substance use" refers to a range of usages, including light, moderate, and heavy use, and abuse. In many cases it is difficult to distinguish use from abuse. For the purposes of this paper, there is little point in trying to make these distinctions, since many of the problems mentioned in parts I and IV can be caused by substance use as well as by abuse.

2. According to one source: ". . . federal spending to combat trafficking and abuse has jumped from \$6.3 billion in 1989 to \$9.5 billion in 1990 to an estimated \$10.4 billion in the current fiscal year." See Clifford Krauss (1991, p. 6). Data recently released by the Bush administration indicate that in 1990 Americans spent \$40.4 billion on cocaine, heroin, marijuana, and other illegal drugs. See David Johnston (1991, p. A11). In the same article, Representative Charles B. Rangel, chair of a House committee on narcotics abuse, is quoted as dismissing the figure of \$40 billion. Rangel estimates that Americans spend approximately \$100 billion a year on illegal drugs. See also Krauss (1991, p. 6). A report in 1989 indicated that 30 million Americans take some kind of illegal drug regularly: 18 million smoke marijuana; 5–6 million take cocaine; 500,000 use heroin or its substitutes; and the rest choose from other illicit drugs. See "Does This War Make Sense?" (1989, p. 25).

or alcohol; unjustly distributed costs of substance use; and poor public health. All of these problems are significant.[3]

An adequate substance use policy for a democratic society should address these ills, yet cohere with the political values of liberalism. In particular, an appropriate balance must be struck between, on one hand, government's duty to prevent persons from causing harm and, on the other, its duties to respect users' autonomy and treat fairly persons' preferences. Practically, the central question is, "Could a policy work?" How well would it regulate substance use and combat the social problems it creates? The philosophical desiderata and practical needs to be addressed by substance use policy give rise to three criteria that any adequate policy should satisfy. It should: (1) be consistent in its regulation of substances; (2) control or prevent the harms created by substance use; and (3) respect personal autonomy. Each criterion is a necessary but not a sufficient condition for the adequacy of a substance use policy.[4] Each can be justified both on grounds of practical need and by coherence with liberal values.

3. For example, half of the murders in Washington D.C., in 1988 were drug-related; during the same year in Detroit, cocaine was implicated in more than 40 percent of reported sudden deaths. See "Does This War Make Sense?" (1989, pp. 25–26). The same report claims, "About two- thirds of the people arrested in the larger cities for felonies such as robbery test positive for illegal drugs, and about half the juveniles in prison are there for a drug offence" (p. 26). Moreover, "In some cities, routine drug indictments make up 50% or more of the criminal work load. . .": Eliot Marshall (1988, p. 1158). Costs of substance use fall on users and nonusers alike, and include the expense of crimes and accidents, strains on the criminal justice system, hospitals and emergency rooms, the costs of drug and alcohol testing, health care subsidies for those made ill by substance use, and lost productivity. The economic costs of America's drug habit are estimated to be between $50 and $100 billion a year; the costs of alcoholism are thought to be even higher. "Does This War Make Sense?" (1989, p. 26). Smoking costs the American economy on net $52–$62 billion per year, primarily in medical costs and lost productivity. See Robert E. Goodin (1989, p. 588). Less tangible costs are emotional stresses borne by the American public, for example, fear and anxiety at the problems caused by substance use, and anger and resentment at being shouldered with unfairly allocated burdens. The health hazards of drug, alcohol, and tobacco use are extensive. The Surgeon General reports that tobacco helps to kill as many as 390,000 Americans a year; alcohol, 100,000; and drugs, 10,000. "Does This War Make Sense?" (1989, p.25).

4. Each requirement is by itself a necessary condition, but none is by itself a sufficient condition, for the adequacy of a policy. The requirements would be necessary and jointly sufficient if another were added: feasibility. Feasibility directly addresses the practical concern of whether a policy would work. It would be difficult, if not impossible, to convincingly establish the feasibility of any policy before it has been tried in this country. The most that can be said in favor of the policy approach defended here is that standard objections to its potential effectiveness can be answered. As used in the text, the criteria do not function to uniquely determine a policy that satisfies necessary and sufficient conditions for adequacy. They function in a weaker way to eliminate undesirable options from a reasonable list of contenders, thereby singling out the policy that, among those on the list, best coheres with liberal values and addresses practical needs.

152

This paper defends the legalization and state-controlled use of drugs, alcohol, and tobacco. Part II surveys the policy options. In Part III, the size of the set of options is reduced by applying the consistency criterion. A non-paternalistic justification of legalization and control is developed in Part IV.

Policy Options[5]

The state has eight apparent alternatives, four options that include legal prohibitions, and four options of legalization and control, as follows:

Prohibition options:

1. Prohibit drugs (including marijuana). Permit use of alcohol and tobacco subject to current restrictions.
2. Prohibit "hard" drugs, e.g., cocaine, heroin, LSD, PCP. Permit the more loosely regulated use of marijuana, alcohol, and tobacco.
3. Completely prohibit drug, alcohol, and tobacco use.
4. Prohibit drugs (including marijuana) and alcohol. Permit tobacco use subject to restrictions.

Legalization and control options:

5. Legalize and strictly control drugs (including marijuana). Permit use of alcohol and tobacco subject to current restrictions.
6. Legalize and strictly control "hard" drug use. Permit the more loosely regulated use of marijuana, alcohol, and tobacco.
7. Legalize and strictly control drug, alcohol, and tobacco use.
8. Legalize and strictly control drugs (including marijuana) and alcohol. Permit tobacco use subject to restrictions.

5. The range of possible options is broad, extending from the complete legal prohibition of drugs, alcohol, and tobacco at one extreme to their legalization and minimally controlled use at the other. Here two extremes are left aside. One is the complete prohibition of all substances on the ground that using them is intrinsically immoral. Prohibiting substances for this reason entails legal moralism – the view that law's legitimate function is to enforce society's moral standards. This is at odds with liberalism's commitment to value neutrality. Moreover, the *de facto* moral pluralism in the United States and, in particular, the evident lack of consensus about the intrinsic immorality of substance use provide ample reason to omit this option. At the other extreme is a position sometimes advocated on libertarian grounds, namely, the legalization and minimal control of substance use. This, too, is omitted. The goal of any plausible policy is to enable the state to control the ills of substance use, yet respect personal autonomy and individual freedom of choice. A policy that increased public availability would hardly enhance state control. The phrase "legalization and control" in each of the four legalization and control options listed in the text refers to the establishment of controlled conditions under which the state can closely regulate substance dispersement and, if possible, subsequent use.

Consistency

The size of the set of options can be reduced by requiring that any policy be consistent in its regulation of substances. That is, if substance X has some property in virtue of which its use is legally prohibited or permitted subject to certain conditions, then, if substance Y has the same or a similar property, the use of Y should be subject to the same kind of regulation as that of X.

Consistency can be justified by appealing to a practical desideratum: the need for user compliance. Any successful option must be able to elicit a reasonable level of compliance from substance users. A policy that appears to some people to be inconsistent in allowing the use of some substances, but prohibiting that of others with a tendency to produce the same or similar effects, is bound to earn the derision of some, who will, most likely, view it as hypocritical. A policy viewed in such a way is unlikely to gain willing acceptance, thereby exacerbating the difficulties of enforcement.

Value neutrality also justifies the consistency requirement. The liberal state must treat citizens impartially; that is, it must not unjustly favor some people's preferences nor unjustly deny others' satisfactions. If someone has a preference for a substance that tends to have certain effects on users, such as marijuana, and someone else prefers to use another substance with a tendency towards similar effects on users, such as alcohol, then, barring further argument, government unfairly discriminates against the former by prohibiting marijuana but permitting alcohol use. Consistency is needed to avoid such unfairness.

Failure to satisfy the consistency requirement disqualifies policies One, Two, Five, and Six from the list of contenders. A reason for prohibiting drugs, including marijuana, as policy One advocates, or for legalizing but strictly controlling their use, as in policy Five, is that these substances tend to produce altered states of consciousness and impaired ability for self-control in users, which can, of course, be hazardous for both users and others.[6] Alcohol tends to have similar effects on self-control, and thus should be subject to the same kind of regulation as other potentially mind-altering substances. Since policies One and Five treat substances with similar properties dissimilarly, they fail to pass the consistency test. Similar failures of consistency disqualify policies Two and Six, which prohibit or legalize and control "hard" drugs, respectively, but

6. On the psychophysical effects of various drugs, including alcohol and marijuana, see Avrum Goldstein and Harold Kalant (1990, p. 1514).

permit the more laxly regulated use of marijuana and alcohol, whose potential for impairing users' self-control is as hazardous as that of many "hard" drugs.

The other policies pass muster. Three, which advocates the complete prohibition of drugs, alcohol, and tobacco, and Seven, which permits their strictly controlled use, do so on the ground that the use of all of these substances tends to cause serious harms to users and others. If this is the property in virtue of which they are legally regulated, all should be regulated in the same way, as indeed they are by these options. Policies Four and Eight also pass the consistency test. They distinguish between the kinds of effects that various substances tend to produce in users. "Hard" drugs, marijuana, and alcohol tend to produce altered states of consciousness and impaired ability for self-control in users, whereas tobacco use tends to produce other kinds of harms.[7] Since impaired self-control presents the possibility of greater social hazards, substances that tend to cause this in users should be subject to more stringent regulation than other substances.

Harm Avoidance and Autonomy: Striking a Balance Through Rational Choice

Requiring a policy to address the ills caused by substance use is justifiable not just on grounds of practical need, but also by reference to the values of liberalism. The liberal state must respect personal autonomy, but may restrict it in order to prevent serious other-regarding harms and interferences in others' pursuit of their significant interests. How can we be sure that a substance use policy appropriately balances the requirements of harm avoidance with respect for personal autonomy? One way of effecting a balance is to informally conceptualize the process of policy selection as a two- party problem of rational choice in which one of the parties is a rational substance user and the other, a rational nonuser. To ensure that the choice process respects the autonomy of each, several assumptions must be made. First, each party is assumed to be rational, well-informed about substance use and its effects, and aware that the other is equally rational and well-informed. Second, each party's preferences should be regarded as rational and autonomous. Third, it is assumed that neither

7. On the harms of smoking, both to self and to others, see Goodin (1989, pp. 575–606). Recent data on other-regarding smoke hazards are summarized in "Secondhand Smoke Blamed for 53,000 Deaths a Year" (1990, p. A9), and "Smoking By Parents Is Found Harmful To Children" (1991, p. A12).

party would be willing to forgo completely the satisfaction of all of her preferences and goals. Each would, however, be willing to make rational compromises for the sake of what she justifiably believes to be a satisfactory outcome. Additionally, it should be assumed that no policy is in effect when the choice is made, but that the parties are choosing a policy for a society that already experiences the negative consequences of extensive substance use. In short, the risks and costs of substance use are such that both parties would acknowledge the need for government regulation. Finally, it is taken for granted that the parties would recognize the need for consistency in the regulation of substances, and so would confine their choice to the four policies remaining on the list of alternatives.

The satisfaction of the preference to use substances is characterized by two relevant features: it can produce pleasure for the user; but it is also a source of possible risks and, for some users, costs. The rational substance user would seek to maximize the pleasures of substance use while minimizing risks and costs.[8] She would therefore seek to avoid risks or costs that are readily avoidable, such as HIV infection from dirty needles. Other risks and costs, however, are difficult to avoid without forgoing use. Some toxic effects are predictably, but not certainly, associated with substance use.[9] For example, liver cirrhosis is associated with the ongoing use of alcohol. The user might willingly incur these risks for the sake of the pleasures substance use brings. She would seek reliable information about these risks in order to adjust preferences, plans, and expectations accordingly.

---

8. Addiction is one of the risks or costs of substance use. Addiction impairs autonomy by gradually eroding a user's capacities for rational self-control. This might be thought to warrant paternalism. However, the effects of addiction vary from user to user. Not all users become addicts, and not all addicts lack control over their substance use. Moreover, the autonomy-impairment caused by some addictions, for example, to nicotine, is local, affecting only preferences for the desired substance. With respect to other substances, such as heroin or "crack," autonomy impairment can easily become more global in scope, affecting more and more of the user's preferences. Consequently, it is difficult to make generalizations about the legitimate applicability and scope of paternalistic restrictions. For the purposes of a non-paternalistic justification of substance abuse policy, it is sufficient to note that the rationally autonomous user values autonomy and would seek, if possible, to avoid the addictive autonomy-impairments that can result from substance use. However, it should be recognized that some rationally autonomous users might be willing to risk becoming addicted to a substance for the sake of the pleasures substance use brings. In all cases, rational users would want to be fully informed of the risks and consequences of becoming addicted to various substances. Full information would, I take it, include not just scientific assessments of the risks and consequences of addiction, but also anecdotal or nonscientific accounts of the experiences of addicts.

9. The occurrence of the toxic effects is related to the quantities of substance ingested and is subject to individual variations in users' sensitivity. Not all effects of a particular substance are expected in every user. See Goldstein and Kalant (1990, p. 1514).

These facts have implications for what it would be rational for the user to want regarding harm avoidance and, consequently, for the choice of a substance use policy. She would be cognizant of three distinct goals regarding crime and physical injuries. First, the higher the price of substances, the more likely it would be that the user would need to turn to crime to support her habit. Crime entails the risk of punishment. Punishment is readily avoidable. To avoid this risk, the user would seek a situation in which she would not have to turn to crime to finance a habit. Second, and for similar reasons, the user would choose a situation in which it would not be a crime to use the substance of choice, thereby avoiding the risk of punishment for use. Third, the user would choose a situation in which she would be neither the victim nor the cause of substance-related crime or physical accidents. Being the victim would itself be a cost; and, since being the cause would create a liability of apprehension and punishment, it would be a risk. Since neither crime nor accidents are necessary occurrences, both the cost of being a victim and the risk of being a cause are avoidable.

In general, the rational user would try to avoid creating any costs that could be socially misallocated. This is because she would realize that the satisfaction of many of her preferences and goals would require social conditions that users, by themselves, probably would be unable to bring about. To realize these ends, the cooperation of nonusers would be needed. Since the misallocated costs of substance use are a source of anger, resentment, fear, and anxiety among nonusers, these costs would have the effect of alienating nonusers from users, thereby rendering the former unsympathetic toward the latter and unwilling to cooperate in efforts to achieve the latter's goals. The rational user would try to avoid this source of friction.

A specific goal of the user overlaps the issues of distributive justice and health. Assuming that the use of at least some substances is rational in the sense that the benefits to the user outweigh the costs, and assuming that, other things being equal, more of a good thing is better than less, the user would seek a situation in which to continue substance use for as long as she chooses. Consequently, she would seek to be assured of competent health care at the lowest possible cost. This raises questions of justice in distribution, since health care would most likely be provided for the user either by the government or through privately underwritten insurance plans. The burden of government-subsidized health care would surely be shared by nonusers as well as by users, although it is possible that users could form insurance groups to provide coverage exclusively for themselves. In either case, some of the cost of each user's health care would be borne by others. Thus, assurance of competent health care would depend upon the willingness of others to share the costs of substance use. The rational user would be aware of this and would seek to create social conditions under which mutual cooperation would be enhanced.

A final goal relating to distributive justice is this: since the user would seek to maximize satisfaction while avoiding costs, she would opt for a social situation in which it would be possible to pay the lowest price for the highest quality substances. Not only would this be cost-efficient for the user, it would prevent substance suppliers from making unjust gains through price gouging.

With respect to health, the user would seek to avoid many readily avoidable risks associated with substance use. For example, she would be unwilling to risk diseases caused by secondhand smoke inhalation, since they are avoidable, and, moreover, are incurred without the concomitant pleasures of using tobacco. Similarly, the user would be unwilling to risk hepatitis or HIV infection from dirty needles used to inject, say, heroin, nor would the user risk overdose or illnesses caused by contaminated substances. However, as suggested, the user would be willing to incur at least some of the risks of substance use that are not readily avoidable, provided that she receives reliable information about them. So, for example, depending on the probability of risk, the nature of the ailment, and the expected pleasures of using a particular substance, the rational user might be willing to risk hypertension or liver cirrhosis, which are chronic effects of alcohol, but not convulsions or prolonged psychotic episodes, associated, respectively, with acute and chronic toxicity of PCP.[10]

The preferences and goals of the rational nonuser must also be considered. Several different preferences could be attributed to the nonuser. She could prefer that no one use substances at all. If this preference were satisfied, problems associated with substance use would simply not arise. Alternatively, the nonuser could prefer not to use substances herself, but would be willing to allow others the freedom to do so. In this case, the nonuser would rationally seek to avoid the problems of crime and physical injuries, distributive justice, and threats to health that are caused by others' substance use. Thus, the nonuser would prefer to live in a society in which certain conditions obtained. First, she would prefer not to risk being the victim of substance-related crimes and accidents. Second, the nonuser would try to avoid, if possible, paying for any misallocated costs, including those of users' health care. However, she would also prefer not to have to work extra hard to compensate for the lagging productivity of

10. See Goldstein and Kalant (1990, p. 1514).

users whose habits have made them ill or unproductive, nor to have to forgo the benefits of living in an economically prosperous society because users have not contributed their fair share. As a consequence, the nonuser would be willing to pay some of the expenses of treatment and rehabilitation for those made ill by substance use in order that they not indefinitely be burdens on society but might someday be productive. The nonuser would regard these costs as short-term investments needed to finance long-term social productivity. Finally, she would seek to escape health hazards, such as secondhand smoke inhalation, that are caused by others' substance use.

The problem of choice can be represented as an assurance game.[11] The rationality of each party's choice depends on beliefs about how it would be rational for the other to behave. Each party can arrive at these beliefs knowing only that the other is equally rational and well-informed about substance use and its effects. As described, the rational user and nonuser have overlapping goals. Both would wish to eliminate the avoidable risks of substance-related crime and accidents, to escape the burden of unjustly allocated costs, and to avoid readily avoidable risks of substance use. For these goals to be attained, it would be necessary and sufficient that each party support the same policy and comply with its requirements. This is because the social problems caused by substance use are so pervasive that neither the user nor the nonuser, acting without the other's cooperation, would be sufficiently powerful to effect the desired changes. Consequently, it would be rational for each party to choose and comply with a policy only if each believed that the other would do so as well, since going it alone would involve costs in the form of unsatisfied preferences and unmet goals.

Suppose that the user were to choose prohibition while the nonuser chose legalization and control. It would be irrational for the nonuser to

---

11. Assurance games are discussed by Ann E. Cudd (1990, pp. 20–21); Jon Elster (1985, pp. 28–29); and Amartya Sen (1982, pp. 78–80). According to Sen, a mutual agreement doesn't need enforcement in an assurance game. Each party ". . . will do the right thing if it is simply assured that the other is doing it too and there is no constant temptation to break the contract." Sen (1982, p. 78). Since a black market would probably arise, there would be a constant temptation for the rational user to break the contract, and so a legalization and control policy would need enforcement. However, the interesting difference between this state of affairs and those represented in prisoner's dilemmas is that, in the latter, enforcement is needed because it could be rational for the parties not to comply with the contract. Given the hazards involved in using illegal substances and the relatively safe conditions for use afforded by legalization and control, it would, arguably, be irrational for the user not to comply with legalization and control restrictions. Consequently, if the user were perfectly rational, the "temptation" of illegal substance use would not be a *bona fide* threat to compliance, and enforcement would not be needed. For imperfectly rational beings, it would, of course, be naive to think enforcement unnecessary.

choose legalization and control if she believed that the user would choose prohibition. In this case, if the nonuser chose legalization and control, she would have sacrificed for nothing the satisfaction of the preference that no one use substances, since the user would, by the choice of prohibition, have expressed a willingness to comply with prohibition requirements. Similarly, it would be irrational for the user to choose prohibition if she believed that the nonuser would choose legalization and control. This is because the user would have sacrificed for nothing the satisfaction of the preference for substance use, since the nonuser would, by the choice of legalization and control, have expressed a willingness to countenance some substance use under controlled conditions.

Suppose, on the other hand, that the user were to choose legalization and control while the nonuser chose prohibition. Given their respective preferences and goals, this might seem to be the rational choice for each party. This would be true if the preferences and goals of each could be satisfied without the cooperation of the other. But such is not the case. Consequently, it would be irrational for the nonuser to choose prohibition if she believed that the user would choose legalization and control. In this case, the nonuser's goals in making that choice, namely, to end completely substance use and its ill effects, would be unmet, since the user would, by her choice, have expressed an unwillingness to comply with prohibition requirements. The user's unwillingness to comply guarantees that some substance use and, with it, its effects would continue. Similarly, it would be irrational for the user to choose legalization and control if she believed that the nonuser would choose prohibition. In this case, the user's goals in making that choice, namely, to use the substances of choice while avoiding, to the greatest extent possible, the negative consequences, would be unmet. This is because the nonuser, by her choice, would have expressed an unwillingness to contribute the resources needed to help create the social conditions under which the user's goals of harm avoidance could be realized. The upshot is that each party needs the other's cooperation for a policy to work to the benefit of either. Either both should choose legalization and control, or both should choose prohibition.

The rational solution is for each party to choose legalization and control. If each were to choose this way, neither would have an incentive not to support and comply with the policy, since it would be better for each if both chose legalization and control than if both chose prohibition. This is because more of the preferences and goals of each would be more likely to be satisfied if both chose and complied with the former than if both did the same with the latter. Since each party is rational and well-informed, each would be willing to choose the policy more likely to maximize the satisfaction of more of her preferences and goals. Since each is aware that the other is equally rational and well-informed, each would believe that the other would choose in like fashion. The crux of the matter is, then, establishing that more of the preferences and goals of each party would indeed be more likely to be satisfied if both chose and complied with legalization and control rather than prohibition.

Would this be true for the user's preferences and goals? Legalization and control would permit the legitimate satisfaction of the preference for substance use and create the conditions under which all of the user's goals could conceivably be attained. It could permit the user to avoid or reduce all of the avoidable risks and costs of substance-related crime and physical injury. If substance prices were controlled, the user would not have to turn to crime to support a habit, nor, if used under legal conditions, would substance use be a crime. Consequently, the risks of punishment that prohibition would associate with these crimes would be avoided. Finally, if the user were to take mind-altering substances only under legally controlled conditions, she would be less likely to cause accidents, thus minimizing the risk of apprehension and punishment associated with causing such misdeeds. And if most or all users complied with legalization and control restrictions, the risk of any particular user being the victim of substance-related accidents, too, would diminish.

Goals relating to distributive justice could also be achieved by legalization and control. Price-controls would enable users to pay reasonable prices for high quality products and would prevent gouging by street pushers. As noted, competent health care for users would most likely be assured if nonusers as well as users were willing to bear some of the costs. All concerned would be more inclined to undertake this burden if they were assured that users bore their fair share of the costs and did not shunt them onto nonusers. Purchases of taxable substances in a legal market would provide such assurance in the form of user-generated revenues that could offset the costs of users' health care. Moreover, users' compliance with legalization and control regulations could be viewed by nonusers as efforts to contain the expenses associated with substance use, and might, consequently, lessen the negative emotions that maldistributed costs are wont to evoke.

A legalization and control policy would also be good preventive medicine. It could enable the user to avoid readily avoidable health risks by providing quality control over substances and paraphernalia and by controlling tobacco use, thereby eliminating the risks of secondhand smoke inhalation. It could also easily provide reliable information about other health risks of substance use.

Compliance with prohibition would, it must be allowed, enable the user to achieve many of these goals, for example, the avoidance of the health risks of substance use as well as the risks associated with crime and physical injury. Regarding distributive justice: effective prohibition would eliminate the illegal market in drugs and thus prevent price gouging by street pushers, but would by itself do nothing to redistribute currently misallocated costs of substance use, nor to promote fair means of financing competent health care for those already made ill by their habits. However, the price of any gains that could accrue to the user from compliance with prohibition would be high: the sacrifice of the satisfaction of the preference for substance use, except, perhaps, for the preference for tobacco use, which would be permitted under restricted conditions by policy Four of the remaining prohibition options.

Would more of the nonuser's preferences and goals be more likely to be satisfied by legalization and control than by prohibition? If her preference were that no one use substances, then prohibition, if completely complied with, would, of course, satisfy this preference, but legalization and control, of course, would not. If the nonuser preferred not to take substances herself but would be willing to permit others to do so, then this preference would not be satisfied by prohibition but would be satisfied by legalization and control. If the nonuser had this latter preference, then she would, it was claimed, want to achieve specific goals with respect to all three areas of harm avoidance: namely, she would want to avoid being the victim of substance-related crime and physical injuries, as well as the health hazards caused by others' substance use. The nonuser would try to escape the misallocated costs of others' substance use, but would be willing to share the costs of rehabilitative health care for the sake of long-term social productivity. Legalization and control would, for some of the reasons previously outlined, enable the nonuser to achieve all of these goals. Prohibition would allow for the realization of some but not all of them. It would, for reasons mentioned above, allow the nonuser to avoid the risks of crime, physical injuries, and health hazards, but would not enable the nonuser to achieve her goals of distributive justice. Thus, if the nonuser's preferences included the willingness to allow some people to use substances, the more rational choice would be legalization and control.

What if the nonuser preferred that no one use substances? If this were her preference, prohibition, it might be thought, would be the rational policy choice. But given the nonuser's beliefs about the user and the effect of these beliefs on the rationality of choice, it would be irrational for the nonuser to choose prohibition in order to secure the social conditions under which this preference could be satisfied. This is because the nonuser would justifiably believe that it would be rational for the user to choose legalization and control, and would know that there are costs associated with going prohibition alone. To choose prohibition under these conditions would be to forgo the satisfaction of the preference in question and, with it, the achievement of any harm avoidance goals that prohibition could secure. Consequently, it would be rational for the nonuser to compromise and seek to satisfy the other preference, which would permit substance use. But if it would be rational for the nonuser to seek to satisfy the other preference, then it would be rational for her to choose legalization and control.

Which of the two legalization and control options remaining on the list of contenders would it be rational for the parties to choose? The difference between the two lies in the stringency with which they regulate tobacco use. Policy Seven, it should be recalled, would permit the strictly controlled use of drugs, alcohol, and tobacco. Policy Eight would strictly control drug and alcohol use but would permit the more loosely regulated use of tobacco, on the ground that drug and alcohol use tends to impair users' abilities for self-control and thus creates the potential for greater social hazards than tobacco use. If users complied with policy Eight, the kinds of harms created by unrestricted tobacco use, for example, the perils of secondhand smoke inhalation, could be reduced or eliminated. Given that the choice of a policy expresses a willingness to comply, the choice of either option would be rational for either party. However, if the rational user's preference for substance use included the desire for tobacco, policy Eight would be the slightly better choice.

Conclusion

The virtue of the foregoing exercise in rational choice is that it provides a non-paternalistic justification of legalization and control that shows how this policy approach addresses the harms caused by substance use, respects the personal autonomy of users, and treats fairly the preferences of all parties to the debate. It shows, too, that legalization and control benefit both users and nonusers. The defense might, however, be accused of the vice of being an "ivory tower" abstraction of academic interest only, with little or no relevance to the real world.

This would, I think, be mistaken. Ultimately, the key to any successful policy is user compliance. Compliance is not unrelated to philosophical issues. Its rationality is intimately bound with the complex topics of the rationality of substance use, the desire for personal autonomy, and the preference for avoiding substance-related harms. The relevance and appeal of legalization and control policies are highlighted by contrasting the psychological presuppositions of this kind of approach with those underlying prohibition options.

Legal prohibitions rely on the "pleasure/pain" principle and the force of the threat of punishment for their effectiveness. To affect personal behavior, the costs of punishment must outweigh the benefits of non-compliance. It is evident that, for many, the advantages of substance use (perhaps mistakenly or irrationally) outweigh the possible costs of punishment. To achieve a parity of cost and benefit that would indeed secure user compliance, it could be necessary to increase legal penalties far beyond a level that is tolerable in a liberal democracy.

Legalization and control policies present the possibility of a more positive, less punitive appeal to the rationality of users. These policies should be viewed as instruments for reshaping the social conventions and attitudes currently associated with substance use in our society. Failure to comply with restrictions could be met with reasonable legal sanctions. Thus, as with prohibition, the potential effectiveness of legalization and control relies, in part, on legal threats. However, at the heart of legalization and control is respect for the rational autonomy of users and the hope that education about the "pros" and "cons" of substance use will enable them to make responsible, informed choices. The success of a legalization and control approach depends on developing a set of rational attitudes toward substance use that is currently lacking among most members of the using population, and on encouraging, among nonusers, a tolerance of what some consider to be truly bad habits. Our current prohibitionist approach fails to reach, in a constructive way, most substance users. Legalization and control, by appealing to the rational interests of all parties involved, provide a way of sending a different message about the pleasures and perils of substance use.

References

Cudd, Ann E. 1990. "Taking Drugs Seriously: Liberal Paternalism and the Rationality of Preferences," *Public Affairs Quarterly*, Vol.4, no. 1, January.

"Does This War Make Sense?" 1989. *The Economist*, Vol. 310, no. 7586, January 21.

Elster, Jon. 1985. *Sour Grapes: Studies in the Subversion of Rationality*, Cambridge University Press, Cambridge.

Goldstein, Avrum and Harold Kalant. 1990. "Drug Policy: Striking the Right Balance," *Science*, Vol. 249, no. 4976, September 28.

Goodin, Robert E. 1989. "The Ethics of Smoking," *Ethics*, Vol. 99, no. 3, April.

Johnston, David. 1991. "Illegal Drug Sales in the U.S. Put at Over $40 Billion in '90," *The New York Times*, June 20.

Krauss, Clifford. 1991. "U.S. Reports Gains in Drug War, But the Battles Keep on Shifting," *The New York Times,* July 14.

Marshall, Eliot. 1988. "Drug Wars: Legalization Gets a Hearing," *Science*, Vol. 241, no. 4870, September 2.

"Secondhand Smoke Blamed for 53,000 Deaths A Year." 1990. *The New York Times*, May 30.

Sen, Amartya. 1982. *Choice, Welfare and Measurement*, Basil Blackwell, Oxford.

"Smoking By Parents Is Found Harmful to Children." 1991. *The New York Times*, June 19.

11

Ethics, Democracy and Foreign Policy: Manipulation or Participation?

Robert J. Myers

Introduction: Is Democracy an Ethical Standard?

The recent collapse of communism and the surges toward democracy in places as disparate as the republics of the former Soviet Union, Africa, and East Asia have elevated the idea of democracy to something akin to an ethical standard. Although there may be some excess in the triumphalism of the "end of history" scenario, the term "democracy" has taken on a newly urgent normative connotation. The democratic ideal has become virtually the only recognized political currency of the 1990s – all governments from Moscow to Addis Abba to Seoul invoke the magic words: "pluralism, liberty, freedom, choice." But how does the ideal of democratic governance translate into practice, particularly in the most complex areas of policymaking such as foreign affairs and particularly in America, the mother-lode of this year's democratic triumphalism?

It is natural to begin by asking why a democratically produced foreign policy might be superior to any other. As de Tocqueville observed:

> Foreign policy does not require the use of any of the good qualities peculiar to democracy but does demand the cultivation of almost all those which it lacks. Democracy favors the growth of the state's internal resources; it extends comfort and develops public spirit, strengthens respect for law in the various classes of society, all of which things have no more than an indirect influence on the standing of one nation in respect to another. But a democracy finds it difficult to coordinate the details of a great undertaking and to fix on some plan and carry it through with determination in spite of obstacles. It has little capacity for combining measures in secret and waiting patiently for the result. Such qualities are more likely to belong in a single man or to an aristocracy. But these are just the qualities which, in the long run, make a nation, and a man too, prevail. ([1835–40], 1969, pp. 228–229)

To answer, democracy is untidy; it is prone to fluctuations of public opinion and the periodic pressures advanced by special interest groups. Coherence and consistency, two traits so vital to the practice of foreign policy, do not come naturally. The leadership in a democratic society must make immense efforts to convince the public of the wisdom of its vision and the soundness of its policies.

Yet here, it might be argued, is why a democratically produced foreign policy might stand on firmer normative ground than those of an aristocracy or a single man. It must stand the test of open debate and not only earn the approval of the governed, but be shaped by it. At a basic level, it demands popular participation: it demands the collective moral judgment of the *demos* and the people's stamp of approval. When a democratic state acts, surely its first avenue of justification is that it acts on behalf of, and in accordance with, the wishes of its people. The Gulf War provides an excellent example of the complex relationship between democracy and the foreign policy process.

What this recent example might mean for the foreign policy process in terms of democratic governance is still undetermined. But what the record shows is that the leadership and the *demos* did, on this occasion, have some important interaction. While the quality of this interaction is open for debate (for example, was the press truly independent in its coverage, or did it slide into a "rally around the flag" mode?; did Congress meet its obligations by exercising timely deliberations?), nonetheless, the public was indeed involved. It was a multi-layered exchange, evolving over time. It was imperfect to be sure, and it is not hard to see room for improvement. But the important point is that in this age of specialization where much is left to the experts, the foreign-policy process in this instance did not escape at least some of the leavening effects of democratic debate.

Democracy Versus Guardianship

The idea of direct democracy in a country the size of the United States was never seriously considered even in the days of the revered Founding Fathers. Representative democracy seemed the sounder choice. Elected representatives, as the founders envisioned them, were to uphold the interests of the *demos* in all governmental activities. This included certain aspects of foreign policy, as stated in the Constitution, as well as additional legislation and resolutions to prod the executive branch, assuming such prodding was considered necessary. Historically, the democratic aspirations residing in the Congress often have found themselves up against the tendency of the executive branch to proceed as it wishes. Secrecy is the most potent weapon of the would-be professional diplomat and the presidential entourage. Congress, on the other hand, profits from transparency because in matters of consequence the public can be informed and respond.

Secrecy and expertise, however, maintain the cult of guardianship in various hidden niches of government. While portraying themselves as helpmates and not adversaries of democracy, these guardians – including those in appointed positions in the national security apparatus – have evolved into something quite apart from the public. Twentieth-century guardians speak special languages (arms control, intelligence estimates, acronym-filled references to international agencies), all in the service of the national interest. Naturally, these guardians have had much to say about how the United States goes to war.

Congress has fought back, with limited results. The War Powers Resolution (Public Law 93–148), passed over President Richard Nixon's veto, has still not stood the ultimate test of constitutionality. The legislation asserted Congress's exclusive authority and denied the president the authority to decide the question of war and peace. Rather than risk a clean-cut decision by the courts as the Gulf crisis was unfolding, both the executive and legislative branches danced an awkward minuet, especially as the troops were all in place and the debate in Congress finally got underway.

The principal question is, simply put, does the president have the right to send United States troops to the next combat zone, and then, if he chooses, send them into action? The answer to point "Λ" is yes, and point "B," not without input, however undefined, from Congress. The public concern and the Congressional debate over the Gulf War highlight again the arguments and concerns as to how democratic societies conduct foreign policy. A still larger question looms, however: is the standard set in the Gulf War debate the standard that America wishes to hold up to the world, especially to the newer democracies that we have encouraged all around the world?

Democracy in Action: Democratic Decisionmaking

It is certainly not practical for every governmental decision to be made by referendum or plebiscite. Some important decisions inevitably will be made in war rooms and field headquarters, and that is as it should be. Yet even decisions that are taken in secret to protect lives are profoundly shaped by the democratic process and the system to which they are held accountable.

The advance of technology in communications, transportation, and in war fighting itself has been used as the justification for entrusting the chief executive with more and more latitude and discretion in using military force, whether a war has been declared or not. There have been in fact only five declarations of war in American history. The length and ferocity of the Vietnam war was the inspiration of the War Powers Act, already mentioned, to brake the president's power to send the nation down the slippery slope of war. If "concern" is the main motivation of political action, as Spengler claimed, it is difficult to assert that many of the people's representatives had a lesser concern than the president.

The case for elite judgment as superior to ordinary judgment is not easy to make in this specific case, nor is it likely to endure as an absolute precedent in the next case. The CIA was roundly blamed for not having top-level spies in Baghdad and too few Arabist case officers in the operations directorate (Perry and Goldberg, 1991, pp. 469–84). And after the event, General Norman Schwartzkopf complained to congressional committees about the inadequacy of theater intelligence before and during the 100-hour battle (*Washington Post*, June 13, 1991, p. 1). The most dramatic demonstration of how the experts can go wrong, however, was an incident recounted in Bob Woodward's book, *The Commanders* (1991). At one briefing of the president before the decision to go to war, Pat Lang of the Defense Intelligence Agency was included because he had predicted the invasion of Kuwait to begin with. Armed with these credentials he advised the president that the Republican Guard "was very well trained, equipped and led ... equivalent to the U.S. Army in these respects." Lang also warned that Saddam Hussein had both control and support of his people and that the war would be "difficult and long." "Other people say differently," Bush said. "Nobody else is telling me that. Shamir, Mubarak, [Syrian President] Assad and [Saudi Ambassador] Bandar all tell me it will be a pushover." Lang had decided he wasn't there to scratch Bush's back, so he replied, "Sir, if I may say, that sounds to me like a collection of the uninformed and self-serving." "Okay," Bush said (1991, p. 360). So much for expertise at that moment in assessing the situation, the order of battle, the strength and disposition of the enemy forces.

One significant lesson emerges in regard to the *demos* and the foreign policy made in its name, and it goes to the heart of the democratic and ethical enterprise. This lesson can best be seen in the statements made to justify American commitment of large forces to the Gulf (and their anticipated actual use). In the fall of 1990, a list of reasons was offered: it began with the imperative of cheap gasoline and followed a line of reasoning leading to Secretary Baker's bald assertion that the reason for intervention in the Gulf boiled down to one word, "jobs." All of these justifications failed. It was only when the president, rising above the "no blood for oil" chant, spoke in the moral tones of the Founding Fathers that support came his way.

How are we to evaluate the role of the people and its Congress in the tussle over foreign policy as exemplified by the Gulf War? Was the country well served, did the system finally work? After World War II Senator Vandenberg, the leading Republican internationalist, said that political bipartisanship should "stop at the water's edge." That idea for a time had become stamped into the national ethos. This may have been one of the reasons why virulent dissent to American foreign policy in Vietnam seemed to many to be anti-patriotic, and why the notion of democratic dissent was put to the test. As Hans J. Morgenthau put it at that time, "The right to dissent derives from the relativist philosophy of democracy. That philosophy assumes that all members of society, being rational, have equal access to the truth, but none of them has a monopoly of it" (1970, p. 40). That observation remains a powerful argument for pluralism, despite the inconvenience.

Finally, what role did ethics play in all these agonies over what was to be done? Before examining selected congressional testimony, it is worth mentioning the detractors of the idea of morality as an arbiter of power. One group says that there is simply no relationship between ethics and foreign policy, while another contents itself by insisting that we are dealing with an oxymoron. Upon analysis of what is really happening in international affairs, however, these are revealed to be simply unreflective views. In international relations, as in other aspects of human activities, it is self-evident that decisions are made. These decisions are posed in terms of ends, means, and consequences. The decisionmaking activity is goal-oriented, and therefore choices are involved and values come into play. Arguments are put forth (in a formal progression or not) revealing preferences weighed on some scale and often the scale of justice. Therefore, the decision often has an ethical content. Over time, these decisions create precedents and traditions for nations which are routinely expressed in the web of rules and habits – regarding many international regimes – that make up the extant normative standards of the international community. Aggression by bad guys (read Saddam Hussein) is bad.

In this broad context, great portions of the American public are involved on an individual basis in activities that touch upon international relations – trade, environment, health, human rights. Information concerning all of these activities and more is available and transparent through the American media to the average citizen. This is a resource that is available for use, and paid heed through polls by our leaders, who in turn add their input.

While President Bush has often been described, particularly in domestic matters, as lacking in leadership, this was not the case in the Gulf, and to the extent his views swayed the public, he undermined the strength of his opposition, largely but not exclusively found in the Democratic party. The contest was thereby joined, and the three days of hearings in the Senate and House in mid-January showed how the issue of war or peace was blurred and finally resolved.

The Debate

A novel factor in the debate in the U.S. Congress over using armed force in the Gulf was that it was in part a response to the UN Security Council resolution authorizing the United Nations Gulf coalition to use "all means necessary" to liberate Kuwait. (China abstained, Cuba and Albania voting against.) The UN Security Council resolution turned out to be easier to accomplish for the Bush administration than the subsequent approval by the American Congress. One does not need to ponder extensively to understand why that was so. There was a momentary convergence of interest in the Security Council, massively so in the General Assembly. Soviet-U.S. cooperation was at a high with Edward Shevardnadze as Soviet foreign minister. The aggression by Saddam Hussein against Kuwait on 2 August 1990 was met by almost universal disapproval. The General Assembly members, many representing countries no larger than Kuwait, were quick to oppose Saddam's annexation, more in terms of their own self-interest than the abstract idea of upholding international law and order. The burden of the resolution, however, weighed heavily on the Congress. It somehow made them look less patriotic than the United Nations, a novel and troubling twist in their debate over the dictates of conscience and sound judgment.

The similarity of the statements about the gravity of the casting of their votes was the hallmark of the somberness of the approach senators and representatives took on the congressional resolutions to support the president's use of force. Mentioned, but not debated, was the constitutional crisis that might have arisen if the resolution had been defeated and if an argument could have been made to proceed based only on the UN Security Council resolution. The administration had been divided on whether to ask for the congressional resolution because (a) despite the War Powers Resolution it was not necessary and (b) it might be rejected. The Department of Justice pressed the first argument. Secretary of Defense Dick Cheney, fearing the resolution might fail, pressed the second. President Bush, however, insisted on trying for the resolution. Senate Majority Leader George Mitchell prepared a bill calling for the continuation of sanctions, while Republican Minority Leader Robert Dole urged a vote for the presidential use of force. At the 10 January hearings, Mitchell addressed the constitutional issue:

> The men who wrote the Constitution had as a central purpose the prevention of tyranny in America. . . . The writers of our Constitution succeeded by creating a government with separate institutions and divided powers. They correctly reasoned that if power were sufficiently dispersed, no institution or individual could gain total power. . . . Acting in his capacity of Commander-in-Chief, President Bush has deployed a vast American military force to the Persian Gulf. He was not required to seek the approval of Congress to order that deployment, and he did not do so. But if he now decides to use those forces in what could plainly be war he is legally obligated to seek the prior approval of Congress. (*Congressional Record*, January 10, 1991, p. S102–103)

To those opposing the Mitchell resolution, Senator John Warner (R-VA) warned that the Iraqis would interpret this debate as indicating a lack of unified support for the president. To this, Senator Sam Nunn (D-GA) said: "I think that the people in the Middle East who are listening to the debate, particularly those in Iraq, particularly Saddam Hussein, should not make any mistake about this debate. This is democracy. This is our system of government" (*CR*, S103). Senator Mitchell's conclusion to his lengthy argument was unequivocal. "The sanctions are being enforced. They are having an effect on Iraq. We should continue their enforcement and seek to enlarge their effect" (*CR*, S102).

The president was not short of supporters, "men of principle," who would expand U.S. involvement in ever additional areas. Said Senator Jesse Helms (R-NC):

> America's stand in the gulf is strong because it is based on strong moral principles. If we fail to extend these same principles to our politics with respect to the Soviet Union, it diminishes our stance in the eyes of Saddam Hussein and the rest of the world. Now is the time for America to keep vigilant and stand with the people of Lithuania as they face down the guns of the Soviet Red Army. (CR, S301)

Senator Albert Gore of Tennessee, the Democratic "Hamlet," had this statement in his testimony:

> Perhaps if the President had not thought this power was his alone, he would not have unilaterally changed the entire strategy of the coalition from defense and curtailment to offense and rollback by force. Perhaps we would then not have to decide between a policy we wish had been left in place and facts that have been created for us without consultation: principally, the fact that the President has brought us and the coalition he skillfully created, and the international community in general, to the very brink of war. (*CR*, January 12, 1991, p. S301)

As for Senator Robert Dole (R–KS), his argument proved to be the most persuasive:

> The Congress of the United States certainly has a role to play. I said last November and December we ought to have been here debating then when the policy was being formulated instead of coming in at the 11th hour after having been AWOL for 3 or 4 months and try to change the direction of the policy President Bush has so patiently and successfully put together. . . . Let us not pull the rug out from under the President at this last moment. . . . (*CR*, p. S367)

As we all witnessed, the vote in the House and Senate came down on the side of the president and the war began and ended with the stated objective of retaking Kuwait. Wider possibilities were not pursued, although a new peace offensive in the Middle East, led by Secretary of State Baker, was begun.

In terms of the democratic ideal, the process of policy consultation and general input from the public, while not perfect, went about as well as can be expected. An informed citizenry participated in its own manipulations. Given the six-month interlude between the invasion of Kuwait and the Allied use of force, there was more than ample time to take the argument to the people through the media and through their legislative representatives. The early false starts in justifying the use of force were clearly related to uninspiring objectives and unjustifiable ends, showing once again how the American democratic society demands inspiring goals, plausible alternatives, and sometimes ethical objectives. Most of all, American society demands an audible voice and active participation in determining what the United States will stand for – a voice in determining what it as a nation believes is "moral, just, and right," as President

Bush pronounced in his 27 January State of the Union Address. This is the preferred American approach to foreign policy. Americans wish to be assured that their country is doing the right thing, even if not the prudent thing.

While the process may have gone as well as can be expected, it is hard to be satisfied with it. The process fell short in terms of confronting the principal ethical dilemma. In fact the process may have done more to obscure than clarify the essential ethical problem: whether or not the use of force was the "just" and "better" policy.

As with many momentous issues put before the public, the language of ethics is often adopted while the substance of the ethical debate is pushed to the side and avoided. In this case, most of the substantive debate focused on the strategic issue of "force or sanctions." The standards or yardsticks used to measure the moral desirability of these actions were never considered systematically. Which yardsticks were operative here: utilitarian calculations of costs and benefits; the moral imperative of "liberating" Kuwait; or some other standard? It seems that the operative standard was uncontested consequentialism. In short, when the policy worked, it became ratified as "moral, just, and right." However, if events had turned sour, the moral high ground certainly would have been called into question.

Democratically produced foreign policy can and should produce even more debate on the specifically ethical dimensions of decisionmaking. More attention needs to be given to the standards by which judgments are made, and those standards need to be linked explicitly to policy decisions such as the one posed by the "force vs. sanctions" choice. "Force vs. sanctions" by itself conveniently finessed the moral issue, which should have been war or peace – the statesman crossing the Rubicon for high purpose – not the politician's callings for half-measures. Fortunately, the leavening effects of democracy make vulgar realpolitik, *raison d'état*, and unmitigated consequentialism impossible for the statesman: the public simply will not tolerate decisions that are at odds with its values and traditions. From the perspective of our thesis of democracy as a superior form of government, the key to improving the debate over the ethics of U.S. foreign policy is to see that tactical considerations and preoccupation with consequences do not push ethics to the margin. We need to set a good example. Where moral choice is concerned, real moral choices should be offered.

References

Albig, William. 1939. *Public Opinion*, McGraw-Hill, New York.

Barzun, Jacques. 1983. *A Stroll With William James*, Harper and Row, New York.

Broder, David. 1991. "A Really Bad Week", in *Congressional Record*, January 11.

de Tocqueville, Alexis. [1835–40] 1969. *Democracy in America*, ed. J.P. Mayer, trans. George Lawrence. Harper and Row, New York.

Evans, Rowland and Robert Novak. 1991. "On Being Wrong," *Washington Post*, March 8.

Morgenthau, Hans J. 1970. *Truth and Power*, Praeger, New York.

Perry, Mark and Jeff Goldberg. 1991. "Will Judge Webster Be Benched?" *The Nation*, April 15.

Woodward, Bob. 1991. *The Commanders*, Simon and Schuster, New York.

12
When Responsive Public Policy Does Not Equal Responsible Government

John Martin Gillroy

The role of the analyst within the democratic policy process is commonly understood as primarily that of responding to the preferences of one's constituents and aggregating these preferences into a cohesive public choice.

> Democratic politics will be improved. . . by a more accurate translation of the preferences of American citizens into public policy. (Jenkins-Smith, 1990, p. 1)

Under this definition of public choice, the responsive policy and responsible policy are one and the same. In many issue areas, however (e.g., environmental risk), a policy analysis that is strictly responsive to preferences may not be responsible to the citizens it is intended to serve. In such cases the need for a morally responsible policy is contingent upon finding a non-preference standard for making the public choice and therefore in defining the responsible policy as distinct from the responsive policy.

Using the public policy issue of environmental risk, I will argue first that the predominant approach to policy analysis, which centers on response to individual preference as the key to a morally sound policy, is dysfunctional in the examination of environmental risk regulation. Second, I will contend that responsive policy still predominates in policy research and analysis because of the association of democracy with responsiveness. Third, I will contend that the anticipatory policy necessary to regulate such issues as environmental risk in the public interest is not antithetical to democratic principles but a necessary component of liberal democracy.

I

Risks from the environment, or more specifically, man-made technologies that transmit risk through environmental media, are a widespread phenomena that perplex policymakers in their discussions of issues as varied as biotechnology, radioactive waste, toxic chemicals, global warming and even the NIMBY (Not In My Back Yard) problems that plague almost every state and province in North America (Page, 1978, Gillroy, 1991, Gillroy, 1992B, 1993). With the growing capacity of natural science to detect and measure risk in the environment, the news has become a day-to-day series of revelations about the potential hazards of what we eat, breath and live in, on, and over (Henderson, 1993). However, the needs of such policy issues and the institutional setting of our "democracy" do not mesh, for while the former requires policy *ex ante* the latter can only produce it *ex post* (Bosso, 1993). For example, the synthetic chemical and nuclear power revolutions of the 1940s and 1950s have turned into the waste disposal nightmares of the 1990s as toxic and radioactive wastes pile up in unsafe dumps while citizens fight the siting of newer and safer facilities (Trost, 1984). Overall, the collective risk we face from our own technological advances has become one of the most troublesome regulatory dilemmas of present policymaking. To understand the roots of this problem, we will first examine the characteristics of environmental risk and then proceed to an argument about how the promise of technological revolution turned predatory.

Talbot Page (1978) has pointed out nine characteristics of environmental risk that separate it from traditional pollution problems and make it understood "so poorly that any management of these problems is truly decision making under uncertainty" (Page, 1978, p. 209). The first characteristic is ignorance of mechanism. "The present state of knowledge of the mechanisms by which a risk is effected is both limited and limiting. *Ignorance of mechanisms* may be present at any number of levels of risk creation, from the generation of the hazard . . . or transmission of the hazard's effect . . . to an organism's response to exposure, particularly health-related responses" (p. 209). Second is the *potential for catastrophic costs*. "What little is known about mechanism in each case establishes that each is a gamble with high stakes. But what is not known about mechanism precludes specification of just how catastrophic and likely the costs might be" (p. 209).

The third characteristic of risk is its *relatively modest benefit* in welfare terms. "Although some may feel that the benefits of nuclear power or recombinant DNA are not small compared with the potential costs, there appears to be at some level a strong asymmetry between potential costs and benefits . . . "(p. 209). Fourth, the policymaker must consider the risk's *low subjective probability for the catastrophic outcome*. When considered with the potential modest benefits the decisionmaker must ask "whether

178

the greater likelihood of the favorable outcome compensates for its smaller relative size. . . . In the extreme case, the problem is called a 'zero-infinity dilemma': a virtually zero probability of a virtually infinite catastrophe" (p. 211).

The fifth and sixth characteristics are the risk's *internal transfer of benefits* and *external transfer of costs*. "In the case of freon propellants, the benefits – added convenience and possibly lower manufacturing costs – are transferred through markets and reflected in product prices [while] . . . the adverse effects of environmental risk gambles usually are transferred directly through the environment rather than through the market" (p. 212). This relates to the seventh characteristic of the situation, its *nature as a collective risk*. . . [M]ajor environmental risk problems have the potential to affect millions of people at the same time. The effectiveness of insurance, liability law, and other traditional compensatory mechanisms in protecting against loss resulting from risk is limited in the case of collective risk" (p. 213).

> The asymmetry between internal benefits and external costs, added to the asymmetry of the potential magnitudes of costs and benefits (zero–infinity dilemma), increases the strain on institutional management of environmental risk. The market failure associated with environmental risk is likely to be more severe than if both benefits and potential costs were external and offsetting, with the same group receiving the benefits also bearing the risks (p. 213).

The eighth characteristic is the *latency* of the risk, that is "the extended delay between the initiation of the hazard, or exposure to it, and the manifestation of its effect" (p. 213). The last characteristic is its *irreversibility*.

> Irreversibility can be essentially absolute, as is the case with plutonium's half-life of 24,000 years. It can also be measured on a scale of tens of generations, as is the case with mutagens. In the freon propellant example, the stratospheric effects of ozone depletion might last a hundred years after fluorocarbon emissions are stopped. Within this essentially irreversible period of stratospheric change, however, the resulting climate modifications could produce further irreversible effects, such as species extinction (p. 214).

The resounding uncertainty of environmental risk problems necessitates that, in conjunction with the now indeterminate "facts" of the situation, the underlying normative system of principles and ideals, or the policymaker's vision of *is* and *ought*, becomes the basis upon which the decisionmaker structures her choices. It is the normative mind-set of the decisionmaker that grants her the power to overcome the uncertainty of empirical "reality" and produce a public choice. Whatever shape these "moral" considerations take, they will determine the standards for judging the successful and "socially better" policy alternative.

> The last two characteristics, latency and irreversibility of effect, have profound ethical and institutional implications. They raise questions concerning fair distribution of risk over time and how institutions can be designed to *anticipate* adverse effects, rather then merely to react to existing, known effects (p. 214, emphasis added).

In the case of environmental risk regulation it is the market paradigm that dominates the field, controlling the approach of American policymakers and setting the standards for what "ought to be" in this area of government regulation. But a close look at the characteristics of environmental risk indicates that once the technology, with potential risk, becomes part of the environment, any hazard is already a zero-infinity dilemma, irreversible and latent in the environment. It is part of our water, air and land, will lie undetectable to our senses and may not physically affect anyone for the duration of its latency period.

I would contend, therefore, that in order to control risk, one must control the introduction of technologies into the environment. The single most important regulatory act is not banning the technology or cleaning up its consequences (which to a greater or lesser extent is useless) but to make the decision about the potential hazard before it is allowed into the environment. The major reason for the troublesome nature of environmental risk is that decisionmakers have been forced to face many problems retroactively. Retroactive attention only allows regulation after these technologies have shown themselves to be harmful and in this way become part of people's preference structures, and subject to the aggregation mechanisms of our democracy as part of the agenda of individual citizens, lobby groups and the electorate in general. At this late point, there is little that can be done to provide security from technology that exhibits the above characteristics.

The original Clean Air and Water Acts were responses to dead fish and visible contamination of air and surface water. The legislation meant to control environmental risk is also responsive to perceived problems that have taken over forty years to become evident. The Resource Conservation and Recovery Act as well as Superfund are attempts to control and clean up existing contamination but largely depend on insurance, liability law and those traditional *ex post* compensatory approaches that Page describes as ineffective in environmental risk cases (p. 213). The only piece of legislation that could be described as at all anticipatory is the 1976 Toxic Substances Control Act (TSCA). This act was passed with the intention of *preventing* "unreasonable risk of injury to health or environment associated with the manufacture, processing, distribution in commerce, use, or disposal of chemical substances" (U.S. Code 2603–f). However, since its passage the act has suffered from a lack of application to the point where "we are still allowing most new chemicals to enter commerce with little or no toxicity testing" (Trost, 1984, p. 276; see also Graham, Green, and Roberts, 1988).

The regulatory record is based on the fear of false positives; that is, the fear that we will condemn a technology that will cause us no harm. It is based on the use of cost–benefit methods that apply the efficiency principle to both the means and ends of environmental policy (Gillroy 1991, Gillroy 1992A) and the dominance of the market as the prior regulator of environmental risk. But if the problems that presently face policymakers can be largely traced back to the reluctance of government to regulate risk-producing technologies when they were first synthesized (Trost 1984, Bosso 1987), and if market-based regulation is responsive and can only employ *ex post* regulation which is dysfunctional to proper policy, then why is it allowed to hold sway?

II

I will argue that the reluctance to establish anticipatory laws, and the propensity to ignore those that are enacted, comes from two mutually supportive and convincing sources: first, the established paradigm of market efficiency, which is supported by the perceived preferences of the electorate for an expanding economy and higher production and, second, the "moral force" of the tie between the market paradigm and our accepted definition of democracy as essentially responsive to individual preferences.

Within the uncertainty surrounding environmental risk policy, the "moral" force of the tie between democratic principles and the market relieves the policymaker from any decisions about the potential hazard of any technology. Instead, facing the uncertainty of environmental risk cases, all she must do is allow the market to regulate the production of the technology and our democratic principles will be secure. The market gives the policymaker the imperative to allow the introduction of any technology for which there exists a consumer, where its capacity to compete is its only qualification for existence. This "moral" argument is based on the ideal that individual consumers know best what they want and that the market is merely responding to the autonomous preferences of these consumers by providing as many choices as possible and, in this way, freedom to the individual and the best possible world for the collective. If consumers want propellants to make spray cans easier to use, they ought to get them; for they are, by definition, in the public interest. If people want red apples and substance X keeps then red, then substance X should be part of the market, for society will be better for its introduction. The only time this pattern is interrupted is if a technology proves, over time, to have more health costs than material benefits and then it may retroactively be stopped from further sales, but only if proof is extensive and "beyond a reasonable doubt."

The argument derived for market democracy is that the production of these technologies provides jobs and a widening economy, which is what the electorate wants. More weight is given to these preferences when these technologies also give the citizen-consumers more choice and a "better life." Here democracy and the institutions it creates take up the market paradigm as the basic expression of the underlying normative assumptions of the electorate and the continued marketing of the technologies of risk become something sanctified by the democratic character of our political institutions. The market provides for the collective interest through the functioning of the invisible hand and for individual freedom by expanding choice to each person.

However, game theory makes us doubt the connection between the invisible hand and the public interest by showing that in a prisoner's dilemma situation, like that established by the cooperation of individuals to provide a collective good like environmental quality, each actor striving for their own personal best outcome renders a non-optimal result for the collective (Goodin, 1976, Hardin, 1983, Gillroy, 1991 and 1992B, 1993). In addition, I am not the only one (Gillroy, 1992A) to see a less than complete definition of freedom in simple quantity of choice in the market. Joe Jackson in his song "It's All Too Much" describes the "poverty" of choice as a complete definition of freedom.

> I hate this supermarket
> But I have to say it makes me think
> A hundred mineral waters
> Its fun to guess which ones are safe to drink
> Two-hundred brands of cookies
> 87 kinds of chocolate chip
> They say that choice is freedom
> I'm so free it drives me to the brink

They say that choice is freedom
I'm so free its driving me insane
It's all too much for me to stand
So much supply and no demand . . .
. . . They say that choice is freedom
I'm so free I'm stuck in therapy
(Joe Jackson, 1991)

The present approach to the analysis of public questions assumes that market principles are the only proper forum for democratic argument and research. The principle of efficiency has been, by far, the most important single imperative of the policy establishment. The environmental risk policy we now have can be seen as a direct outgrowth of the priority of market efficiency in the policy process. The question is whether the responsive policy that has put us in our present position can be said to be the responsible policy. The present regulatory structure, based on the principle of efficiency, must answer in the affirmative, for it elevates the responsive policy and claims it as the responsible one.

If the answer here could possibility be negative, then we need to reassess our criteria of choice and our definition of democracy. If it is possible that the responsive policy is not necessarily the responsible one, then it is incumbent on those interested in policy argument and research to routinize the inclusion of other principles that might define the responsible and anticipatory policy, independently from the policy that is responsive to individual preferences.

III

The overwhelming prejudice of our present regulatory structure is to prevent a false positive (finding an innocent technology a hazard) rather than protect individuals and the community from false negatives (finding a guilty technology innocent) (Page, 1978, pp. 221–249). To responsibly address environmental risk issues we must concentrate on the prevention of false negatives and have anticipatory institutions in place that will regulate to maintain a sound level of environmental quality and accept risks only in the collective interest. But are these institutions democratic? Will they not violate both the principles of individual freedom and collective equality?

I have two arguments to support the position that anticipatory democracy is indeed democracy. First I will contend that the definition of liberal democracy bears within it the assumption of anticipatory institutions. Second, I will maintain that if the principle justifying these anticipatory institutions involves the autonomy of the individual, then they cannot be anti-democratic.

Although liberal democracy is based on the concept of neutrality (Kymlicka, 1989, Chapter 5) this concept has both a "thin" and "thick" definition. The thin definition of liberal democracy makes it coextensive with self-sufficiency and based on the assumption that the only way to insure individual freedom and collective equality is to maintain strictly responsive institutions.

> In a liberal society, the common good is the result of a process of combining preferences, all of which are counted equally. . . . All preferences have equal weight 'not in the sense that there is an agreed public measure of intrinsic value or satisfaction with respect to which all these conceptions come out equal, but in the sense that they are not evaluated at all from a [public] standpoint.' (Kymlicka, 1989, pp. 76–77 [quoting Rawls])

But it is precisely the question of "intrinsic value," ignored within this definition of liberal democracy, that makes it a "thin" connotation of the concept. Here we find the roots of the "thick" concept of liberal democracy in its more classical definition.

The classic definition of a democracy is structured on the idea that it fulfill two functions. The first function of a democracy is to be responsive to electoral majorities. The second function is that it protect the basic rights of each and every citizen, regardless of their place in a majority or minority. The liberal democratic imperative is to construct "a political system in which individual rights are given special constitutional protection against majorities . . ." (Barry, 1989, p. 258) and this relates directly to the Kantian definition of the democratic republic found in Part I of his *Metaphysics of Morals* (Kant, [1797] 1991, pp. 160–163). In Kant's democratic republic the democratic component is characterized by its responsiveness to the changing will of the majority or plurality, while the republican character of the state sets certain matters apart from majority will as necessary to the moral character of each citizen and therefore more universal and necessary to the polity. Kant maintains that the republic is a necessary precondition for just liberal democracy (Kant, 1991, p. 162).

The predominant role of market efficiency within our democracy can be rightly traced to the first of these characteristics of liberal democracy. Freedom as choice and the neutrality of democratic institutions in the process of preference aggregation is no doubt one component of liberal democracy, with its own definition of freedom. But what about the other component of liberal democracy and its responsibility toward the *ex ante* protection of individual rights and the good of the community? On what can we justify a "thick" definition of liberal democracy that can act as a foundation for anticipatory institutions?

I will argue that one possible foundation for a "thick" definition of liberal democracy is the intrinsic value of the individual understood as an autonomous agent. Moral autonomy, defined as the "higher-order control over the moral quality of one's life" (Kuflik, 1984, p. 273) defines an intrinsic value for the individual, which is the basis for all rights and duties and is therefore worthy of protection within a "thick" definition of liberal democracy. One could say that these *ex ante* protections are necessary to the development of those preferences to which the other components of liberal democracy will be set up to respond and, as such, are the basis for responsible public policy and a prior condition for the just aggregation of preferences.

Therefore, in addition to negative freedom of choice, one must also consider the internal positive freedom of the individual (Kant, 1991, Berlin, 1969, Kymlicka, 1989). We must acknowledge that along with the want-regarding principles, like efficiency, which presently form the major part of the decisionmaker's calculus, there are also ideal-regarding principles. The latter can provide the *ex ante* respect for individual autonomy that environmental risk policy requires if decisionmakers are to anticipate hazards to the quality of our lives and prevent them. Brian Barry sets up this distinction.

> A want-regarding evaluation is one that takes account of the extent of want satisfaction and nothing else, counting all satisfied wants equally regardless of their nature. An ideal-regarding evaluation, in contrast, is one that discriminates among want-satisfactions, assigning a greater value to some than to others, perhaps assigning to some a zero or even a negative value. (Barry, 1990, pp. xliv–xlv)

Currently the decisionmaker has largely been limited to the application of want-regarding principles to policy issues like environmental risk. This restricts the field of policy argument and limits the definition of responsible policy to that of responsive policy. However, this approach commits the democratic decisionmaker to the devaluation of the intrinsic character of the individual as well as any intrinsic value that one might attribute to the natural environment. But, the autonomy and empowerment of the individual can now act as a basis for the definition of a responsible policy as distinct from a responsive policy. Efficiency as an imperative of the policymaker now has a competitive principle, autonomy, with which to contend.

IV

But what are the possible counter-arguments to anticipatory institutions as part of liberal democracy? I will isolate three. First, that autonomy as a basis for anticipatory democracy is violated by any action of the state that would take the choice away from the individual. This I will call the self-sufficiency argument. Second, that any anticipatory action by the state would be paternalistic and therefore anti-democratic; and third, that anticipatory action to protect the environment and regulate the economy is "green totalitarianism."

The self-sufficiency argument (Nozick, 1974, Wolff, 1970) contends that autonomous choice means that the individual must be self-sufficient and have no interference from third parties in her decision or choice process. Therefore, it is maintained that anticipatory action by the state is the anti-democratic violation of individual autonomy. This definition of autonomy, as isolated choice, is very narrow and assumes that it is the choice that is important and not the internal capacity that informs that choice; that is, that capacity which actually defines the intrinsic value of the individual. The "thick" definition of liberal democracy, based on a foundation of individual autonomy, moves past the assumptions about the self-sufficiency of the individual and her preferences that are characteristic of efficiency analysis.

> In addition, the ideal of autonomy is perfectly compatible with a 'division of moral labor.' Autonomy is not to be equated with self-sufficiency. Indeed, in a complex world it is difficult to believe that anyone is always the best judge of every possible matter. Thus the morally reflective person is prepared to acknowledge that in certain cases someone else may be in a better position to gather morally relevant information or even to give disinterested attention to the facts, once they have been assembled (Kuflik, 1984, p. 273)

Second, it could be argued that any anticipatory policy is by definition paternalistic as decisions are made by the state for the individual. I will offer two counter-arguments to this proposition. First, I don't believe the action of the state can be paternalistic if it makes a choice (e.g., to regulate toxic chemicals) which is beyond the power of the individual to make for herself but which is also necessary for a capacity to be autonomous that is prior to having any preference order at all. Second, if

Mill ([1859] 1978) is correct that the state can act non-paternalistically to prevent collective harm, then acting to regulate toxic chemicals and prevent a collective hazard is indeed not paternalistic.

The third argument against anticipatory action by the state is that, in the case of environmental risk, it is "green totalitarianism." The state is totalitarian if it controls individual behavior to achieve a collective ideal. The argument comes from the "myth" surrounding the efficiency analysis of markets that imagines them as neutral, supporting individual liberty and the collective good simultaneously. The claim is that to regulate the free trade of individuals, for any reason, would be to violate individual autonomy and the democratic nature of markets and is therefore totalitarian. I reject the argument that efficiency supports more than a "thin" sense of autonomy as choice (see Gillroy, 1992A) and counter this approach on the same basis as I reject the paternalism argument. If the intervention of anticipatory institutions is to protect the intrinsic value of each individual as an autonomous person, then how can it be totalitarian? The action of the state is to protect that without which one can have no preference order or will to trade. The protection of rights is the imperative of anticipatory institutions and does not mean the diminution of democracy but its enhancement. With autonomy as the basis of anticipatory institutions, democracy is protected against the forced choices of those who, because of externalities, cannot maintain or satisfy the preferences they would otherwise have. In any case, the intervention of the state to enforce market principles through cost-benefit analysis also inhibits the choices of those who are victimized by environmental risk and in this way have their choices restricted. In this way the "green" variety is no more totalitarian than the "market" variety.

Overall, I contend that a responsible policy is distinct from a responsive policy and that the former can be justified by the principle of autonomy to support a complete and "thick" definition of liberal democracy that includes anticipatory institutions.

References

Barry, Brian. 1990. *Political Argument*, University of California Press, Berkeley.

Barry, Norman P. 1989. *An Introduction to Modern Political Theory*, 2nd Ed., St. Martin's Press, New York.

Berlin, Isaiah. 1969. *Four Essays on Liberty*, Clarendon Press, Oxford.

Bosso, Christopher J. 1987. *Pesticides & Politics*, University of Pittsburgh Press, Pittsburgh.

_______1993. "Environmental Values and Democratic Institutions," *Environmental*

Risk, Environmental Values and Political Choices, John Martin Gillroy (ed.) Westview Press, Boulder, CO.

Gillroy, John Martin. 1991. "Moral Considerations and Public Policy Choices: Individual Autonomy and the NIMBY Problem", *Public Affairs Quarterly*, Vol. 5.

—— 1992A. "The Ethical Poverty of Cost-Benefit Methods," *Policy Science*, 25: 83–102.

—— 1992B. "Public Policy and Environmental Risk," *Environmental Ethics*, 14: 217–237.

—— 1993. "Integrity, Intrinsic Value and the Analysis of Environmental Risk," *Environmental Values and Political Choices*, John Martin Gillroy (ed.) Westview Press, Boulder, CO.

Goodin, Robert E. 1976. *The Politics of Rational Man*, John Wiley, London.

Graham, John D., Laura C. Green and Mark J. Roberts. 1988. *In Search of Safety*, Harvard University Press, Cambridge.

Hardin, Russell. 1983. *Collective Action*, The Johns Hopkins University Press, Baltimore.

Henderson, David. Forthcoming. "Science, Environmental Values and Policy Prescriptions," *Environmental Risk, Environmental Values and Political Choices*, John Martin Gillroy (ed.) Westview Press, Boulder, CO.

Jenkins-Smith, Hank C. 1990. *Democratic Politics and Policy Analysis*, Brooks/Cole, Pacific Grove, CA.

Kant, Immanuel. [1797] 1991. *Political Writings*, Hans Reiss (ed.) Cambridge University Press, Cambridge.

Kuflik, Arthur. 1984. "The Inalienability of Autonomy," *Philosophy and Public Affairs*, Vol. 13. Reprinted in John Martin Gillroy and Maurice Wade (eds.) 1992. *The Moral Dimensions of Public Policy Choice: Beyond the Market Paradigm*, University of Pittsburgh Press, Pittsburgh.

Kymlicka, Will. 1989. *Liberalism, Community, and Culture*, Clarendon Press, Oxford.

Mill, John Stuart. [1859] 1978. *On Liberty*, Elizabeth Rapaport (ed.) Hackett, Indianapolis.

Nozick, Robert. 1974. *Anarchy, State, and Utopia*, Basic Books, New York.

Page, Talbot. 1978. "A Generic View of Toxic Chemicals and Similar Risks," *Ecology Law Quarterly*, Vol. 7.

Trost, Cathy. 1984. *Elements of Risk,* New York Times Books, New York.

Wolff, Robert Paul. 1970. *In Defense of Anarchism*, Harper and Row, New York.

About the Contributors

David Anderson received his doctorate in philosophy from the University of Michigan. He has taught at the University of Cincinnati and is presently teaching at the College of Charleston and Trident Technical College in Charleston, South Carolina. His research interests include psychoanalytic feminist social theory, Rawls's theory of justice, and topics in the foundations of moral and political theory.

Robert Paul Churchill received his PhD in philosophy from The Johns Hopkins University in 1975. He is currently professor of philosophy at The George Washington University. In addition to a textbook in logic (in second edition), he has published articles concerning the philosophy of law, Just War theory, national defense policy, nuclear deterrence, pacifism, nonviolence, and Gandhi and Vaclav Havel. He is presently working on a book about the philosophy of nonviolence.

James S. Fishkin holds the Darrell K. Royal Regents Chair in government, law, and philosophy at the University of Texas at Austin where he is also chair of the department of government. He earned both a PhD in philosophy from Cambridge University (England) and a PhD in political science from Yale University. He is the author of four books including *Democracy and Deliberation: New Directions for Democratic Reform* (Yale, 1991) and The Dialogue of Justice (Yale 1992). He is associate editor of the journal *Ethics* and coeditor with Peter Laslett of volume 5 and the forthcoming volume 6 of *Philosophy, Politics and Society*.

John Martin Gillroy is assistant professor and Dana Faculty Fellow in the department of political science and director of the public policies study program at Trinity College in Hartford, Connecticut. He received his PhD in political theory from the University of Chicago. His primary interest is in the relationship between (normative and positive) political thought and public policy choice with special emphasis on the use of Kant's ethical and political theory in the formation and prosecution of policy arguments. His recent publications include *The Moral Dimensions of Public Policy Choice* (Pittsburgh, 1992) edited with Maurice Wade.

Gordon Graham is a graduate of the Universities of St. Andrews (Scotland) and Durham (England). He is currently reader in moral philosophy at the University of St. Andrews, and he has held visiting positions at colleges and universities in Colorado, Malta, Maryland, and Minnesota. He is the author of five books on moral and political philosophy, including the textbook, *Contemporary Social Philosophy* (Basil Blackwell, 1987).

Russell Hardin is Professor and Chair of Politics at New York University. He is currently working on issues in ethics and public life and on the foundations of rational choice and social order. He is the author of *Morality Within the Limits of Reason* (Chicago, 1988) and *Collective Action* (Johns Hopkins, 1982), and is the past editor of *Ethics: An International Journal of Social, Political and Legal Philosophy*.

Lisa M. Heldke received her PhD in philosophy from Northwestern University and is presently associate professor of philosophy at Gustavus Adolphus College in St. Peter, Minnesota. She teaches and writes in the area of pragmatist feminism. Among her recent works are *Cooking, Eating, Thinking: Transformative Philosophies of Food* (Indiana, 1992) co-edited with Deane Curtin.

Ron Hirschbein is professor of philosophy at California State University, Chico, where he coordinates the concentration in war and peace studies. He has also served as a visiting research philosopher at the University of California's Institute on Global Conflict and Cooperation. He has presented numerous papers on issues in social philosophy and peace studies; many of these papers have appeared in various anthologies. His recent book, *Newest Weapons/Oldest Psychology*, hazards a novel account of the arms race, and he is currently completing a hermeneutical study of international crises.

Michael W. Howard received his PhD in philosophy from Boston University and is presently associate professor of philosophy at the University of Maine. His area of specialization is social and political philosophy and he has published articles on justice, democracy, worker self-management, and nuclear deterrence. He is currently working on self-management, postmodernism, and the media.

Robert J. Myers studied international relations at the University of Chicago where he served as a research assistant for Hans J. Morgenthau and where he received his PhD in 1959 in the history of Indonesian socialism. Following distinguished service with the Army, the Department of State, and the Far East Division of the CIA, he cofounded and published *The Washingtonian* until 1968, when he accepted responsibilities for publishing *The New Republic*. Since 1980, he has been president of the Carnegie Council on Ethics and International Affairs in New York City. In the past few years, he has had more than a dozen books and articles published. Recent conferences at which he has directed seminars or presented papers have involved travel to Germany, Japan, Korea, the People's Republic of China, and the former Soviet Union, as well as within the United States.

Matt Silliman received his PhD in philosophy from Purdue University and is currently assistant professor of philosophy at North Adams State College in Massachusetts. The paper on civil disobedience included in this volume represents his efforts to reconcile his work as an academic philosopher with his interest in grassroots political organizing, and his efforts to come to terms philosophically with some of his experiences in community politics. He is presently writing about Locke's views on the family and Plato on censorship.

Nancy E. Snow received her PhD in philosophy from the University of Notre Dame and is presently assistant professor of philosophy at Marquette University, Milwaukee. Her research interests are in ethics, applied ethics, and social and political philosophy. Among her recent publications is her article "Compassion" in the *American Philosophical Quarterly*, Vol. 28 (July 1991). She is currently working on conceptions of moral personhood, humility, and self-respect.

Maurice L. Wade received his PhD in philosophy from Stanford University in 1982 and joined the philosophy faculty at Trinity College in 1983 where he is currently associate professor of philosophy. His areas of research and publication include contemporary political philosophy, applied ethics (particularly ethics and medical technology), and the philosophy of David Hume. He is currently editing an anthology of essays on nonhuman rights and a collection of commentary on Rawls's work after *A Theory of Justice*.

Index

collectivities. *See* communities
Collins, Larry, 140, 144
Commission on Party Structure and
   Delegate Selection, 110
common good. *See* good; common good
communism, 52
communitarianism, 2, 7, 15, 16–17, 72, 74
   n.6, 81–92 passim
   critique of liberalism, 2, 6, 15, 16–17,
      32, 72, 81, 82, 86–89 passim, 92
   defects of theory, 33
   democracy and, 32–33
   ethics and, 72, 89–90
   individual identity, 89–90. *See also*
      Taylor, Charles
   institutionalism, 32
communication. *See* speech
communities, 7, 12, 77. *See also* social life
   speech and, 112, 113, 114, 115, 118,
      119, 121 n. 21, 122, 123, 125, 126.
      See also speech
Congress, 101, 147, 168–75 passim
   debate over Gulf Crisis, 147, 169, 171,
      172–74
   Gulf War. *See* foreign policy; Gulf War
   War Powers Resolution, 169, 173
conscience, 7, 99–100, 137, 138–39, 140,
      141, 144
   civil disobedience. *See* civil disobedi-
      ence; conscience
   moral character, 138. *See also* individu-
      als; moral development
   personal conviction, 138, 139,
   public responsibility, 138–39, 140
   social aspects, 138, 141, 144
   socially constructed, 99–100
consent, 4, 32, 98, 99, 131
   Locke, John and. *See* Locke, John
   tacit consent, 99
consequentialism, 147, 175. *See also* utili-
      tarianism
consumers, 148, 181, 182–83
consistency criterion, 153, 154–55, 156
Consitution (U.S.), 168, 172, 173, 184
constitutional government, 3, 175
contractarianism, 12–13, 14, 15, 31, 32,
      37–39, 43, 61–62, 63, 64, 65–66, 75,
      76
   autonomy and. *See* autonomy; contrac-
      tarian theory
   concept of person, 31, 38
   contractualist principle, 38
   democratic participation, 38
   Hobbes, Thomas, 74, 75
   individuals and, 38. *See also* individuals

institutionalism, 32, 37–38
Locke, John, 32. *See also* Locke, John
   morality and. *See* ethics; contractarian-
      ism
   Rawls, John, 32. *See also* Rawls, John
cost-benefit analysis, 181, 187
critical theory, 66
Cuba, 172
Cudd, Ann E., 159 n.11, 164
Curtin, Deane, 119 n.16

Dahl, Robert A., 3, 4, 6, 8, 102, 110
Dalton, Peter, 125 n.29
Daniels, Norman, 51 n.6, 67
Darwell, Stephen, 51 n.6, 56 n.11, 58
   n.12, 67
Davion, Victoria M., 61 n.14, 67
decision theory, 13
Defense Intelligence Agency, 170
deliberation, 4, 7, 26, 65, 95, 103, 104,
      105, 106, 107, 108. *See also* participa-
      tion; non-deliberation, deliberative
      opinion polls. *See* representation;
      deliberative opinion polls
deliberative rationality, 65
democratic politics and, 101–09 passim
democracy, 1–8, 11, 12, 13, 16, 22–23,
      24, 27, 31–34, 43, 45, 72, 96, 97, 129,
      132, 148–49, 175, 184
   alternative forms, 102–03
      ceremonial, 97, 129–36 passim. *See
         also* voting; rites
      deliberative, 95, 103, 105, 106–09.
         See also deliberation
      direct democracy, 101, 102, 105–09,
         168
      liberal democracy. *See* liberal
         democracy
      Madisonian, 102, 103
      majoritarian, 3, 7, 95, 101, 102, 106.
         See also majorities
      mass democracy, 95, 97, 101, 103,
         105, 106, 109. *See also* mass society
      participatory, 13, 132. *See also* par-
         ticipation; democratic
      plebiscitary, 105, 106, 108, 109
      populist. *See* populism
      representative, 3, 5, 7, 95, 98,
         101–03, 105, 106, 108, 168
      teledemocracy, 101, 105
   anticipatory institutions, 183–86, 187
   autonomy and. *See* autonomy; democra-
      cy
   best form of government, 7, 13, 19, 98
   character development and, 4, 34. *See*